T0100162

Podman in Action

SECURE, ROOTLESS CONTAINERS
FOR KUBERNETES, MICROSERVICES, AND MORE

DANIEL WALSH

MANNING

SHELTER ISLAND

For online information and ordering of this and other Manning books, please visit
www.manning.com. The publisher offers discounts on this book when ordered in quantity.
For more information, please contact

> Special Sales Department
> Manning Publications Co.
> 20 Baldwin Road
> PO Box 761
> Shelter Island, NY 11964
> Email: orders@manning.com

Manning Publications Co.	Development editor: Toni Arritola
20 Baldwin Road	Technical development editor: Joshua White
PO Box 761	Technical editor: Roman Zhuzha
Shelter Island, NY 11964	Review editor: Aleksandar Dragosavljević
	Production editor: Andy Marinkovich
	Copy editor: Christian Berk
	Proofreader: Katie Tennant
	Technical proofreader: Alain Lompo
	Typesetter: Dennis Dalinnik
	Cover designer: Marija Tudor

ISBN: 9781633439689
Printed in the United States of America

In memory of my mother, Joan P. Walsh

brief contents

contents

preface

I have been working on computer security for close to 40 years, and for the past 20 years, I've focused on container technologies. When Docker showed up about 10 years ago, it triggered a revolution in the way the people distributed and ran applications on the internet. As I worked on Docker, I felt it could have been designed better. Working with a root-running daemon and then adding more and more daemons felt like the wrong approach. Instead, I felt we could use low-level operating systems concepts to create a tool that ran the same containerized applications in the same manner but with more security and requiring fewer privileges. With this in mind, my team at Red Hat set out to build a series of tools to help developers and administrators run containers in the most secure way possible. Out of this effort came Podman.

I started blogging on subjects like SELinux in the early 2000s and have been writing articles ever since. I have written hundreds of articles on containers and security over the years, but I wanted to consolidate the ideas and describe the technology of Podman in a single book I could point users and customers to.

This book introduces Podman and how to use it. It also dives deep into the technology and the different parts of the Linux operating system that we take advantage of. Since I am a security engineer, I also spend a couple of chapters describing how the security of containers works. Reading this book should give you a better understanding of what containers are, how they work, and how to work with different features of Podman. You will even learn a lot more about Docker. As Podman grows in popularity and infiltrates your infrastructure, this book will be a handy reference to guide your way.

acknowledgments

I extend thanks to all the people who helped me write this book. This includes members of the Podman team, who have written articles that helped me understand some of the technology I did not fully comprehend and have helped build a great product. Thank you, Brent Baude, Matt Heon, Valentin Rothberg, Giuseppe Scrivano, Urvashi Mohnani, Nalin Dahyabhai, Lokesh Mandvekar, Miloslav Trmac, Jason Greene, Jhon Honce, Scott McCarty, Tom Sweeney, Ashley Cui, Ed Santiago, Chris Evich, Aditya Rajan, Paul Holzinger, Preethi Thomas, and Charlie Doern. I also want to thank the countless open source contributors who have made Linux containers and Podman possible.

I thank the entire team at Manning, but especially Toni Arritola. Toni taught me how to better focus my ideas and has been a great partner on this journey. She's had to deal with me, an old mathematics major who was never great at writing, and she helped make this book possible.

To all the reviewers—Alain Lompo, Alessandro Campeis, Allan Makura, Amanda Debler, Anders Björklund, Andrea Monacchi, Camal Cakar, Clifford Thurber, Conor Redmond, David Paccoud, Deepak Sharma, Federico Kircheis, Frans Oilinki, Gowtham Sadasivam, Ibrahim Akkulak, James Liu, James Nyika, Jeremy Chen, Kent Spillner, Kevin Etienne, Kirill Shirinkin, Kosmas Chatzimichalis, Krzysztof Kamyczek, Larry Cai, Michael Bright, Mladen Knežić, Oliver Korten, Richard Meinsen, Roman Zhuzha, Rui Liu, Satadru Roy, Seung-jin Kim, Simeon Leyzerzon, Simone Sguazza, Syed Ahmed, Thomas Peklak, and Vivek Veerappan—thank you, your suggestions helped make this a better book.

about this book

Podman in Action describes how users can build, manage, and run containers. My goal in writing it was to explain how easy it is to transfer skills you might have learned in Docker to Podman as well as how easy it is to use Podman if you have never used a container engine before. *Podman in Action* also teaches you how to use advanced features like pods and guides you on your journey toward building applications ready to run on the edge of or inside Kubernetes. Finally, *Podman in Action* explains all of the security features of the Linux kernel used to isolate containers from the system as well as from other containers.

Who should read this book?

Podman in Action is written for software developers who are looking to understand, develop, and work with containers, as well as system administrators who need to run containers in production. Reading this book will give you a deeper understanding of what containers are. Having knowledge of Linux processes and familiarity working with the Linux shells is necessary to get the full benefit of the book.

The book should have something for everyone on their quest to use containers. Users with a deep understanding of Docker will learn about advanced features of Podman not available from Docker and will get an even deeper understanding of how Docker works. Novice users will learn the basics of containers and pods.

How this book is organized: A roadmap

Podman in Action is split into four parts and six appendixes:

- Part 1, "Foundations," comprises four chapters and provides readers an introduction to Podman. Chapter 1 explains what Podman does, why it was created, and why it is important. The next two chapters introduce the command-line interface and how to use volumes within containers. Finally, chapter 4 introduces the concept of pods and how Podman works with them. There should be something for everyone in these chapters, but if you have great experience with Docker, you should be able to skim over much of the content in chapter 2.

- Part 2, "Design," comprises two chapters in which I dig deep into Podman's design. You will learn about rootless containers and how they work and will come out of these chapters with a better understanding of user namespaces and the security of rootless containers. You will also learn how to customize the configuration of your Podman environment.

- Part 3, "Advanced topics," comprises three chapters and moves beyond the basics of Podman. In chapter 7 you will see how Podman can work in production through its integration with systemd. It covers running systemd inside a container and how you can use it as a container manager. You will learn how to set up edge servers with Podman containers, where systemd manages the life cycle of the container. Podman makes it easy to generate systemd unit files to help you put your containerized applications into production. In chapter 8 you will learn how Podman can be used to help you move containers into Kubernetes. Podman supports launching containers with the same YAML files that Kubernetes uses as well as the ability to generate Kubernetes YAML from your current containers. In chapter 9 you will see Podman running as a service, allowing remote access to Podman containers. Using Podman as a service allows you to use other programming languages and tools to manage Podman containers. You will see how docker-compose can work with Podman containers. You will also learn how to use the Python libraries like podman-py and docker-py to communicate with the Podman service for managing containers.

- Part 4, "Container security," comprises two chapters, in which I discuss important security considerations. Chapter 10 covers features used to ensure container isolation. This chapter covers security subsystems of Linux, like SELinux, seccomp, Linux capabilities, kernel file systems, and namespaces. Chapter 11 then examines the security considerations I consider best practices for running your containers in as secure a manner as possible.

Additionally, there are six appendixes covering Podman-related subjects:

- Appendix A covers all of the Podman-related tools, including Buildah, Skopeo, and CRI-O.

- Appendix B dives into the different OCI runtimes available to Podman as well as Docker. It covers `runc`, `crun`, Kata, and gVisor.
- Appendix C describes how you can get Podman onto your local system, whether that system is a Linux, Mac, or Windows box.
- Appendix D describes the Podman open source community and how you can join.
- Appendixes E and F dive into running Podman on Mac and Windows boxes.

liveBook discussion forum

Each purchase of *Podman in Action* includes free access to liveBook, Manning's online reading platform. Using liveBook's exclusive discussion features, you can attach comments to the book globally or to specific sections or paragraphs. It's a snap to make notes for yourself, ask and answer technical questions, and receive help from the author and other users. To access the forum, go to https://livebook.manning.com/book/podman-in-action/discussion. You can also learn more about Manning's forums and the rules of conduct at https://livebook.manning.com/discussion.

Manning's commitment to our readers is to provide a venue where a meaningful dialogue between individual readers and between readers and the author can take place. It is not a commitment to any specific amount of participation on the part of the author, whose contribution to the forum remains voluntary (and unpaid). We suggest you try asking him some challenging questions lest his interest stray! The forum and the archives of previous discussions will be accessible from the publisher's website as long as the book is in print.

Author online

You can follow Dan Walsh on Twitter and GitHub @rhatdan. He regularly blogs at https://www.redhat.com/sysadmin/users/dwalsh as well as on several other sites. There are many videos of talks Dan has presented available on YouTube as well.

about the author

DANIEL WALSH leads the team that created Podman, Buildah, Skopeo, CRI-O, and their related tools. Dan is a senior distinguished engineer at Red Hat, having joined in August 2001. He has worked in the computer security field for over 40 years. Dan is sometimes referred to as Mr. SELinux after leading the development of SELinux at Red Hat prior to leading the container team. Dan has a BA in mathematics from the College of the Holy Cross and an MS in computer science from Worcester Polytechnic Institute. On Twitter and GitHub you can find him @rhatdan. You can email him at dwalsh@redhat.com.

about the cover illustration

The figure on the cover of *Podman in Action* is captioned "La vandale," or "The vandal," and is taken from a collection by Jacques Grasset de Saint-Sauveur, published in 1797. Each illustration is finely drawn and colored by hand.

In those days, it was easy to identify where people lived and what their trade or station in life was just by their dress. Manning celebrates the inventiveness and initiative of the computer business with book covers based on the rich diversity of regional culture centuries ago, brought back to life by pictures from collections such as this one.

Part 1

Foundations

In part 1 of the book, I introduce you to several ways you can use Podman from the command line. In chapter 2 you learn how to create and work with containers and how containers work with images. You also learn the difference between a container and an image, how to save a container into an image, and then to push the image to a registry, so it can be shared with other users.

In chapter 3 I introduce the concept of a *volume*. Volumes are the mechanisms most users of your containerized applications use to store their data and keep it isolated from the application. The first two chapters really concentrate on the use of containers and images, which is very similar to the way containers work in Docker.

Chapter 4 adds the concept of *pods*, similar to Kubernetes Pods, a feature Docker does not support. Pods allow you to share one or more containers within the same resource, namespaces, and security constraints. Pods can allow you to write more complex applications and manage them as a single entity.

Podman:
A next-generation
container engine

This chapter covers

- What Podman is
- The advantages of using Podman over Docker
- Examples of using Podman

Starting this book is difficult because so many people come to it with different expectations and experiences. You likely have some experience with containers, Docker, or Kubernetes—or at least are interested in learning more about Podman because you've heard about it. If you've used or evaluated Docker, you'll find that Podman works the same as Docker in most cases, but it solves some problems inherent in Docker; most significantly, Podman offers enhanced security and the ability to run commands with non-root privileges. This means you can manage containers with Podman without root access or privileges. Because of Podman's design, it can run with much better security than Docker by default.

In addition to being open source (and therefore free), Podman's commands, run from the command-line interface (CLI), are quite similar to Docker's. This book shows how you can use Podman as a local container engine to launch containers on a single node, either locally or through a remote REST API. You'll also learn how to find, run, and build containers using Podman with open source tools such as Buildah and Skopeo.

1.1   *About all these terms*

Before you go further, I think it is important to define the terminology that will be used throughout this book. In the container world, terms like *container orchestrator, container engine,* and *container runtime* are often used interchangeably, which commonly leads to confusion. The following list is a summary of what each of these terms refers to in the context of this text:

- *Container orchestrators*—Software projects and products that orchestrate containers onto multiple different machines or nodes. These orchestrators communicate with container engines to run containers. The primary container orchestrator is Kubernetes, which was originally designed to talk to the Docker daemon container engine, but using Docker is becoming obsolete because Kubernetes primarily uses CRI-O or containerd as its container engine. CRI-O and containerd are purpose built for running orchestrated Kubernetes containers (CRI-O is covered in appendix A). Docker Swarm and Apache Mesos are other examples of container orchestrators.
- *Container engines*—Primarily used for configuring containerized applications to run on a single local node. They can be launched directly by users, administrators, and developers. They can also be launched out of systemd unit files at boot as well as launched by container orchestrators like Kubernetes. As previously mentioned, CRI-O and containerd are container engines used by Kubernetes to manage containers locally. They really are not intended to be used directly by users. Docker and Podman are the primary container engines used by users to develop, manage, and run containerized applications on a single machine. Podman is seldom used to launch containers for Kubernetes; therefore, Kubernetes is not generally covered in this book. Buildah is another container engine, although it is only used for building container images.
- *Open Container Initiative (OCI) container runtimes*—Configure different parts of the Linux kernel and then, finally, launch the containerized application. The two most commonly used container runtimes are `runc` and `crun`. Kata and gVisor are other examples of container runtimes. See appendix B to understand the differences between the OCI container runtimes.

Figure 1.1 shows into which categories these open source container projects fit.

Podman is short for *Pod Manager.* A *pod,* a concept popularized by the Kubernetes project, is one or more containers sharing the same namespaces and `cgroups` (resource constraints). Pods are covered in greater depth in chapter 4. Podman runs individual containers as well as pods. The Podman logo in figure 1.2 is a group of Selkies, the Irish concept of a mermaid. Groups of Selkies are called pods.

The Podman project describes Podman as "a daemonless container engine for developing, managing, and running OCI Containers on your Linux System. Containers can either be run as root or in rootless mode" (https://podman.io). Podman is often summarized with the simple line *alias Docker = Podman* because Podman does

Figure 1.1 Different open source projects dealing with containers within the categories of orchestrators, engines, and runtimes.

almost everything that Docker can do with the same command line as Docker. But as you will learn in this book, Podman can do so much more. Understanding Docker is not critical to understanding Podman, but it is helpful.

Figure 1.2 Podman's logo

NOTE   The Open Container Initiative (OCI) is a standards body with the primary goal of creating open industry standards regarding container formats and runtimes. For more information, see https://opencontainers.org.

The Podman upstream project resides at github.com in the Containers project, (https://github.com/containers/podman) shown in figure 1.3, along with other

Figure 1.3   Containers is the developer site for Podman and other related container tools (see https://github.com/containers).

container libraries and container management tools like Buildah and Skopeo. (See appendix A for a description of some of these tools.)

Podman runs images with the newer OCI format, described in section 1.1.2, as well as the legacy Docker (v2 and v1) format images. Podman runs any image available at container registries, like docker.io and quay.io, as well as the hundreds of other container registries. Podman pulls these images to a Linux host and launches them in the same way as Docker and Kubernetes. Podman supports all OCI runtimes, including runc, crun, kata, and gvisord (appendix B), just like Docker.

This book is intended to aid Linux administrators in understanding the advantages of using Podman as their primary container engine. You will learn how to configure your systems as securely as possible but still allow your users to work with containers. One of Podman's primary use cases is running containerized applications on single-node environments, such as edge devices. Podman and systemd allow you to manage the entire life cycle of the application on nodes without human intervention. Podman's goal is running containers naturally on a Linux box, taking advantage of all the features of the Linux platform.

> **NOTE** Podman is available for many different Linux distributions and on Mac and Windows platforms. Please refer to appendix C to see how to get Podman on your platform.

Application developers are also an intended audience for this book. Podman is a great tool for developers looking to containerize their applications in a secure manner. Podman allows developers to create Linux containers on all Linux distributions. In addition, Podman is available on the Mac and Windows platforms, where it can communicate with the Podman service running within a VM or on a Linux box available on the network. *Podman in Action* shows you how to work with containers, build container images, and then convert their containerized applications into either single-node services to run on edge devices or into Kubernetes-based microservices.

Podman and the container tools are open source projects with contributors from many different companies, universities, and organizations. Contributors come from all over the world. The projects are always looking to add new contributors to improve them; please refer to appendix D to see how you can join the effort. In this chapter, I first provide a brief overview of containers, and then I explain some key features that make Podman a great tool for working with containers.

1.2 *A brief overview of containers*

Containers are groups of processes running on a Linux system that are isolated from each other. Containers make sure one group of processes does not interfere with other processes on the system. Rogue processes can't dominate system resources, which might prevent other processes from performing their task. Hostile containers are also prevented from attacking other containers, stealing data, or causing denial of service attacks. A final goal of containers is allowing applications to be installed with their own versions of shared libraries that do not conflict with applications requiring different versions of the same libraries. Instead they allow applications to live in a virtualized environment, giving the impression that they own the entire system.

Containers are isolated via the following:

- *Resource constraints (cgroups)*—The cgroup man page (https://man7.org/linux/man-pages/man7/cgroups.7.html) defines cgroups as the following: "Control groups, usually referred to as cgroups, are a Linux kernel feature which allow processes to be organized into hierarchical groups whose usage of various types of resources can then be limited and monitored."

  Examples of resources controlled by cgroups include the following:

  - The amount of memory a group of processes can use
  - The amount of CPU processes can use
  - The amount of network resources a process can use

  The basic idea of cgroups is preventing one group of processes from dominating certain system resources in such a way that another group of processes can't make progress on the system.

- *Security constraints*—Containers are isolated from each other using many security tools available in the kernel. The goal is blocking privilege escalation and preventing a rogue group of processes from committing hostile acts against the system, including the following examples:

  - Dropped Linux capabilities limit the power of root.
  - SELinux controls access to the filesystem.
  - There is read-only access to kernel filesystems.
  - Seccomp limits the system calls available in the kernel.
  - A user namespace to map one group of UIDs in the host to another allows access to limited root environments.

Table 1.1 gives further information and provides links with more detail about some of these security features.

Table 1.1   Advanced Linux security features

Component	Description	Reference
Linux capabilities	Linux capabilities subdivide the power of root into distinct capabilities.	The capabilities man page is a good overview of the available capabilities (https://bit.ly/3A3Ppeg).
SELinux	Security-Enhanced Linux (SELinux) is a Linux kernel mechanism that labels every process and every filesystem object on the system. A SELinux policy defines the rules on how labeled processes interact with label objects. The Linux kernel enforces the rules.	I wrote the *SELinux Coloring Book*, which is a fun way to help you understand SELinux (https://bit.ly/33plEbD). If you really want to study the subject, check out the SELinux notebook (https://bit.ly/3GxGhkm).

Table 1.1 Advanced Linux security features *(continued)*

Component	Description	Reference
Seccomp	seccomp is a Linux kernel mechanism that limits the number of syscalls to a group of processes on the system. You can remove potentially dangerous syscalls from being called by the processes.	The seccomp man page is a good source of additional information on seccomp (https://bit.ly/3rnnim1).
User namespace	The user namespace allows you to have Linux capabilities within the group of UIDs and GIDs assigned to the namespace, without having root capabilities on the host.	The user namespace is fully explained in chapter 3.

- *Virtualization technologies (namespaces)*—The Linux kernel employs a concept called *namespaces*, which creates virtualized environments, where one set of processes sees one set of resources, while another set of processes sees a different set of resources. These virtualized environments eliminate processes' views into the rest of the system, giving them the feel of a virtual machine (VM) without the overhead. Examples of namespaces include the following:
  - *Network namespace*—Eliminates the access to the host network but gives access to virtual network devices
  - *Mount namespace*—Eliminates the view of all the filesystem, except the containers filesystem
  - *PID namespace*—Eliminates the view of other processes on the system; container processes only see the processes within the container

These container technologies have existed in the Linux kernel for many years. Security tools for isolating processes started in Unix back in the 1970s, and SELinux started in 2001. Namespaces were introduced around 2004, and cgroups were introduced around 2006.

> **NOTE** Windows container images exist, but this book concentrates on Linux-based containers. Even when running Podman on Windows, you are still working with Linux containers. Podman on Mac is covered in appendix E. Podman on Windows is covered in appendix F.

1.2.1 Container images: A new way to ship software

Containers really didn't take off until the Docker project introduced the concept of the container image and container registry. Basically, they created a new way to ship software.

Traditionally, installing multiple software applications on a Linux system has led to a problem of dependency management. Before containers, you packaged software using package managers like RPM and Debian packages. These packages are installed on a host and share the content on the host, including shared libraries. When developers test their code, everything might work fine when run on the host machine. The quality engineering team then might test the software on a different machine with different packages and see failures. Both teams would need to work together to generate the proper requirements. Finally, the software is shipped to customers, who have many different configurations and software installed, leading to further breakage of the application.

Container images solve the dependency management problem by bundling all the software needed to run your application together into a unit. You ship all the libraries, executables, and configuration files together. The software is isolated from the host via container technology. Usually the only part of the host system that your application interacts with is the host kernel.

The developer, quality engineers, and customer all run the exact same containerized environment along with the application. This helps guarantee consistency and limits the number of bugs caused by misconfiguration.

Containers are often compared to VMs in that they both can run multiple isolated applications on a single node. When using VMs, you need to manage the entire VM operating system as well as the isolated application. You need to manage the life cycle of the different kernel, init system, logging, security updates, backups, and so on. The system also has to deal with the overhead of the entire running operation system, not just the application. In the container world, all you run is the containerized application—there is no overhead and no additional OS management. Figure 1.4 shows three applications running in three different VMs.

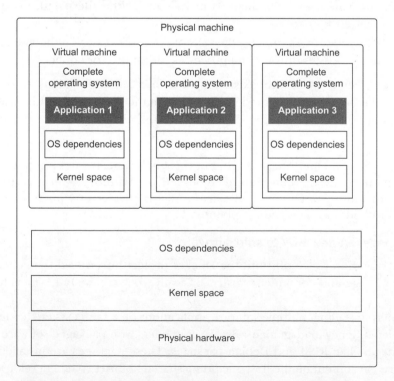

Figure 1.4   Physical machine running three applications in three VMs

With VMs you end up needing to manage four operations systems, whereas with containers the three applications run with just their required user spaces. You end up managing just one operating system, as shown in figure 1.5.

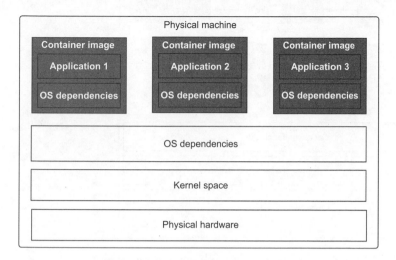

Figure 1.5   Physical machine running three applications in three containerized applications

1.2.2   Container images lead to microservices

Packing applications inside of container images allows the installation of multiple applications with conflicting requirements on the same host. For example, one application might require a different version of the C library than another, which prevents them from being installed at the same time. Figure 1.6 shows a traditional application running within an operating system without use of containers.

Containers can have the correct C library within their container image, with each image potentially having different versions of the library specific to the container's application. You can run applications from totally different distributions.

Containers make it easy to run multiple instances of the same application, as shown in figure 1.7. Container images encourage the packaging of a single service or application into a single container. Containers allow you to easily wire multiple applications together via the network.

Instead of designing monolithic applications in which you have a web frontend, a load balancer, and a database, you can build three different container images and then wire them together to build microservices. Microservices allow you and other users to experiment with running multiple databases and web frontends, then orchestrate them together. Containerized microservices make the sharing and reuse of software possible.

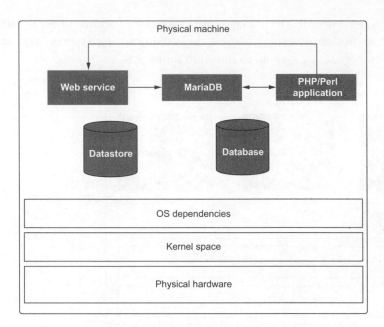

Figure 1.6   Traditional LAMP stack (Linux, Apache, MariaDB, and PHP/PERL application) running on a server

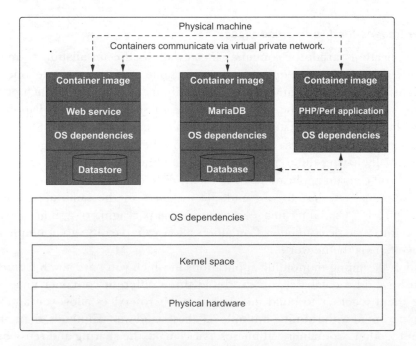

Figure 1.7   LAMP stack packaged individually into microservice containers. As containers communicate via the network, they can be easily moved to other VMs, making reuse much easier.

1.2.3   Container image format

A container image consists of three components:

- A directory tree containing all the software required to run your application
- A JSON file that describes the contents of the rootfs
- Another JSON file called a manifest list that links multiple images together to support different architectures

The directory tree is called a *rootfs* (root filesystem). The software is laid out like it was the root (/) of a Linux system.

The executable to be run within the rootfs, the working directory, the environment variables to be used, the maintainer of the executable, and other labels to help identify the content of the image are defined in the first JSON file. You can see this JSON file using the podman inspect command:

```
$ podman inspect docker://registry.access.redhat.com/ubi8
{
    ...
    "created": "2022-01-27T16:00:30.397689Z",
    "architecture": "amd64",
    "os": "linux",
    "config": {
        "Env": [

            "PATH=/usr/local/sbin:/usr/local/bin:/usr/sbin:/usr/bin:/sbin:/bin",
                "container=oci"
        ],
        "Cmd": [
                    "/bin/bash"
        ],
        "Labels": {
                "architecture": "x86_64",
                "build-date": "2022-01-27T15:59:52.415605",
        ...
}
```

Architecture for this image → "architecture"

Operating system for this image → "os"

Date the image was created → "created"

Environment variables that the developer of the image wants to be set within the container → "Env"

Default command to be executed when the container starts → "Cmd"

Labels to help describe the contents of the image. These fields can be free-form and do not affect the way images are run but can be used to search for and describe the image. → "Labels"

The second JSON file, the manifest list, allows users on an arm64 machine to pull an image with the same name as they would if they were on an arm64 machine. Podman pulls the image based on the default architecture of the machine, using this manifest list. Skopeo is a tool that uses the same underlying libraries as Podman and is available at github.com/containers/skopeo (see appendix A). Skopeo provides lower-level output examining the structures of a container image. In the following example, use the skopeo command with the --raw option to examine the registry.access.redhat.com/ubi8 image manifest specification:

```
$ skopeo inspect --raw docker:/ /registry.access.redhat.com/ubi8
{
    "manifests": [
      {
```

```
          "digest": "sha256:cbc1e8cea              Digest of the exact image pulled when
  ➥ 8c78cfa1490c4f01b2be59d43ddbb                 the architecture and OS match
  ➥ ad6987d938def1960f64bcd02c",              ◁
          "mediaType": "application/vnd.docker.distribution.manifest.v2+json",  ◁
          "platform": {                                                              mediaType
 The OS of       "architecture": "amd64",  ◁                                    describes the type
this image       "os": "linux"                    The architecture             of the image, OCI,
digest: Linux    },                               of this image                Docker, and so on.
          "size": 737                             digest: amd64
          },
          {                                   This stanza points to a different image
          "digest":                       ◁   for a different architecture: arm64.
  ➥ "sha256:f52d79a9d0a3c23e6ac4c3c8f2ed8d6337ea47f4e2dfd46201756160ca193308",
          "mediaType": "application/vnd.docker.distribution.manifest.v2+json",
          "platform": {
          "architecture": "arm64",
          "os": "linux"
          },
          "size": 737
          },
  ...
  }
```

Images use the Linux tar utility to pack the rootfs and the JSON files together. These images are then stored on web servers called container registries (e.g., docker.io, quay.io, and Artifactory). Container engines like Podman can copy these images to a host and unpack them onto the filesystem. Then the engine merges the image's JSON file, the engine's built-in defaults, and the user's input to create a new container OCI runtime specification JSON file. The JSON file describes how to run the containerized application.

In the last step, the container engine launches a small program called a container runtime (e.g., `runc`, `crun`, `kata`, or `givisord`). The container runtime reads the container's JSON and instruments, kernel cgroups, security constraints, and namespaces before finally launching the primary process of the container.

1.2.4 Container standards

The OCI standards body defined the standard formats for storing and defining container images. They also defined the standard for container engines running containers. The OCI created the OCI Image Format, which standardizes the format of the container images and the images' JSON file. They also created the OCI Runtime Specification, which standardized the container's JSON file to be used by OCI runtimes. The OCI standards allow other container engines, like Podman,[1] to follow the standards and be able to work with all the images stored at container registries and to run them in the exact same way as all other container engines, including Docker (see figure 1.7).

---

[1] Other container engines include Buildah, CRI-O, containerd, and many others.

1.3   Why use Podman when you have Docker?

I often get asked the question, "Why do you need Podman when you already have Docker?" Well one reason is that *open source is all about choice*. Operating systems have more than one editor, more than one shell, more than one filesystem, and more than one internet web browser. I believe that Podman's design is fundamentally better than Docker's and offers features that advance the security and use of containers.

1.3.1   Why have only one way to run containers?

One of Podman's advantages was that it was created long after Docker existed. Podman developers looked at ways to improve on Docker's design from a totally different perspective. Because Docker was written as open source, Podman shares some of the code and takes advantage of new standards, like the Open Container Initiative. Podman works with the open source community to concentrate on developing new features.

In the rest of this section, I cover some of these improvements. Table 1.2 describes and compares features available in Podman and Docker.

Table 1.2   Podman and Docker feature comparison

Feature	Podman	Docker	Description
Supports all OCI and Docker images	✓	✓	Pulls and runs container images from container registries (i.e., quay.io and docker.io). See chapter 2.
Launches OCI container engines	✓	✓	Launches `runc`, `crun`, Kata, gVisor, and OCI container engines. See appendix B.
Simple command-line interface	✓	✓	Podman and Docker share the same CLI. See chapter 2.
Integration with systemd	✓	✗	Podman supports running systemd inside the container as well as many systemd features. See chapter 7.
Fork/exec model	✓	✗	The container is a child of the command.
Fully supports user namespace	✓	✗	Only Podman supports running containers in separate user namespaces. See chapter 6.
Client-server model	✓	✓	Docker is a REST API daemon. Podman supports REST APIs via a systemd socket-activated service. See chapter 9.
Supports `docker-compose`	✓	✓	Compose scripts work against both REST APIs. Podman works in rootless mode. See chapter 9.
Supports docker-py	✓	✓	Docker-py Python bindings work against both REST APIs. Podman works in rootless mode. Podman also supports podman-py for running advanced features. See chapter 9.
Daemonless	✓	✗	The Podman command runs like a traditional command-line tool, while Docker requires multiple root-running daemons.

Table 1.2   Podman and Docker feature comparison *(continued)*

Feature	Podman	Docker	Description
Supports Kubernetes-like pods	✓	✗	Podman supports running multiple containers within the same pod. See chapter 4.
Supports Kubernetes YAML	✓	✗	Podman can launch containers and pods based on Kubernetes YAML. It can also generate Kubernetes YAML from running containers. See chapter 8.
Supports Docker Swarm	✗	✓	Podman believes the future for orchestrated multinode containers is Kubernetes and does not plan on implementing Swarm.
Customizable registries	✓	✗	Podman allows you to configure registries for short-name expansion. Docker is hardcoded to docker.io when you specify a short name. See chapter 5.
Customizable defaults	✓	✗	Podman supports fully customizing all of its defaults, including security, namespaces, and volumes. See chapter 5.
macOS support	✓	✓	Podman and Docker support running containers on a Mac via a VM running Linux. See appendix E.
Windows support	✓	✓	Podman and Docker support running containers on a Windows WSL 2 or a VM running Linux. See appendix F.
Linux support	✓	✓	Podman and Docker are supported on all major Linux distributions. See appendix C.
Containers aren't stopped on software upgrade.	✓	✗	Podman is not required to remain running when containers are running. Since the Docker daemon is monitoring containers, by default, when it stops, all containers stop.

1.3.2   *Rootless containers*

Probably the most significant feature of Podman is its ability to run in rootless mode. In many situations, you do not want to give full root access to your users, but users and developers still need to run containers and build container images. Requiring root access prevents lots of security-conscious companies from widespread adoption of Docker. Podman, on the other hand, can run containers with no additional security features in Linux other than a standard login account.

You can run the Docker client as a normal user by adding the user to the Docker user group (/etc/group), but I believe granting this access is one of the most dangerous things you can do on a Linux machine. Access to the docker.sock allows you to gain full root access on the host by running the following command. In the command, you are mounting the entire host operating system / on the /host directory within the container. The `--privileged` flag turns off all container security, and then you `chroot` to /host. After the `chroot`, you are in a root shell at / of the operating system, with full root privileges:

```
$ docker run -ti --name hacker --privileged -v /:/host ubi8 chroot /host
#
```

At this point, you have full root privileges on the machine, and you can do whatever you want. When you are done hacking the machine, you can simply execute the `docker rm` command to remove the container and all records of what you did:

```
$ docker rm hacker
```

When Docker is configured with default file logging, all records of your launching the container are erased. I believe this is far worse than setting up `sudo` without root, in that at least with `sudo`, you have the chance to see that `sudo` was run in your log files.

With Podman the processes running on the system are always owned by the user and have no capabilities greater than a normal user. Even if you break out of the container, the process is still running as your UID, and all actions on the system are recorded in the audit logs. Users of Podman cannot simply remove the container and cover up their tracks. See chapter 6 for more information.

> **NOTE** Docker now has the ability to run rootless similarly to Podman, but almost no one runs it that way. Starting up multiple services in your home directory just to launch a single container has not caught on.

1.3.3   Fork/exec model

Docker is built as a REST API server. Fundamentally Docker is a client-server architecture including multiple daemons. When a user executes the Docker client, they execute a command-line tool that connects to the Docker daemon. The Docker daemon then pulls images to its storage and then connects to the containerd daemon, which finally executes an OCI runtime that creates the container. The Docker daemon, then, is a communication platform that communicates reads and writes of `stdin`, `stdout`, and `stderr` from the initial process (PID1) created in the container. The daemon relays all of the output back to the Docker client. Users imagine the container's processes are just children of the current session, but there is a lot of communication going on behind the scenes. Figure 1.8 shows the Docker client-server architecture.

The bottom line is the Docker client communicates with the Docker daemon, which then communicates with the containerd daemon, which finally launches an OCI runtime like `runc` to launch PID1 of the container. There is a lot of complexity involved in running containers in this way. Over the years, failures in any of the Daemons have led to all containers shutting down, and it is often difficult to diagnose what happened. The core Podman engineering team comes from an operating system background grounded in the Unix philosophy.

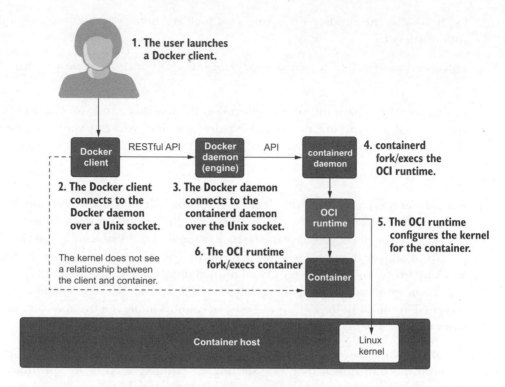

Figure 1.8   Docker client-server architecture. The container is a direct descendant of containerd, not the Docker client. The kernel sees no relationship between the client program and the container.

Unix and C were designed with the fork/exec model of computing. Basically, when you execute a new program, a parent program like the Bash shell forks a new process and then executes the new program as a child of the old program. The Podman engineering team thought they could make containers simpler by building a tool that pulls container images from a container registry, configures container storage, and then launches an OCI runtime, which starts the container as a child of your container engine.

In the Unix operating system, processes can share content via the filesystem and inter-process communication (IPC) mechanisms. These features of the operating system enable multiple container engines to share storage without requiring a daemon to be running to control access and share content. The engines do not need to communicate together aside from using locking mechanisms provided by the operating system's filesystems. Future chapters examine the advantages and disadvantages of this mechanism. Figure 1.9 shows the Podman architecture and communication flow.

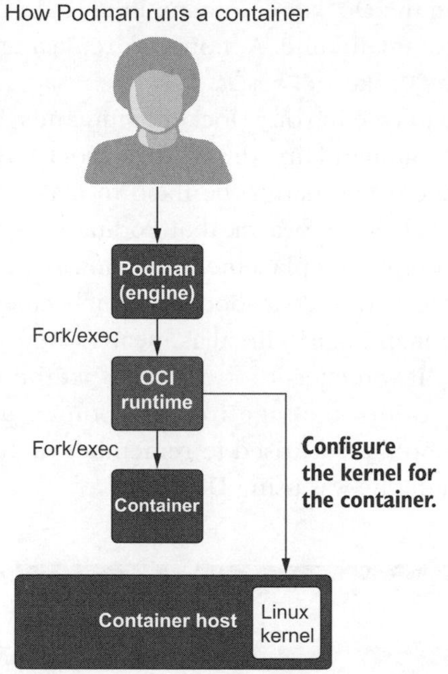

How Podman runs a container

Fork/exec

Fork/exec

Configure the kernel for the container.

Figure 1.9   Podman fork/exec architecture. The user launches Podman, which executes the OCI runtime, which then launches the container. The container is a direct descendant of Podman.

1.3.4 *Podman is daemonless*

Podman is fundamentally different from Docker because it is daemonless. Podman can run all of the same container images as Docker and launch containers with the same container runtimes. However, Podman does this without having multiple continuously root-running daemons.

Imagine you have a web service that you want to run at boot time. The web service is packaged in a container, so you need a container engine. In the Docker case, you need to set it up to be running on your machine with each of the daemons running and accepting connections. Next, launch the Docker client to start the web service. Now you have your containerized application running as well as all of the Docker daemons. In the Podman case, use the Podman command to launch your container, and Podman will go away. Your container will continue to run without the overhead of running the multiple daemons. Less overhead is incredibly popular on low-end machines like IOT devices and edge servers.

1.3.5 *User-friendly command line*

One of the great features of Docker is the simple command-line interface. There have been other container command lines like RKT, lxc, and lxcd, but they have their own command-line interfaces. The Podman team realized early on that it wouldn't gain market share if Podman had its own command-line interface. Docker was the dominant tool, and almost everyone who had played with containers had done it with its CLI. In addition, if you were to search how to do something with a container online, invariably you would get an example using the Docker command line. Right from the start, Podman had to match the Docker command line. A motto for replacing Docker with Podman was quickly developed: `alias Docker = Podman`.

With this command, you can continue to type in your Docker commands, but Podman runs your containers. If the Podman command line differs from Docker, it is considered a bug in Podman, and users demand Podman to be fixed to make the tools match. There are a few commands, such as Docker Swarm, that Podman doesn't support, but for the most part, Podman is a complete replacement for the Docker CLI.

Many distributions supply a package called `podman-docker`, which changes the alias from *docker* to *podman* and links the man page. The alias means when you type `docker ps`, the `podman ps` command runs. If you execute `man docker ps`, the Podman `ps` man pages show up. Figure 1.10 is a twitter message from a Podman user who aliased the `docker` command to `podman`, and was surprised to remember he had been using Podman for two months while thinking he was using Docker.

Figure 1.10   Tweet about "alias docker='podman'"

Back in 2018, Alan Moran tweeted, "I completely forgot that ~2 months ago I set up 'alias docker="podman"' and it has been a dream. #nobigfatdaemons…". Joe Thomson responded, "So, what reminded you?" and Alan Moran answered "docker help." And Podman help showed up.

1.3.6   Support for REST API

Podman can be run as a socket-activated REST API service. This allows remote clients to manage and launch Podman containers. Podman supports the Docker API as well as the Podman API for advanced Podman features. Through the use of the Docker API, Podman supports `docker-compose` and other users of the docker-py Python bindings. This means that even if you built your infrastructure around using the Docker socket for launching containers, you can simply replace Docker with the Podman service and continue to use your existing scripts and tools. Chapter 9 covers the Podman service.

The Podman REST API also allows remote Podman clients on Mac, Windows, and Linux systems to interact with Podman containers on a Linux machine. Appendixes E and F cover Podman use on Mac and Windows machines.

1.3.7   Integration with systemd

Systemd is the fundamental init system in the operating systems. The init process on a Linux system is the first process that is started by the kernel on boot. Therefore, the init system is the ancestor of all processes and can monitor them all. Podman wants to fully integrate the running of containers with the init system. Users want to use systemd to start and stop containers at boot time. Containers should do the following:

- Support systemd within a container
- Support socket activation
- Support systemd notifications that a containerized application is fully activated
- Allow systemd to fully manage the cgroups and lifespan of a containerized application

Basically, containers work as services in systemd unit files. Many developers want to run systemd within a container to run multiple system-defined services within a container.

However, the upstream Docker community disagrees with this and has denied all pull requests that attempt to integrate systemd into Docker. They believe Docker should manage the life cycle of the container, and they do not want to accommodate users who want to run systemd in a container.

The upstream Docker community believes the Docker daemon, as opposed to systemd, should be the controller of processes, it should manage the life cycle of containers, and it should start and stop them at boot time. The problem is there are many more features in systemd than in Docker, including startup ordering, socket activation, service ready notifications, and so on. Figure 1.11 is an actual badge of a Docker employee at the first DockerCon, illustrating their hostility towards systemd.

When Podman was designed, the developers wanted to make sure it fully integrated with systemd. When you run systemd inside a container, Podman sets up the container the way systemd expects and allows it to simply run as PID1 of the container with limited privileges. Podman allows you to run services within the container the

Figure 1.11   Docker employee badge at DockerCon EU

same way they run on a system or in a VM: via systemd unit files. Podman supports socket activation, service notifications, and many other systemd unit file features. Podman makes it simple to generate systemd unit files with best practices for running containers within a systemd service. For more information, see chapter 7 on systemd integration.

The Containers project (https://github.com/containers) where Podman, container libraries, and other container management tools reside, wants to embrace all features of the operating system and fully integrate it. Chapter 7 explains Podman integration with systemd.

1.3.8   Pods

One advantage of Podman is described in its name. As mentioned earlier, *Podman* is actually short for *Pod Manager*. As the official Kubernetes documentation puts it, "A pod (as in a pod of seals, hence the logo, or pea pod) is a group of one or more containers, with shared storage/network resources, and a specification for how to run the containers." Podman works with either a single container at a time, like Docker, or it can manage groups of containers together in a pod. One of the design goals of containers is to separate services into single containers: microservices. Then you combine containers together to build larger services. Pods allow you to group multiple services together to form a larger service managed as a single entity. One of the goals of Podman is allowing you to experiment with pods. Figure 1.12 shows two pods running on a system, each pod containing three containers.

Podman has the `podman generate kube` command, which allows you to generate Kubernetes YAML files from running containers and pods, as you can see in chapter 7.

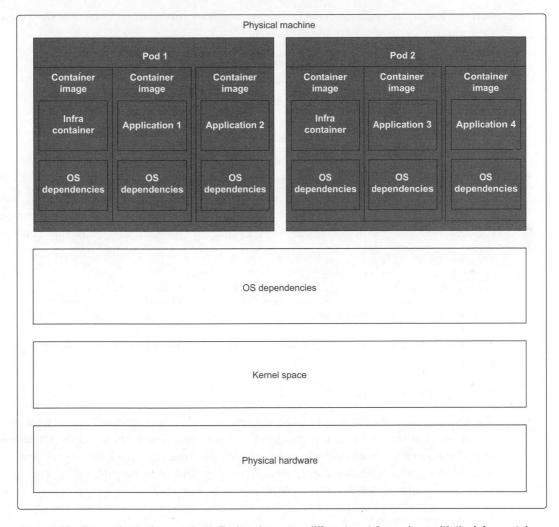

Figure 1.12   Two pods running on a host. Each pod runs two different containers along with the infra container.

Similarly, it has the `podman play kube` command, which allows you to play Kubernetes YAML files and generate pods and containers on your host. I suggest using Podman for running pods and containers on a single host and using Kubernetes to take your pods and containers and run them on multiple machines and all through your infrastructure. Other projects, like kind (https://kind.sigs.k8s.io/docs/user/rootless), are experimenting with running pods with Podman under the guidance of Kubernetes.

1.3.9   *Customizable registries*

Container engines like Podman support the concept of pulling images using short names, such as ubi8, without specifying the registry in which they reside: registry.access .redhat.com. Complete image names include the name of the container registry they were pulled from: registry.access.redhat.com/library/ubi8:latest. Table 1.3 shows the components of the image name broken out.

Table 1.3   Short name to container image name table

Name	Registry	Repo	Name	Tag
Short name			ubi8	
Complete name	registry.access.redhat.com	library	ubi8	latest

Docker is hardcoded to always pull from https://docker.io when using a short name. If you want to pull an image from a different container registry, you must fully specify the image. In the following example, I attempt to pull ubi8/httpd-24, and it fails because the container image is not on docker.io. The image is on registry.access.redhat.com:

```
# docker pull ubi8/httpd-24
Using default tag: latest
Error response from daemon: pull access denied for ubi8/httpd-24,
repository does not exist or may require 'docker login': denied: requested
access to the resource is denied
```

So if I want to use ubi8/httpd-24, I am forced to type the entire name, including the registry:

```
# docker pull registry.access.redhat.com/ubi8/httpd-24
```

The Docker engine gives docker.io an advantage over other container registries as the preferred registry. Podman was designed to allow you to specify multiple registries, like what you can do with `dnf`, `yum`, and `apt` tools for installing packages. You can even remove docker.io from the list. If you attempt to pull ubi8/httpd-24 with Podman, Podman presents you with a list of registries to choose from:

```
$ podman pull ubi8/httpd-24
? Please select an image:
    registry.fedoraproject.org/ubi8/httpd-24:latest
      ▸ registry.access.redhat.com/ubi8/httpd-24:latest
    docker.io/ubi8/httpd-24:latest
    quay.io/ubi8/httpd-24:latest
```

Once you make your decision, Podman records the short-name alias and no longer prompts and uses the previously selected registry. Podman supports lots of other features, like blocking registries, only pulling signed images, setting up image mirrors, and specifying hardcoded short names, so specific short names map directly to the long names (see chapter 5).

1.3.10 Multiple transports

Podman supports many different container image sources and targets called *transports* (see table 1.4). Podman can pull images from container registries and from local containers storage but also supports images stored in OCI format, OCI TAR format, legacy Docker TAR format, directory format, and images directly from the Docker daemon. Podman commands can easily run images from each of the formats.

Table 1.4   Podman-supported transports

Transport	Description
Container registry (`docker`)	References a container image stored in a remote container image registry website. Registries store and share container images (e.g., docker.io and quay.io).
`oci`	References a container image compliant with OCI layout specifications. The manifest and layer tarballs are located in the local directory as individual files.
`dir`	References a container image compliant with the Docker image layout, similar to the `oci` transport but storing the files using the legacy `docker` format.
`docker-archive`	References a container image in a Docker image layout that is packed into a TAR archive.
`oci-archive`	References a container image compliant with OCI layout specifications that is packed into a TAR archive.
`docker-daemon`	References an image stored in the Docker daemon's internal storage.
`container-storage`	References a container image located in a local storage. Podman defaults to using container storage for local images.

1.3.11 Complete customizability

Container engines tend to have lots of built-in constants, like the namespaces they run with, whether or not SELinux is enabled, and which capabilities containers run with. With Docker, most of these values are hardcoded and cannot be changed by default. Podman, on the other hand, has a very customizable configuration.

Podman has its built-in defaults but defines three locations for its configuration files to be stored:

- */usr/share/containers/containers.conf*—Where a distribution can define the changes the distribution likes to use
- */etc/containers/containers.conf*—Where they can set up system overrides
- *$HOME/.config/containers/containers.conf*—Can be specified only in rootless mode

The configuration files allow you to configure Podman to run the way you want by default. You can even run with more security by default if you choose.

1.3.12 User-namespace support

Podman is fully integrated with the user namespace. Rootless mode relies on user namespaces, which allows for multiple UIDs to be assigned to a user. User namespaces provide isolation between users on a system, so you can have multiple rootless users running containers with multiple user IDs, all isolated from each other.

A user namespace can be used to isolate containers from each other. Podman makes it simple to launch multiple containers, each with a unique user namespace. The kernel then isolates the processes from host users as well as each other based on UID separation.

Docker only supports running containers in a single, separate, user namespace, meaning all containers run within the same user namespace. Root in one container is the same as root in another container. It does not support running each container in a different user namespace, which means containers attack each other from a user-namespace perspective. Even though Docker supports this mode, almost no one runs containers with Docker in a separate user namespace.

1.4   When not to use Podman

Like Docker, Podman is not a container orchestrator. Podman is a tool for running container workloads on a single host in either rootless or rootful mode. Higher-level tools are required if you want to orchestrate running containers on multiple machines.

I believe the best tool for doing this now is Kubernetes. Kubernetes won the container orchestrator war when it comes to mind share. Docker has an orchestrator called Swarm, which had some popularity, but it now seems to be out of favor. Because the Podman team believes Kubernetes is the way to go for containers on multiple machines, Podman does not support Swarm functionality. Podman has been used for different orchestrators and is used for grid/HPC computing, and open source developers have even added it to Kubernetes frontends.

Summary

- Containers technology has been around for many years, but the introduction of container images and container registries allows developers a better way to ship software.
- Podman is an excellent container engine, suitable for almost all of your single-node container projects. It is useful for developing, building, and running containerized applications.
- Podman is as simple to use as Docker, with the exact same command-line interface.
- Podman supports a REST API, which allows remote tools and languages, including `docker-compose`, to work with Podman containers.
- Unlike Docker, Podman includes such notable features as user-namespace support, multiple transports, customizable registries, integration with systems, the fork/exec model, and out-of-the-box rootless mode.
- Podman is a more secure way to run containers.

Command line

2

This chapter covers

- The Podman command line
- Running an OCI application
- Comparing containers and images
- Building an OCI-based image

Podman is an excellent tool for running and building containerized applications. In this chapter, you'll get started by building a simple web application to demonstrate commonly used features of the Podman command line.

If you don't have Podman installed on your machine, you can jump to appendix C, and then return here. This chapter assumes that Podman 4.1 or later is already installed. Older versions of Podman probably work fine, but all examples were tested with Podman 4.1. The example base image I use is the registry.access.redhat.com/ubi8/httpd-24 image.

> **NOTE** Universal Base Images (UBI) can be used anywhere, but container software maintained and vetted by Red Hat as well as run on a Red Hat operating system is fully supported. There are hundreds of Apache images that work similarly to this image that you can also try out.

27

Chapter 2 shows how Podman is a great tool for working with containers. In this chapter, I walk you through running the scenario you might use to build a containerized application. You launch a container, modify its contents, create an image, and ship it to a registry. Then I explain how you can do this in an automated way to maintain the security of your container image. Through it all, you will be exposed to many of the Podman command-line interfaces and get a good understanding of how to work with Podman.

If you are an experienced Docker user, you probably just want to skim through this chapter. You will know a lot of it, but there are many features unique to Podman, such as the ability to mount container images (section 2.2.10) and different transports (section 2.2.4). Let's start by running our first container.

NOTE Podman is an open source project under heavy development. Podman is packaged and provided on many different Linux distributions as well as Mac and Windows. These distributions might be shipping older versions of Podman without some of the current features covered in this book. Some examples in this book assume you are using Podman 4.1 or later. If an example does not work, please update your version of Podman to the latest version. Refer to appendix C for further information on installing Podman.

2.1 *Working with containers*

There are thousands of different container images sitting at container registries. Developers, administrators, quality engineers, and general users primarily use the `podman run` command to pull down and run, test, or explore these container images. To start building out containerized applications, the first thing you need to do is start working with a base image. In our examples, you pull and run the registry.access.redhat.com/ubi8/httpd-24 image to container storage in your home directory and start exploring inside the container.

2.1.1 *Exploring containers*

In this section, you will examine a typical Podman command, step by step. You will execute the `podman run` command, which reaches out to the registry.access.redhat.com container registry and begins pulling down the image and storing it locally in your home directory:

```
$ podman run -ti --rm registry.access.redhat.com/ubi8/httpd-24 bash
```

Now I will break down the command you just executed. By default the `podman run` command executes the containerized command in the foreground until the container exits. In this case, you end up at a Bash prompt running within the container and showing the `bash-4.4$` prompt. When you exit this Bash prompt, Podman stops the container.

In this example, you used two options: -t and -i, as -ti, which tells Podman to hook up to the terminal. This connects to the input, output, and error stream of the bash process within the container to your screen, which allows you to interact within the container:

```
$ podman run -ti --rm registry.access.redhat.com/ubi8/httpd-24 bash
```

The --rm option tells Podman to delete the container as soon as the container exits, freeing up all of the container's storage:

```
$ podman run -ti --rm registry.access.redhat.com/ubi8/httpd-24 bash
```

Next, specify the container image, registry.access.redhat.com/ubi8/httpd-24, you are working with. The podman command reaches out to the container registry at registry.access.redhat.com and begins copying down the ubi8/httpd-24:latest image. Podman copies multiple layers (aka blobs), as shown in the following listing, and stores them in the local container storage. You see the progress as the image layers are pulled down. Some images are rather large and can take a long time while being pulled down. If you later run a different container on the same image, Podman skips the image-pulling step, since you already have the correct image in local container storage.

Listing 2.1 Pulling and running a container image from a registry

```
$ podman run -ti --rm registry.access.redhat.com/ubi8/httpd-24 bash
Trying to pull registry.access.redhat.com/
⮕ ubi8/httpd-24:latest...                    ◄──┐ Contact with
Getting image source signatures                 │ the registry
Checking if image destination supports signatures
Copying blob 296e14ee2414 skipped: already exists
Copying blob 356f18f3a935 skipped: already exists
Copying blob 359fed170a21
⮕ [=========================>---------] 11.8MiB / 16.2MiB        Layer
Copying blob 226cafc3a0c6                                       pulling is
⮕ [=====>---------------------------]                           skipped.
⮕ 10.1MiB / 61.1MiB
```

Finally, specify the executable to be run within the container, in this case, bash:

```
$ podman run -ti --rm registry.access.redhat.com/ubi8/httpd-24 bash
...
bash-4.4$
```

> **NOTE** Images almost always have default commands they execute. You only have to specify a command if you want to override the default application the image runs with. In the case of the registry.access.redhat.com/ubi8/httpd-24 image, it runs the Apache web server.

While inside the bash shell container, cat /etc/os-release, and notice it is likely a different OS or a different version than the /etc/os-release outside the container. Explore around in the container, and notice how different it is from your host environment:

```
bash-4.4$ grep PRETTY_NAME /etc/os-release
PRETTY_NAME="Red Hat Enterprise Linux 8.4 (Ootpa)"
```

On my host on a different terminal, the same command outputs

```
$ grep PRETTY_NAME /etc/os-release
PRETTY_NAME="Fedora Linux 35 (Workstation Edition Prerelease)"
```

Back inside the container, you will notice there are a lot fewer commands available:

```
bash-4.4$ ls /usr/bin | wc -l
525
```

However, on the host you see

```
$ ls -l /usr/bin | wc -l
3303
```

Execute the ps command to see what processes are running inside of the container:

```
$ ps
PID TTY          TIME CMD
1 pts/0      00:00:00 bash
2 pts/0      00:00:00 ps
```

You only see two processes: the bash script and the ps command. Needless to say, on my host machine, there are hundreds of processes running (including these two processes). You can further explore the inside of the container to gain an understanding of what is going on within a container.

When you are done, you exit the bash script, and the container shuts down. Since you ran with the --rm option, Podman removes all the container storage and deletes the container. The container image remains in container/storage. Now that you have explored the inner workings of a container, it is time to start working with the default application within the container.

2.1.2   *Running the containerized application*

In the previous example, you pulled and ran bash within a containerized application, but you did not run the application the developer intended you to run. In this next example, you will run the actual application by removing the command and running with a couple of new options.

First, remove the -ti and the --rm options, since you want the container to remain running when the podman command exits. You are not a shell running within the container interactively, since it is just running the containerized web service:

```
$ podman run -d -p 8080:8080 --name myapp registry.access.redhat.com/ubi8/httpd-24
37a1d2e31dbf4fa311a5ca6453f53106eaae2d8b9b9da264015cc3f8864fac22
```

The first option to notice is the -d (--detach) option, which tells Podman to launch the container and then detach from it. Basically, run the container in the background. The Podman command actually exits and leaves the container running. Chapter 6 goes much deeper into what is going on behind the scenes:

```
$ podman run -d -p 8080:8080 --name myapp
     registry.access.redhat.com/ubi8/httpd-24
```

The -p (--publish) option tells Podman to publish or bind the container port 8080 to the host port 8080 when the container is running. With the -p option, the field before the colon refers to the host port, while the field after the colon refers to the container port. In this case, you see that the ports are the same. If you specify only one port, Podman considers this port a container port and randomly picks a host port on which the container port is bound. You can use the podman port command to discover which ports are bound to a container.

> **Listing 2.2 Example of the podman port command**

```
$ podman port myapp
8080/tcp -> 0.0.0.0:8080   ◁——
```
Shows that port 8080/tcp inside the container is bound to all of the host networks (0.0.0.0) at port 8080

By default, containers are created within their own network namespace, meaning they are not bound to the host network but to their virtualized network. Suppose I execute the container without the -p option. In that case, the Apache server within the container binds to the network interface within the container's network namespace, but Apache is not bound to the host network.

Only processes within the container are able to connect to port 8080 to communicate with the web server. By executing the command with the -p option, Podman connects the port from inside the container to the host network at the specified port. The connection allows external processes like a web browser to read from the web service.

> **NOTE** If you are running containers in rootless mode, covered in chapter 3, Podman users are by default not permitted to bind to ports < 1024 by the kernel. Some containers want to bind to lower ports like port 80, which is allowed inside the container, but -p 80:80 fails, since 80 is less than 1024. Using -p 8080:80 causes Podman to bind the host's port 8080 to port 80 within the container. The upstream Podman repo contains troubleshooting information on problems like binding to ports less than 1024 and many others (see http://mng.bz/69ry).

The -p option can map port numbers inside the container to different port numbers outside the container:

```
$ podman run -d -p 8080:8080 --name myapp
    registry.access.redhat.com/ubi8/httpd-24
```

In the example name, the container myapp is using the --name myapp option. Specifying a name makes it easier to find the container, and it allows you to specify a name that can then be used for other commands (e.g., podman stop myapp). If you don't specify a name, Podman automatically generates a unique container name along with a container ID. All of the Podman commands that interact with containers can use either the name or the ID:

```
$ podman run -d --name myapp -p 8080:8080
    registry.access.redhat.com/ubi8/httpd-24
```

When the podman run command completes, the container is running. Since this container is running in detached mode, Podman prints out the container ID and exits, but the container remains running:

```
$ podman run -d -p 8080:8080 --name myapp
    registry.access.redhat.com/ubi8/httpd-24
37a1d2e31dbf4fa311a5ca6453f53106eaae2d8b9b9da264015cc3f8864fac22
```

Now that the container is running, you can launch a web browser to communicate with the web server inside of the container at localhost port 8080 (see figure 2.1):

```
$ web-browser localhost:8080
```

Congratulations! You have launched your first containerized application.

Now imagine you want to start another container. You can execute a similar command with just a couple of changes:

```
$ podman run -d -p 8081:8080 --name myapp1 \
➥ registry.access.redhat.com/ubi8/httpd-24
fa41173e4568a8fa588690d3177150a454c63b53bdfa52865b5f8f7e4d7de1e1
```

Notice you need to change the name of the container to myapp1; otherwise, the podman run command fails with the myapp name because the container previously existed. Also you need to change the -p option to use 8081 for the host port because the previous container, myapp, is currently running and is bound to port 8080. The second container isn't allowed to bind to port 8080 until the first container exits:

```
$ podman run -d -p 8081:8080 --name myapp1
    registry.access.redhat.com/ubi8/httpd-24
```

The podman create command is almost identical to the podman run command. The create command pulls the image if it is not in container storage and configures the

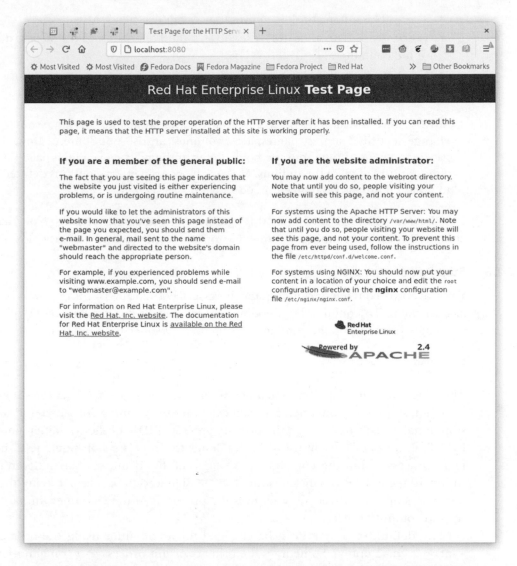

Figure 2.1   Web browser window connecting to the ubi8/httpd-24 container running in Podman

container information to make it ready to run but never executes the container. It is often used together with the `podman start` command described in section 2.1.4. You might want to create a container and then later use a systemd unit file to start and stop the container.

Some notable `podman run` options include the following:

- `–user USERNAME`—This tells Podman to run the container as a specific user defined in the image. By default, Podman will run the container as root, unless the container image specifies a default user.

- `--rm`—This automatically removes the container when it exits.
- `--tty -(t)`—This allocates a pseudo `-tty` and attaches it to the standard input of the container.
- `--interactive (-i)`—This connects `stdin` to the primary process of the container. These options give you an interactive shell within the container.

NOTE There are dozens of `podman run` options available, allowing you to change security features, namespaces, volumes, and so on. Some of these I use and explain throughout the book. Refer to the `podman-run` man page for a description of all of the options. Most of the `podman create` options defined in table 2.1 are also available for `podman run`.

Use the `man podman-run` command for information about all options. Now that the container is up and running, it is time to stop the container and go to the next step.

2.1.3 *Stopping containers*

You have two containers running and have tested them by running a web browser against them. To continue the development by actually adding some content to the web page, you can stop the containers using the `podman stop` command:

```
$ podman stop myapp
```

The `stop` command stops the container started with the previous `podman run` command.

When stopping a container, Podman examines the running container and sends a stop signal, usually `SIGTERM`, to the primary process (PID1) of the container, and then by default it waits 10 seconds for the container to stop. The stop signal tells the primary process within the container to exit gracefully. If the container doesn't stop within 10 seconds, Podman sends the `SIGKILL` signal to the process, forcing the container to stop. The 10-second wait gives the processes in the container time to clean up and commit changes.

The default stop signal can be changed for a container using the `podman run --stop-signal` option. Sometimes the primary or init process of a container ignores `SIGTERM` (e.g., containers that use systemd as the primary process inside a container). systemd ignores `SIGTERM` and specifies that it shuts down using the `SIGRTMIN+3` (signal #37) signal. The stop signal can be embedded in container images, as I describe in section 2.3.

Some containers ignore the `SIGTERM` stop signal, which means you have to wait 10 seconds for the container to exit. If you know the container ignores the default stop signal, and you don't care about the container cleaning up, you can just add the `-t 0` option to `podman stop` to send the `SIGKILL` signal right away:

```
$ podman stop -t 0 myapp1
myapp1
```

Podman has a similar command, `podman kill`, which sends the specified kill signal. The `podman kill` command can be useful when you want to send signals into the container without actually stopping the container.

Some notable Podman stop options include the following:

- `--timeout (-t)`—This sets the timeout; `-t 0` sends the `SIGKILL` without waiting for the container to stop.
- `--latest (-l)`—This is a useful option to allow you to stop the last created container rather than having to use the container name or container ID. Most Podman commands that require you to specify a container name or ID also accept the `--latest` option. This is only available on Linux machines.
- `--all`—This tells Podman to stop all running containers. Similarly to `--latest`, Podman commands that require a container name or container ID parameter also take the `--all` option.

Use the `man podman-stop` command for information about all options.

Eventually, your system will have lots of stopped containers, and sometimes you will need to restart them (e.g., if the system was rebooted). Another common use case is to first create a container and later start it. The next section explains how to start a container.

2.1.4 Starting containers

The container you created has now been stopped. Next, you may want to start it back up again using the command in the following listing.

Listing 2.3 Example of starting a container

```
$ podman start myapp          The start command prints the names
myapp                         of the containers that were started.
```

The `podman start` command starts one or more containers. This command will output the container ID, indicating that your container is up and running. You can now reconnect to it with a web browser. One common use case for `podman start` is starting a container after a reboot to start all of the containers that were stopped during shutdown.

Some favorite Podman start options include these:

- `--all`—This starts all of the stopped containers in container storage.
- `--attach`—This attaches your terminal to the output of the container.
- `--interactive (-i)`—This attaches the terminal input to the container.

Use the `man podman-start` command for information about all options.

After you've been using Podman for a while and have pulled down and run many different container images, you might want to figure out which containers are running or which containers you have in local storage. You will need to be able to list these containers.

2.1.5   *Listing containers*

You can list the running containers and all of the containers that were previously created. Use the `podman ps` command to list containers:

```
$ podman ps
CONTAINER ID IMAGE                            COMMAND        CREATED \
    STATUS         PORTS         NAMES
b1255e94d084 registry.access.redhat.com/ubi8/httpd-24:latest /usr/bin/run-\
    http... 6 minutes ago Up 4 minutes ago 0.0.0.0:8080->8080/tcp myapp
```

Notice the `podman ps` command by default lists the running containers. Use the `--all` option to see all of the containers:

```
$ podman ps --all
CONTAINER ID IMAGE                            COMMAND        CREATED \
    STATUS         PORTS         NAMES
b1255e94d084 registry.access.redhat.com/ubi8/httpd-24:latest /usr/bin/run-\
    http... 9 minutes ago Up 8 minutes ago    0.0.0.0:8080->8080/tcp myapp
3efee4d39965 registry.access.redhat.com/ubi8/httpd-24:latest /usr/bin/run-\
    http... 7 minutes ago Exited (0) 3 minutes ago 0.0.0.0:8081->8080/tcp myapp1
```

Some notable `podman ps` options include the following:

- `--all`—This tells Podman to list all containers rather than just running containers.
- `--quiet`—This tells Podman to only print the container IDs.
- `--size`—This tells Podman to return the amount of disk space currently used for each container other than the images they are based on.

Use the `man podman-ps` command for information about all options. Now that you know all of the containers you have on the system, you might want to inspect their internals.

2.1.6   *Inspecting containers*

To fully understand a container, sometimes you want to know which image a container was based on, which environment variables a container gets by default, or what the security settings used for a container are. The `podman ps` command gives us some data about the containers, but if you want to really examine information about the container, you can use the `podman inspect` command.

The `podman inspect` command can also be used to inspect images, networks, volumes, and pods. The `podman container inspect` command is also available and specific to containers. But most users just type the shorter `podman inspect` command:

```
$ podman inspect myapp
[
  {
    "Id":
    "240271ae90480d3836b1477e5c0b49fbd3883846ca474e3f6effdfb271f4ff54",
    "Created": "2021-09-27T05:27:47.163828842-04:00",
    "Path": "container-entrypoint",
```

```
    "Args": [
        "/usr/bin/run-httpd"
    ],
...
]
```

As you can see, the `podman inspect` command outputs a large JSON file—307 lines on my machine. All of this information is eventually handed down the OCI runtime to launch the container. When using the `inspect` command, it is often better to pipe its output to `less` or `grep` to find particular fields you are interested in. Alternatively, you can use the format option. If you want to examine the command executed when you start the container, execute the following.

Listing 2.4   Inspecting a specified command to execute the container

```
$ podman inspect --format '{{ .Config.Cmd }}' myapp
[/usr/bin/run-httpd]
```
◁—— **inspect is displaying data from the OCI image specification.**

Or if you want to see the stop signal, execute the following.

Listing 2.5   Inspecting the stop signal to be used when stopping the container

```
$ podman inspect --format '{{ .Config.StopSignal }}' myapp
15
```
◁——┐ **The default stop signal for all containers is 15 (SIGTERM).**

Some notable `podman inspect` options include the following:

- `--latest` (`-l`)—This is handy in that it allows you to quickly inspect the last created container rather than specifying the container name or container ID.
- `--format`—This is useful, as shown previously, to extract particular fields out of the JSON.
- `--size`—This adds the amount of disk space the container is using. Gathering this information takes a long time, so it is not done by default.

Use the `man podman-inspect` command for information about all options. After you inspect a container, you might realize you no longer need that container taking up storage, so you need to remove it.

2.1.7   Removing containers

If you are done using a container, you may want to remove the container to free up disk space or reuse the container name. Remember when you started a second container called `myapp1`? You no longer need it, so you can remove it. Make sure to stop the container (section 2.1.3) before removing it. Then use the `podman rm` command to remove container:

```
$ podman rm myapp1
3efee4d3996532769356ffea23e1f50710019d4efc704d39026c5bffd6aa18be
```

Some notable `podman rm` options include the following:

- `--all`—This option is useful if you want to remove all your containers.
- `--force`—This option tells Podman to stop all the running containers when removing.

Use the `man podman-rm` command for information about all options. Now that you understand a few commands, it is time to start modifying the running container.

2.1.8   *exec-ing into a container*

Often, when a container is running, you might want to start another process within the container to debug or examine what is going on. In some cases, you may want to modify some of the content the container is using.

Imagine you want to go into your container and modify the web page it is showing. You can `exec` into the container using the `podman exec` command. Use the `--interactive` (`-i`) option to allow you to execute commands within the container. You need to specify the name of the container `myapp` and execute the Bash script while in the container. If you stopped the `myapp` container, you need to restart it, since `podman exec` only works on running containers.

In the following example, you will `exec` a `bash` process into the container to create the /var/www/html/index.html file. You will write HTML content that causes the containerized website to display `Hello World`:

```
$ podman exec -i myapp bash -c 'cat > /var/www/html/index.html' << _EOF
<html>
 <head>
 </head>
 <body>
  <h1>Hello World</h1>
 </body>
</html>
_EOF
```

exec-ing back into the container a second time, you can see that the file was successfully modified. This shows that modifications to a container via `exec` are permanent to the container and will remain even if you stopped and restarted the container. A key difference between `podman run` and `podman exec` is that `run` creates a new container off of an image with processes running inside, while `exec` starts processes inside of existing containers:

```
$ podman exec myapp cat /var/www/html/index.html
<html>
 <head>
 </head>
 <body>
  <h1>Hello World</h1>
 </body>
</html>
```

Now let's connect a web browser to the container to see if the content has changed (see figure 2.2):

```
$ web-browser localhost:8080
```

Figure 2.2   Web browser window connecting to the ubi8/httpd-24 container running in Podman with updated Hello World HTML

Some notable podman exec options include the following:

- --tty—This connects a -tty to the exec session.
- --interactive—The -i option tells Podman to run in interactive mode, meaning you can interact with an exec-ed program, like a shell.

Use the man podman-exec command for information about all options.

Now that you have created an application, you might want to share it with others. First, you need to commit the container to an image.

2.1.9   Creating an image from a container

Developers often run containers from a base image to create a new container environment. Once they are done, they pack this environment into a container image to be able to share it with other users. Those users can then use Podman to launch the containerized application. You can do this with Podman by committing the container to an OCI image.

First, stop or pause the container to make sure nothing gets modified while you are committing it:

```
$ podman stop myapp
```

Now you can execute the podman commit command to take your application container, myapp, and commit it, creating a new image named myimage:

```
$ podman commit myapp myimage
Getting image source signatures
Copying blob e39c3abf0df9 skipped: already exists
Copying blob 8f26704f753c skipped: already exists
Copying blob 83310c7c677c skipped: already exists
Copying blob 654b3bf1361e skipped: already exists
Copying blob 9e816183404c done          Copying config e38084bb8a done
Writing manifest to image destination
Storing signatures
e38084bb8a76104a7cac22b919f67646119aff235bb1cfcba5478cc1fbf1c9eb
```

Now you can continue running the existing myapp container by calling podman start, or you can create a new container based on myimage:

```
$ podman run -d --name myapp1 -p 8080:8080 myimage
0052cb32c8e63b845ac5dfd5ba176b8204535c2c6cafa3277453424de601263f
```

> **NOTE** Using the podman commit command to create an image is not a common method. The entire process of building container images can be scripted and automated using podman build. See section 2.3 for more information on this process.

Some notable podman commit options include the following:

- --pause—This pauses a running container during the commit. Notice I stopped the container before doing the commit, while I could have simply paused it. The podman pause and podman unpause commands allow you to pause and unpause containers directly.
- --change—This option allows you to commit instructions on using the image. The instructions are CMD, ENTRYPOINT, ENV, EXPOSE, LABEL, ONBUILD, STOPSIGNAL, USER, VOLUME, and WORKDIR. These instructions match up with the directives in the Containerfile or Dockerfile.

Use the man podman-commit command for information about all options. Table 2.1 lists all the Podman container commands.

Now that you have committed your container to an image, it is time to show how Podman can work with images.

> **NOTE** You have examined a few of the Podman container commands, but there are many more. Use the podman-container(1) man pages to explore all of them as well as a full description of commands specified in this section.

Table 2.1 Podman container commands

Command	Man page	Description
attach	podman-container-attach(1)	Attach to a running container.
checkpoint	podman-container-checkpoint(1)	Checkpoint a container.
cleanup	podman-container-cleanup(1)	Clean up network and mount points of a container.
commit	podman-container-commit(1)	Commit a container into an image.
cp	podman-container-cp(1)	Copy files or folders into and out of containers.
create	podman-container-create(1)	Create a new container.
diff	podman-container-diff(1)	Inspect changes in a container's filesystem.
exec	podman-container-exec(1)	Run a process in a container.

Table 2.1 Podman container commands *(continued)*

Command	Man page	Description
exists	podman-container-exists(1)	Check if a container exists.
export	podman-container-export(1)	Export a container's filesystem as a TAR archive.
init	podman-container-init(1)	Init a container.
inspect	podman-container-inspect(1)	Display detailed information on a container.
kill	podman-container-kill(1)	Send a signal to the primary process in the container.
List (ps)	podman-container-list(1)	List all of the containers.
logs	podman-container-logs(1)	Fetch logs for a container.
mount	podman-container-mount(1)	Mount a container's root filesystem.
pause	podman-container-pause(1)	Pause container.
port	podman-container-port(1)	List port mappings for a container.
prune	podman-container-prune(1)	Remove all non-running containers.
rename	podman-container-rename(1)	Rename an existing container.
restart	podman-container-restart(1)	Restart a container.
restore	podman-container-restore(1)	Restore a checkpointed container.
rm	podman-container-rm(1)	Remove a container.
run	podman-container-run(1)	Run a command in a new container.
runlabel	podman-container-runlabel(1)	Execute the command described by an image label.
start	podman-container-start(1)	Start a container.
stats	podman-container-stats(1)	Display statistics for a container.
stop	podman-container-stop(1)	Stop a container.
top	podman-container-top(1)	Display running process in a container.
unmount	podman-container-unmount(1)	Unmount a container's root filesystem.
unpause	podman-container-unpause(1)	Unpause all the containers in a pod.
wait	podman-container-wait(1)	Wait for a container to exit.

2.2 Working with container images

In the previous section, you tried basic operations with containers, including inspecting and committing to a container image. In this section, you will try working with container images, learn how they differ from containers, and learn how to share them through container registries.

2.2.1 *Differences between a container and an image*

One of the problems with computer programming is that the same names are constantly used for different purposes. In the container world, there is no more overused term than *container*. Often *container* refers to the running processes launched by Podman. But *container* can also refer to container data as the non-running objects sitting in container storage. As you saw in the previous section, `podman ps --all` shows running and non-running containers.

Another example is the term *namespace*, which is used in many different ways. I often get confused when people talk about namespaces within Kubernetes. Some people hear the term and think of *virtual clusters*, but when I hear it I think of Linux namespaces used with Pods and Containers. Similarly, *image* can refer to a VM image, a container image, an OCI image, or a Docker image stored at a container registry.

I think of containers as executing processes within an environment or something that is being prepared to run. In contrast, images are *committed containers*, which are prepared to be shared with others. Other users or systems can use these images to create new containers.

Container images are just committed containers. The OCI defines the format of an image. Podman uses the container/image library (https://github.com/containers/image) for all of its interaction with images. Container images can be stored in different types of storage or transports, as *container/image* refers to them. These transports can be container registries, Docker archives, OCI archives, `docker-daemon`, as well as containers/storage. See section 2.2.4 for more information on transports.

In the context of Podman, I usually refer to images as the content stored locally in a container storage or in container registries like docker.io and quay.io. Podman uses the GitHub container/storage library (https://github.com/containers/storage) for handling locally stored images. Let's take a closer look at it.

The container/storage library provides the concept of a storage container. Basically, storage containers are intermediate storage content that hasn't been committed yet. Think of them as files on disk and some JSON describing the content. Podman has its own datastore of data related to a Podman container, and Podman needs to deal with multiple users of its containers at the same time. It relies on filesystem locking provided by containers/storage to make sure hundreds of Podman executables can reliably share the same datastore.

When you commit a container to storage, Podman copies the container storage to the image storage. Images are stored in a series of layers, with every commit creating a new layer.

I like to think of an image like a wedding cake (figure 2.3). In our previous example, you used the ubi8/httpd-24 image, which is two layers: the base layer is ubi8, and then the image provided added the `httpd` package and a few others to create the ubi8/httpd-24. Now when you commit your container in the previous section, Podman adds another layer on top of the ubi8/httpd-24 image called `myimage`.

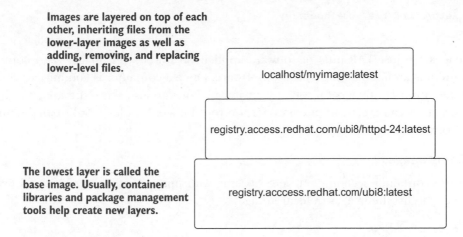

Images are layered on top of each other, inheriting files from the lower-layer images as well as adding, removing, and replacing lower-level files.

localhost/myimage:latest

registry.access.redhat.com/ubi8/httpd-24:latest

The lowest layer is called the base image. Usually, container libraries and package management tools help create new layers.

registry.acccess.redhat.com/ubi8:latest

Figure 2.3   A wedding cake display showing the images making up our Hello World application.

One handy Podman command for showing the layers of an image is the `podman image tree` command:

```
$ podman image tree myimage
Image ID: 2c7e43d88038
Tags:    [localhost/myimage:latest]
Size:    461.7MB
Image Layers
├── ID: e39c3abf0df9 Size: 233.6MB
├── ID: 42c81bd2b468 Size: 20.48kB Top Layer of:
│    [registry.access.redhat.com/ubi8:latest]
├── ID: 51a7beaa0b88 Size: 57.43MB
├── ID: 519e681b5702 Size: 170.6MB Top Layer of:
│    [registry.access.redhat.com/ubi8/httpd-24:latest]
└── ID: bc3dcdefdac3 Size: 69.63kB Top Layer of: [localhost/myimage:latest
     localhost/myapp:latest]
```

You can see that the image `myimage` consists of five layers.

Another useful Podman command, `podman image diff`, allows you to see the actual files and directories that have been changed (C), added (A), or deleted (D) compared to another image or the lower layer:

```
$ podman image diff myimage ubi8/httpd-24
C /etc/group
C /etc/httpd/conf
C /etc/httpd/conf/httpd.conf
C /etc/httpd/conf.d
C /etc/httpd/conf.d/ssl.conf
C /etc/httpd/tls
C /etc
C /etc/httpd
A /etc/httpd/tls/localhost.crt
```

```
A /etc/httpd/tls/localhost.key
...
```

Images are just TAR diffs of software applied on lower-level images, and container content is an uncommitted layer of software. Once a container is committed, you can create other containers on top of your image. You can also share the image with others, so they can create other containers on your image. Now let's look at all the images in your container storage.

2.2.2   Listing images

In the container section, you were working with images and used command `podman images` to list the images in local storage:

```
$ podman images
REPOSITORY                TAG        IMAGE ID        CREATED        SIZE
localhost/myimage         latest     2c7e43d88038    46 hours ago   462 MB
registry.access.redhat
➥.com/ubi8/httpd-24       latest     8594be0a0b57    5 weeks ago    462 MB
registry.access.redhat
➥.com/ubi8               latest     ad42391b9b46    5 weeks ago    234 MB
```

Let's look at the different fields in the default output. Table 2.2 describes the different fields and data available with the `podman images` command. You will use the `podman images` command throughout this section.

Table 2.2   Default fields listed by the `podman images` command

Heading	Description
Repository	Complete name of the image.
TAG	Version (tag) of the image. Image tagging is covered in section 2.2.6.
IMAGE ID	Unique identifier of the image. It is generated by Podman as a SHA256 hash of the image's JSON configuration object.
CREATED	Elapsed time since the image was created. Images are sorted by this field by default.
SIZE	The amount of storage being used by the image.

NOTE   Over time, the amount of storage used by all the images you pull grows. It is relatively common for users to run out of disk space, so you should monitor the size of images and containers, removing them when you are no longer using them. Use the `man podman-system-prune` command for more information on cleaning up.

One notable `podman image` option is the following:

- `--all`—This option is useful for listing all images. By default, `podman-images` lists only the images currently in use. When an image is replaced by a newer image with the same tag, the previous image is tagged as <none><none>; These images are called dangling images. I cover dangling images in section 2.3.1.

Use the `man podman-images` command for information about all options. Similarly to containers, you will likely want to examine the configuration information associated with an image by inspecting it.

2.2.3 Inspecting images

In the previous sections, I mentioned a couple of commands to examine images. I used the `podman image diff` to examine files and directories created or deleted between images. I also showed you a way to see the image hierarchy or wedding cake layers of images using the `podman image tree` command.

Sometimes you may want to examine the configuration of an image; use the `podman image inspect` command for this. The `podman inspect` command can also be used to inspect images, but the names can conflict with containers, so I prefer to use the specific image command:

```
$ podman image inspect myimage
[
    {
        "Id": "3b8fcf9081b4c4e6c16d763b8d02684df0737f3557a1e03ebfe4cc7cd6562135",
        "Digest":
"sha256:ff49aa6253ae47569d5aadbd73d70e7d0431bcf3a2f57b1b56feecdb531029a3",
        "RepoTags": [
            "localhost/myimage:latest"
        ],
        "RepoDigests": [
            "localhost/myimage@sha256:ff49aa6253ae47569d5aadbd73d70e7d0431bcf3a2f57b1b\
    ➥ 56feecdb531029a3"
        ],
    ...
]
```

As you can see, this command outputs a large JSON array—153 lines in the previous example—that includes the data used for the OCI Image Format specification. When you create a container from an image, this information is used as one of the inputs to create the container.

When using the `inspect` command, it is often better to pipe its output to `less` or `grep` to find particular fields you are interested in. Alternatively, you can use the `--format` option.

If you want to to examine the default command to be executed from this image, execute the following:

```
$ podman image inspect --format '{{ .Config.Cmd }}' myimage
[/usr/bin/run-httpd]
```

Or if you want to see the stop signal, execute

```
$ podman image inspect --format '{{ .Config.StopSignal }}' myimage
```

As you can see, nothing is output, meaning the developer of the application did not specify a `STOPSIGNAL`. When you build a container off of this image, the `STOPSIGNAL` is the default, 15, unless you override it via the command line.

One notable `podman image inspect` option is the following:

- `--format`—This is useful as you see above to extract particular fields out of the json.

Use the `man podman-image-inspect` command for information about the command.

Once you are happy with a container and commit it to an image, the next step is sharing it with others or perhaps running it on another system. You need to push the image out to other types of container storage, usually a container registry.

2.2.4   *Pushing images*

In Podman, you use the `podman push` command to copy an image and all of its layers out of container storage and push it to other forms of container image storage, like a container registry. Podman supports a few different types of container storage, which it calls transports.

CONTAINER TRANSPORTS

Podman uses the containers/image library (https://github.com/containers/image) for pulling and pushing images. I describe the containers/image project as a library for copying images between different types of container storage. One storage, as you have seen, is containers/storage.

When pushing an image, the `[destination]` is specified using `transport:Image-Name` format. If no transport is specified, the `docker` (container registry) transport is used by default.

One of the novel things that Docker did, as I explained earlier, was invent the container registry concept—basically, a web server that contains container images. The docker.io, quay.io, and Artifactory web servers are all examples of container registries. The Docker engineering team defined a protocol for pulling and pushing these images from the container registries, which I refer to as the container registry or docker transport.

When I want to run a container of an image, I can fully specify the image name, including the transport like the following command:

```
$ podman run docker://registry.access.redhat.com/ubi8/httpd-24:latest echo hello
hello
```

For Podman, `docker://` transport is the default; it can be skipped for convenience:

```
$ podman run registry.access.redhat.com/ubi8/httpd-24:latest echo hello
hello
```

The `myimage` image you created in the previous section was created locally, which means it doesn't have a registry associated with it. By default, locally created images have the localhost registry associated with them. You can see the images in the containers/storage using the podman `images` command:

```
$ podman images
REPOSITORY                       TAG      IMAGE ID       CREATED       SIZE
localhost/myimage                latest   2c7e43d88038   46 hours ago  462 MB
registry.access.redhat
➡ .com/ubi8/httpd-24             latest   8594be0a0b57   5 weeks ago   462 MB
registry.access.redhat
➡ .com/ubi8                      latest   ad42391b9b46   5 weeks ago   234 MB
```

If the image has a remote registry associated with it (e.g., registry.access.redhat.com/ubi8), it can be pushed without specifying the [destination] field. On the contrary, since localhost/myimage does not have a registry associated with it, remote registry needs to be specified (e.g., quay.io/rhatdan):

```
$ podman push myimage quay.io/rhatdan/myimage
Getting image source signatures
Copying blob 164d51196137 done
Copying blob 8f26704f753c done
Copying blob 83310c7c677c done
Copying blob 654b3bf1361e [==================>------------------] 82.0MiB /
    162.7MiB
Copying blob e39c3abf0df9 [================>---------------------] 100.0MiB /
    222.8MiB
```

NOTE Before executing the podman push command, I logged into the quay.io/rhatdan account using podman login, which is covered in the next section.

After the push command is finished, the image becomes available for pull for other users, given they have access to this container registry. Table 2.3 describes the supported transports for different types of container's storage.

Table 2.3 Podman-supported transports

Transport	Description
Container registry (Docker)	Default transport. This references a container image stored in a remote container image registry. Container registry is a place for storing and sharing container images (e.g., docker.io or quay.io).
oci	References a container image, compliant with the Open Container Image Layout Specification. The manifest and layer tarballs as individual files are located in the local directory.
dir	References a container image, compliant with the Docker image layout. It is very similar to the oci transport but stores the files using the legacy Docker format. It is a nonstandardized format, primarily useful for debugging or non-invasive container inspection.
docker-archive	References a container image in Docker image layout, which is packed into a TAR archive.

Table 2.3   Podman-supported transports *(continued)*

Transport	Description
`oci-archive`	References an image compliant with the Open Container Image Layout Specification, which is packed into a TAR archive. It is very similar to the `docker-archive` transport, but it stores an image in OCI format.
`docker-daemon`	References an image stored in the Docker daemon's internal storage. Since the Docker daemon requires root privileges, Podman has to be run by the root user.
`container-storage`	References an image located in a local container storage. It is not a transport but more of a mechanism for storing images. It can be used to convert other transports into `container-storage`. Podman defaults to using `container-storage` for local images.

You want to push your image to a container registry, but if you try to push it, the container registry rejects your push, since you have not provided login authorization information. You need to execute `podman login` to create the authorization.

2.2.5   *podman login: Logging into a container registry*

In the previous section, I pushed the image to my container registry by executing the following:

```
$ podman push myimage quay.io/rhatdan/myimage
```

However, I left out a key step: logging into a container registry using correct credentials. This is a necessary step for pushing a container image. It is also required for pulling a container image from a private registry.

To follow along in this section, you need to set up an account at a container registry; there are several container registries available to choose from. The https://quay.io and https://docker.io registries both provide free accounts and storage. Your company might have a private registry, where you can also get an account.

For the examples, I will continue to use my rhatdan account at quay.io. Log in to get your credentials:

```
$ podman login quay.io
Username: rhatdan
Password:
Login Succeeded!
```

Notice the Podman command prompts you for your username and password at the registry. The `podman login` command has options to pass the username/password information on the command line to avoid the prompt, allowing you to automate the login process.

To store authentication information for the user, the `podman login` command creates an auth.json file. By default, this is stored in the /run/user/$UID/containers/auth.json file:

```
cat /run/user/3267/containers/auth.json
{
  "auths": {
    "quay.io": {
      "auth": "OBSCURED-BASE64-PASSWORD"
    }
  }
}
```

The auth.json file contains your registry password in a Base64-encoded string; there is no cryptography involved. Therefore, the auth.json file needs to be protected. Podman defaults to storing the file in /run because it is a temporary filesystem and is destroyed when you log out or the system is rebooted. The /run/user/$UID/containers directory is not accessible by other users on the system.

It is possible to override the location by specifying the --auth-file option. Alternatively, you can use the REGISTRY_AUTH_FILE environment variable to modify its location. If both are specified, the --auth-file option is used. All container tools use this file to access the container registry.

It is possible to run the podman login command multiple times to log in to multiple registries, storing the login information in the same authorization file with a different stanza.

> **NOTE** Podman supports other mechanisms for storing the password information. These are called *credential helpers.*

After you are done using the registry, you can log out by executing podman logout. This command deletes the cached credentials stored in the auth.json file:

```
$ podman logout quay.io
Removed login credentials for quay.io
```

Some notable podman login and logout options include the following:

- --username, (-u—This provides the Podman username to use when logging into the registry.
- --authfile—This tells Podman to store the authorization file in a different location. You can also use the REGISTRY_AUTH_FILE environment variable to change the location.
- --all—This allows you to log out of all of the registries.

Use the man podman-login and man podman-logout commands for information about all options.

Notice when you pushed the image to a container registry, you renamed myimage to quay.io/rhatdan/myimage:

```
$ podman push myimage quay.io/rhatdan/myimage
```

It'd be nice to just have the local image named quay.io/rhatdan/myimage, in which case you could have just executed

```
$ podman push quay.io/rhatdan/myimage
```

In the next section, you will learn how to add names to images.

2.2.6   *Tagging images*

Earlier in this chapter, I pointed out that locally created images are created with a localhost registry. Images get created with the localhost registry when you commit a container to an image or if you use podman build to build an image. Podman has a mechanism to add additional names to images; it calls these names tags, and the command is podman tag.

Using the podman images command, list the image(s) in container/storage:

```
$ podman images
REPOSITORY                     TAG        IMAGE ID          CREATED          SIZE
localhost/myimage              latest     2c7e43d88038    46 \hours ago     462 MB
registry.access.redhat
➥.com/ubi8/httpd-24            latest     8594be0a0b57     5 weeks ago      462 MB
registry.access.redhat
➥.com/ubi8                     latest     ad42391b9b46     5 weeks ago      234 MB
```

You will want the final image you plan on shipping to be referred to as quay.io/rhatdan/myimage. To achieve this, add that name with the following podman tag command:

```
$ podman tag myimage quay.io/rhatdan/myimage
```

Now run podman images again to examine the images. You will see that the name is now quay.io/rhatdan/myimage. Notice that the localhost/myimage and quay.io/rhatdan/myimage have the same image ID of 2c7e43d88038:

```
$ podman images
REPOSITORY                     TAG        IMAGE ID          CREATED          SIZE
localhost/myimage              latest     2c7e43d88038    46 hours ago      462 MB
quay.io/rhatdan/myimage        latest     2c7e43d88038    46 hours ago      462 MB
registry.access.redhat
➥.com/ubi8/httpd-24            latest     8594be0a0b57     5 weeks ago      462 MB
registry.access.redhat
➥.com/ubi8                     latest     ad42391b9b46     5 weeks ago      234 MB
```

Since the images have the same image ID, they are the same image with multiple names. Now you can interact directly with quay.io/rhatdan/myimage. First, you need to log back in to quay.io:

```
$ podman login --username rhatdan quay.io
Password:
Login Succeeded!
```

Now push without requiring the destination name:

```
$ podman push quay.io/rhatdan/myimage
Getting image source signatures
…
Storing signatures
```

That was much simpler.

Let's tag the previously used image with a version, 1.0:

```
$ podman tag quay.io/rhatdan/myimage quay.io/rhatdan/myimage:1.0
```

Once again, examine the images; notice that `myimage` now has three different names/tags. All three have the same image ID of `2c7e43d88038`:

```
$ podman images
REPOSITORY                     TAG        IMAGE ID        CREATED         SIZE
localhost/myimage              latest     2c7e43d88038    46 hours ago    462 MB
quay.io/rhatdan/myimage        1.0        2c7e43d88038    46 hours ago    462 MB
quay.io/rhatdan/myimage        latest     2c7e43d88038    46 hours ago    462 MB
registry.access.redhat
➥.com/ubi8/httpd-24            latest     8594be0a0b57    5 weeks ago     462 MB
registry.access.redhat
➥.com/ubi8                     latest     ad42391b9b46    5 weeks ago     234 MB
```

Now you can push the 1.0 version of the `myimage` (application) to the registry:

```
$ podman push quay.io/rhatdan/myimage:1.0
Getting image source signatures
Copying blob 8f26704f753c skipped: already exists
Copying blob e39c3abf0df9 skipped: already exists
Copying blob 654b3bf1361e skipped: already exists
Copying blob 83310c7c677c skipped: already exists
Copying blob 164d51196137 [--------------------------------------] 0.0b / 0.0b
Copying config 2c7e43d880 [--------------------------------------] 0.0b / 4.0KiB
Writing manifest to image destination
Storing signatures
```

Users can pull either the latest image or the 1.0 version. Later, when you build version 2.0 of your application, you can store both images at the registry. You can run both version 1.0 and 2.0 of your application on the host at the same time.

Use a web browser (e.g., Firefox, Chrome, Safari, Internet Explorer, or Microsoft Edge) to look at the images at quay.io. You can see 1.0 and the latest image in figure 2.4:

```
$ web-browser quay.io/repository/rhatdan/myimage?tab=tags
```

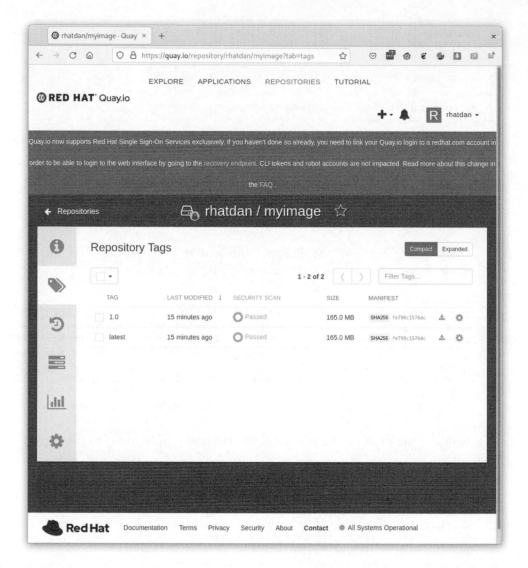

Figure 2.4   List of `myimage` tags on quay.io (https://quay.io/repository/rhatdan/myimage/?tab=tags)

Now that you have pushed your image to a container registry, you may want to free up storage from your home directory by removing the images.

NOTE   Contrary to common sense, the tag `latest` does not refer to the most up-to-date image in the repository. It is just another tag with no magic involved. Even worse, because it is being used as a default tag for images pushed without tags, it could refer to any random version of an image. There could be newer images in the container registry than your local container's storage

with this tag. Thus, it is always better to refer to the specific version of the
image you want to use, rather than relying on the latest.

2.2.7   Removing images

Over time, images can take up a lot of disk space. Thus, it will be a good idea to
remove images you no longer use. Let's list local images first:

```
$ podman images
REPOSITORY                      TAG      IMAGE ID        CREATED       SIZE
localhost/myimage               1.0      2c7e43d88038    46 hours ago  462 MB
quay.io/rhatdan/myimage         1.0      2c7e43d88038    46 hours ago  462 MB
quay.io/rhatdan/myimage         latest   2c7e43d88038    46 hours ago  462 MB
registry.access.redhat
➥.com/ubi8/httpd-24             latest   8594be0a0b57    5 weeks ago   462 MB
registry.access.redhat
➥.com/ubi8                      latest   ad42391b9b46    5 weeks ago   234 MB
```

Use the podman rmi command to remove local images:

```
$ podman rmi localhost/myimage
Untagged: localhost/myimage:latest
```

Listing the local images again, you will see that the command didn't actually remove
the image but only the localhost tag from the image. Podman still has two references
to the same image ID: the actual content of the image has not been removed. None of
the disk space was freed up:

```
$ podman images
REPOSITORY                      TAG      IMAGE ID        CREATED       SIZE
quay.io/rhatdan/myimage         1.0      2c7e43d88038    46 hours ago  462 MB
quay.io/rhatdan/myimage         latest   2c7e43d88038    46 hours ago  462 MB
registry.access.redhat
➥.com/ubi8/httpd-24             latest   8594be0a0b57    5 weeks ago   462 MB
registry.access.redhat
➥.com/ubi8                      latest   ad42391b9b46    5 weeks ago   234 MB
```

You can remove the other tags using a short name (see section 2.2.8). Podman uses
the short name and finds the first name in local storage that matches the short name
without a registry and removes it, which is why I need to remove it twice to get rid of
both images. Tags other than latest need to be specified explicitly:

```
$ podman rmi myimage
Untagged: quay.io/rhatdan/myimage:latest
$ podman rmi myimage:1.0
Untagged: quay.io/rhatdan/myimage:1.0
Deleted: 2c7e43d88038669e8cdbdff324a9f9605d99697215a0d21c360fe8dfa8471bab
```

It is only when the last tag is removed that the actual disk space is reclaimed:

```
$ podman images
REPOSITORY                     TAG        IMAGE ID       CREATED       SIZE
registry.access.redhat
⮡ .com/ubi8/httpd-24           latest     8594be0a0b57   5 weeks ago   462 MB
registry.access.redhat
⮡ .com/ubi8                    latest     ad42391b9b46   5 weeks ago   234 MB
```

Alternatively, you can try removing the images by specifying the image ID:

```
$ podman rmi 14119a10abf4
Error: unable to delete image\
⮡ "2c7e43d88038669e8cdbdff324a9f9605d99697215a0d21c360fe8dfa8471bab" by\
⮡ ID with more than one tag ([quay.io/rhatdan/myimage:1.0\
⮡ quay.io/rhatdan/myimage:latest]): please force removal
```

But that fails because there are multiple tags for the same image. Adding the `--force` option removes the image and all of its tags:

```
$ podman rmi 14119a10abf4 --force
Untagged: quay.io/rhatdan/myimage:1.0
Untagged: quay.io/rhatdan/myimage:latest
Deleted: 2c7e43d88038669e8cdbdff324a9f9605d99697215a0d21c360fe8dfa8471bab
```

As your image sizes and numbers grow and more containers are created, it becomes harder to figure out which images are no longer needed. Podman has another useful command—`podman image prune`—for removing all dangling images. *Dangling images* are images that no longer have a tag associated with them or a container using them. The `prune` command also has the `--all` option, which removes all images that are currently not in use by any containers, including dangling images:

```
$ podman image prune -a
WARNING! This command removes all images without at least one container \
⮡ associated with them.
Are you sure you want to continue? [y/N] y
6d633c2626113fb4e5aa75babb2af39268948497893f7bb5b4c2043d7a986ba0
B9097177b416944cabdcfcab0e74a319223ad1acaed38ac57a262b2421732355
```

> **NOTE** Having no containers running the `podman image prune` command removes all of the local images. This frees up all of the disk space in the home directory. You can use the `podman system df` command to show all of the storage in your home directory used by Podman.

```
$ podman images
REPOSITORY                              TAG        IMAGE ID    CREATED     SIZE
```

Some notable `podman image prune` options include the following:

- `--all`—This tells Podman to remove all images, freeing up all storage. Images that have containers running on them are not removed.

- `--force`—This tells Podman to stop and remove any containers that are running on them and remove any images dependent on the image you are attempting to remove.

Use the `man podman-image-prune` command for information about all options.

Images pushed to the registry could also be pulled for various reasons, including but not limited to sharing your applications with others, testing other versions, getting back removed local versions, and working on a new version of an image.

2.2.8   Pulling images

Although you previously removed all local images, you can pull the previously pushed image at quay.io/rhatdan/myimage. Podman has the `podman pull` command to pull images from container registries (transports) into local container storage:

```
$ podman pull quay.io/rhatdan/myimage
Trying to pull quay.io/rhatdan/myimage:latest...
Getting image source signatures
Copying blob dfd8c625d022 done
Copying blob e21480a19686 done
Copying blob 68e8857e6dcb done
Copying blob 3f412c5136dd done
Copying blob fbfcc23454c6 done
Copying config 2c7e43d880 done
Writing manifest to image destination
Storing signatures
2c7e43d880382561ebae3fa06c7a1442d0da2912786d09ea9baaef87f73c29ae
```

Does the output look familiar? You probably remember similar output from the `podman run` command from section 2.1.2:

```
$ podman run -d -p 8080:8080 --name myapp\
➥ registry.access.redhat.com/ubi8/httpd-24
Trying to pull registry.access.redhat.com/ubi8/httpd-24:latest...
Getting image source signatures
Checking if image destination supports signatures
Copying blob 296e14ee2414 skipped: already exists
Copying blob 356f18f3a935 skipped: already exists
Copying blob 359fed170a21 done
Copying blob 226cafc3a0c6 done
Writing manifest to image destination
Storing signatures
37a1d2e31dbf4fa311a5ca6453f53106eaae2d8b9b9da264015cc3f8864fac22
```

Many Podman commands implicitly execute the `podman pull` command if the required image is not present locally.

So executing `podman images` shows the image back in container storage, ready to be used for containers:

```
$ podman images
REPOSITORY                     TAG       IMAGE ID       CREATED     SIZE
quay.io/rhatdan/myimage        latest    2c7e43d88038   2 days ago  462 MB
```

Up until now, you have been typing the image with the full names as registry.access .redhat.com/ubi8/httpd-24 or quay.io/rhatdan/myimage, but if you are like me and not a great typist, this can be a pain. You really need a way to refer to the images via short names.

SHORT NAMES AND CONTAINER REGISTRIES

When Docker first hit the scene, they defined an image reference as a combination of the container registry where the image was stored, repository, image name, and a tag or version of the image. In our examples, we have been using quay.io/rhatdan/myimage. In table 2.4, you can see this image name breakdown; note that the latest tag was used implicitly, as the image version wasn't specified.

Table 2.4   Container image name table

Registry	Repository	Name	Tag
quay.io	rhatdan	myimage	latest

The Docker command line has internally set the docker.io registry as the only registry, thus making every short image name refer to images at docker.io. There is also a special repository library, which is used for certified images.

So rather than typing

```
# docker pull docker.io/library/alpine:latest
```

You can just execute

```
# docker pull alpine
```

Conversely, if you want to pull an image from a different registry, you need to specify the full name of the image:

```
# docker pull registry.access.redhat.com/ubi8/httpd-24:latest
```

Table 2.5 shows the difference between the image name used in a short name versus the fully specified image name. Notice that when using the short name, the registry, repository, and tag were not specified.

Table 2.5   Short name to container image name table

Registry	Repository	Name	Tag
		alpine	
docker.io	library	alpine	latest

Since I am lazy and hate to type extra characters, I almost always use short names. With Podman, the developers did not want to hardcode one registry, docker.io, into the tool. Podman allows distributions, companies, and you to control which registries to use and to be able to configure multiple registries. At the same time, Podman provides support for the easier-to-use short names.

Podman usually comes with multiple registries defined, controlled by the distribution that packaged Podman. You can use the `podman info` command to see what registries are defined for your Podman installation:

```
$ podman info
...
registries:
  search:
  - registry.fedoraproject.org
  - registry.access.redhat.com
  - docker.io
  - quay.io
```

The list of registries can be modified in the registries.conf file, which is described in section 5.2.1.

Let's discuss the security side of things using these commands:

```
$ podman pull rhatdan/myimage
$ podman pull quay.io/rhatdan/myimage
```

From a security perspective, it is always better to specify the full image name when pulling it from a registry. That way, Podman guarantees that it pulls from the specified registry. Imagine you are attempting to pull rhatdan/myimage. Using the previous search order, there is a chance someone could set up an account on docker.io/rhatdan and trick you into mistakenly pulling docker.io/rhatdan/myimage.

To help protect against this, on the first pull of an image, Podman prompts you to select an exact image from the list of found images in configured registries:

```
$ podman create -p 8080:8080 ubi8/httpd-24
? Please select an image:
    registry.fedoraproject.org/ubi8/httpd-24:latest
  ▸ registry.access.redhat.com/ubi8/httpd-24:latest
    docker.io/ubi8/httpd-24:latest
    quay.io/ubi8/httpd-24:latest
```

Once you have selected and pulled an image successfully, Podman records the short name mapping. In the future, when you run a container with this short name, Podman uses the short name mapping to pick the correct registry and does not prompt.

Linux distributions also ship mappings of the most commonly used short names, as they want you to pull from their supported registries. You can find these short name configuration files in the /etc/containers/registries.conf.d directory on the Linux host. Companies can also drop short name alias files in this directory:

```
$ cat /etc/containers/registries.conf.d/000-shortnames.conf
[aliases]
```

```
# centos
"centos" = "quay.io/centos/centos"
# containers
"skopeo" = "quay.io/skopeo/stable"
"buildah" = "quay.io/buildah/stable"
"podman" = "quay.io/podman/stable"
...
```

Some notable `podman pull` options include the following:

- `--arch`—This tells Podman to pull an image for a different architecture. For example, on my x86_64 machine, I can pull an arm64 image. By default, `podman pull` pulls images for the native architecture.
- `--quiet (-q)`—This tells Podman not to print out all the progress information. It just prints the image ID when it completes.

Use the `man podman-pull` command for information about all options.

I have mentioned a few images in this book, but there are thousands and thousands of images available. You need a mechanism to be able to search through these images for the perfect match.

2.2.9   *Searching for images*

You might not know the name of a particular image you want to run or use as a base for your own image. Podman provides the command `podman search`, which allows you to search container registries for matching names:

```
$ podman search registry.access.redhat.com/httpd
INDEX      NAME
⇒    DESCRIPTION                          redhat.com
⇒ registry.access.redhat.com/rhscl/httpd-24-rhel7
⇒ Apache HTTP 2.4\ Server
redhat.com  registry.access.redhat.com/ubi8/httpd-24\
⇒ Platform for running Apache httpd 2.4 or bui...
redhat.com  registry.access.redhat.com/rhscl/varnish-6-rhel7        Varnish\
⇒ available as container is a base pla...
...
```

In this example, we are searching for images that include the string *httpd* in their name on the repository registry.access.redhat.com.

Some notable `podman search` options include the following:

- `--no-trunc`—This tells Podman to show the full description of the image.
- `--format`—This allows you to customize which fields are displayed by Podman.

Use the `man podman-search` command for information about all options.

Up until now, you have seen several ways of managing and manipulating container images, including inspecting, pushing, pulling, and searching for them. But you have only been able to look at the contents of an image by running it as a container. One way to simplify the process is mounting a container image.

2.2.10   *Mounting images*

Often you might want to examine the contents of a container image, and one way to do this is launching a shell inside a running container from the image. The problem with this is that the tools you use to examine the container image might not be available within the container. There is also a security risk that the application in the container is malicious, making use of this container undesirable.

To help with these problems, Podman provides the podman image mount command to mount an image's root filesystem in a read-only mode without creating a container from it. The mounted image becomes immediately available on the host system, allowing you to examine its contents.

Now try mounting the image you pulled previously:

```
$ podman mount quay.io/rhatdan/myimage
Error: cannot run command "podman mount" in rootless mode, must execute
    `podman unshare` first
```

The reason for this error is that rootless mode does not allow mounting images. You need to enter a user namespace and separate mount namespace. Chapter 5 explains how most rootless Podman commands enter the user namespace and mount namespace when they execute. For now, it is enough to know that the podman unshare command enters the user and mount namespaces and will shut down when you execute the exit command of your shell.

> **NOTE** The name unshare comes from the Linux syscall unshare (man 2 unshare). Linux also includes an unshare tool (man 1 unshare), which allows you to create namespaces by hand. Another low-level tool called nsenter, or namespace enter (man 1 nsenter), allows you to join processes to different namespaces. Podman unshare uses the same kernel features. It simplifies the process of creating and configuring namespaces and inserting processes into the namespaces.

The podman unshare command leaves you at a # prompt, where you can actually mount an image:

```
$ podman unshare
#
```

Mount the image, and save the location of the mounted filesystem in an environment variable:

```
# mnt=$(podman image mount quay.io/rhatdan/myimage)
```

Now you can actually examine the content of the image. Let's print the contents of a file on the terminal:

```
# cat $mnt/var/www/html/index.html
<html>
```

```
<head>
</head>
<body>
 <h1>Hello World</h1>
</body>
</html>
```

When you are done, unmount the image, and exit the unshare session:

```
# podman image unmount quay.io/rhatdan/myimage
# exit
```

> **NOTE** You have examined about a half of the `podman image` subcommands, arguably the most used ones. Refer to the Podman man pages for a full explanation of these and other subcommands of the `podman image` command:
> `$ man podman-image`.

Now that you have a better understanding of containers and images, the next important step is updating your image. The main reasons for this are the need to update your application and the availability of new versions for the base image you use. You can build scripts to manually run the commands to build the image, but luckily, Podman optimized the experience.

2.3 Building images

So far you have been working with images, which were already created and uploaded to a container registry. The process of creating a container image is called *building*.

When building container images, you manage not only your application but also the image content used by this application. In the days prior to containers, you shipped applications as an RPM or DEB package, and then it was up to the distribution to make sure the other parts of the OS were kept up to date and secure. But in the container world, the container image includes the application along with a subset of the OS. It is the developers' responsibility to keep all of the image contents up to date and secure.

A coworker of mine, Scott McCarty (smccarty@redhat.com, @fatherlinux), has a saying, "Container images don't age like wine but more like cheese. As the image gets older it gets stinky."

This means that if the developer doesn't keep up with the security updates, the number of vulnerabilities in the image will grow at an alarming rate. Luckily for developers, Podman has a special mechanism for helping you with image building for your applications. The `podman build` command uses the Buildah tool (https://github.com/containers/buildah) as a library to build container images; Buildah is covered in appendix A.

The `podman build` uses a special text document called Containerfile or Dockerfile to automate the building of container images. This document lists commands used to build a container image.

NOTE The concept of a Dockerfile and its syntax was originally created for the Docker tool, developed by Docker, Inc. Podman defaults to using Containerfile for the name, which uses the exact same syntax. Dockerfile is supported as well for legacy purposes. The Docker build command does not support Containerfile by default but can use the Containerfile. You can specify the `-f` option: # `docker build -f Containerfile`.

2.3.1 Format of a Containerfile or Dockerfile

Containerfiles take many directives. I break these down into two categories, adding content to the container image and describing and documenting how to use the image.

ADDING CONTENT TO AN IMAGE

Recall back in section 1.1.2 that I described a container image as a tdirectory on disk that looks like root on a Linux system. This directory is called a rootfs. Several of the directives in a container job are adding content to this rootfs. This rootfs eventually contains all of the content used to create your container image.

Every Containerfile must include a `FROM` line. The `FROM` line specifies the image that the new image is based off, often called a base image. The `podman build` command supports a special image named `scratch`, which means to start your image with no content. When Podman sees the `FROM scratch` directive, it just allocates space in containers/storage for an empty rootfs, then `COPY` can be used to populate the rootfs. More often, the `FROM` directive uses an existing image. For example, `FROM registry.access.redhat.com/ubi8` causes Podman to pull the ubi8 image from the registry.access.redhat.com container registry and copy it to container storage. `podman build` pulls the same image as the `podman pull` command you learned about in section 2.2.8. When the image is pulled, Podman uses container storage to mount the image on the rootfs directory, using a copy on the write filesystem, like OverlayFS, where the other directives can start to add content. This image becomes the base layer of the rootfs.

The `COPY` directive is often used to copy files, directories, or tarballs off of the local host into the newly created rootfs. The `RUN` directive is one of the most commonly used Containerfile directives. `RUN` tells Podman to actually run a container on the image. Package management tools, like DNF/YUM and `apt-get`, are run to install packages from distributions onto your new image. The `RUN` directive runs any command within the container image as a container. The `podman build` command runs the commands with the same security constraints as the `podman run` command.

As an example, imagine you want to add the `ps` command to a container image; you can create a directive like the following. The `RUN` command executes a container, which updates all of the packages from the base image, and then installs the `procps-ns` package, which includes the `ps` command. Finally the containerized command executes yum to clean up after itself, so cruft is removed from the container image:

```
RUN yum -y update; yum -y install procps-ng; yum -y clean all
```

Adding content to the container image is only half of what you need to do when creating a container image. You also need to describe and document how the image will be used when other users download and run your image.

DOCUMENTING HOW TO USE THE IMAGE

Recall that back in section 1.1.2, I also described the JSON file that included the image specification. This specification describes how the container image is to be run, the command, which user to run it with, and other requirements of the image. The Containerfile also supports many directives, which tells Podman how to run containers. These include the following:

- *The* ENTRYPOINT *and* CMD *directives*—These instrument the image with the default command to be executed when users execute the image with Podman run. CMD is the actual command to run. ENTRYPOINT can cause the entire image to execute as a single command.
- *The* ENV *directive*—This sets up the default environment variables to run when Podman runs a container on the image.
- *The* EXPOSE *directive*—This records the network ports for Podman to expose in containers based on the image. If you execute podman run --publish-all ..., Podman looks inside of the image for the EXPOSE network ports and connects them to the host.

Table 2.6 explains the directives used in a Containerfile to add content to a container image.

Table 2.6   Containerfile directives that update the image

Directive examples	Explanation
FROM quay.io/rhatdan/myimage	Sets the base image for subsequent instructions. Containerfiles must have FROM as their first instruction. The FROM may appear multiple times within a single Containerfile to create multiple build stages.
ADD start.sh /usr/bin/start.sh	Copies new files, directories, or remote file URLs to the filesystem of the container at a specified path.
COPY start.sh /usr/bin/start.sh	Copies files to the filesystem of the container at a specified path.
RUN dnf -y update	Executes commands in a new layer on top of the current image and commits the results. The committed image is used for the next step in the Containerfile.
VOLUME /var/lib/mydata	Creates a mount point with the specified name and marks it as holding externally mounted volumes from the native host or from other containers. For more on volumes, see chapter 3.

Table 2.7 explains the directives used in a Containerfile to populate the OCI Runtime Specifications with information that tells container engines like Podman information

about the image and how to run the image. You can find much more information on Containerfiles in the `containerfile(5)` man page.

Table 2.7 Containerfile directives that define the OCI Runtime Specification

Directive examples	Explanation
CMD /usr/bin/start.sh	Specifies the default command to run when launching a container off this image. If CMD is not specified, the parent image's CMD is inherited. Note that RUN and CMD are very different. RUN runs the commands during the build process, while CMD is only used when a user launches the image without specifying a command.
ENTRYPOINT "/bin/sh -c"	Allows you to configure a container to run as an executable. The ENTRYPOINT instruction is not overwritten when arguments are passed to podman run. This allows arguments to be passed to the entrypoint—for instance, podman run <image> -d passes the -d argument to the ENTRYPOINT.
ENV foo="bar"	Adds an environment variable to be used during both the image build and container execution.
EXPOSE 8080	Announces the port that containerized applications will be exposing. This does not actually map or open any ports.
LABEL Description="Web browser which displays Hello World"	Adds metadata to an image.
MAINTAINER Daniel Walsh	Sets the Author field for the generated images.
STOPSIGNAL SIGTERM	Sets the default stop signal sent to the container to exit. The signal can be a valid unsigned number or a signal name in the format SIGNAME.
USER apache	Sets the user name (or UID) and group name (or GID) to use for any RUN, CMD, and ENTRYPOINT specified after it.
ONBUILD	Adds a trigger instruction to the image to be executed at a later time, when the image is used as the base for another build.
WORKDIR /var/www/html	Sets the working directory for RUN, CMD, ENTRYPOINT, and COPY directives. A directory will be created if it doesn't exist.

COMMITTING THE IMAGE

When `podman build` finishes processing the Containerfile, it commits the image, using the same code as `podman commit` you learned about in section 2.1.9. Basically, Podman TARs up all of the differences between the new content in the rootfs and the base image, pulled down by the FROM directive. Podman also commits the JSON file and saves this as an image in container storage. Now you can take the steps used to build out containerized applications and automate them using a Containerfile and Podman build.

> **TIP** Use the `--tag` option to name the new image you are creating with `podman build`. This tells Podman to add the specified tag or name to the image in container storage in the same way as the `podman tag` command.

2.3.2   *Automating the building of our application*

First, create a directory to put your Containerfile and any other content for the container image in. The directory is called a context directory:

```
mkdir myapp
```

Next, create the index.html file you plan to use in the containerized application in the myapp directory:

```
$ cat > myapp/index.html << _EOF
<html>
 <head>
 </head>
 <body>
 <h1>Hello World</h1>
 </body>
</html>
_EOF
```

Next, create a simple Containerfile to build your application in the `myapp` directory. The first line of the Containerfile is the `FROM` directive to pull the ubi8/httpd-24 image you are treating as your base image. Then add a `COPY` command to copy the index.html file into the image. The `COPY` directive tells Podman to copy the index.html file out of the context directory (./myapp) and copy it to the /var/www/html/index.html file within the image:

```
$ cat > myapp/Containerfile << _EOF
FROM ubi8/httpd-24
COPY index.html /var/www/html/index.html
_EOF
```

Finally, use `podman build` to build your containerized application. Specify the `--tag` (-t) to name the image quay.io/rhatdan/myimage. You also need to specify the context directory ./myapp:

```
$ podman build -t quay.io/rhatdan/myimage ./myapp
STEP 1/2: FROM ubi8/httpd-24
STEP 2/2: COPY index.html /var/www/html/index.html
COMMIT quay.io/rhatdan/myimage
--> f81b8ace4f1
Successfully tagged quay.io/rhatdan/myimage:latest
F81b8ace4f134d08cedb20a9156ae727444ae4d4ec1ceb3b12d3aff23d18128b
```

When the `podman build` command completes, it commits the image and tags (-t) it with the quay.io/rhatdan/myimage name. It is now ready to be pushed to the container registry using the `podman push` command.

Now you can set up a CI/CD system or even a simple cron job to regularly build and replace `myapplication`:

```
$ cat > myapp/automate.sh << _EOF
#!/bin/bash
podman build -t quay.io/rhatdan/myimage ./myapp
podman push quay.io/rhatdan/myimage
_EOF
$ chmod +x myapp/automate.sh
```

Add some test scripts as well to make sure your application works the way it was designed before replacing the previous version. Let's take a look at the images that were built:

```
$ podman images
REPOSITORY                        TAG       IMAGE ID        CREATED         SIZE
quay.io/rhatdan/myimage           latest    f81b8ace4f13    2 minutes ago   462 MB
<none>                            <none>    2c7e43d88038    2 days ago      462 MB
registry.access.redhat
➡.com/ubi8/httpd-24               latest    8594be0a0b57    5 weeks ago     462 MB
```

Notice the old version of quay.io/rhatdan/myimage, image ID `2c7e43d88038`, still exists in container storage but now has a `REPOSITORY` and `TAG` of <none> <none>. Images like these are called dangling images. Since I have created a new version of quay.io/rhatdan/myimage with the `podman build` command, the previous image loses that name. You can still use the Podman commands with the image ID, or if the new image doesn't work, simply use `podman tag` to rename the old image back to quay.io/rhatdan/myimage. If the new image works correctly, you can remove the old image with `podman rmi`. These <none><none> images tend to build up over time, wasting space, but you can periodically use the `podman image prune` command to remove them.

The `podman build` could really use a chapter or even a book to itself. People build images in thousands of different ways using the commands briefly described here.

`--tag` is a notable `podman build` option that specifies the image tag or name for the image. Remember that you can always add additional names after you create the image with the `podman tag` command you used in section 2.2.6. Use the `man podman-build` command for information about all options (see table 2.8).

Table 2.8 Podman image commands

Command	Man page	Description
build	podman-image-build(1)	Builds an image using instructions from Containerfiles
diff	podman-image-diff(1)	Inspects changes in image's filesystem
exists	podman-image-exists(1)	Checks whether an image exists
history	podman-image-history(1)	Shows a history of a specified image

Table 2.8   Podman image commands *(continued)*

Command	Man page	Description
import	podman-image-import(1)	Imports a tarball to create a filesystem image
inspect	podman-image-inspect(1)	Displays the configuration of an image
list	podman-image-list(1)	Lists all of the images
load	podman-image-load(1)	Loads image(s) from a tarball
mount	podman-image-mount(1)	Mounts an image's root filesystem
prune	podman-image-prune(1)	Removes unused images
pull	podman-image-pull(1)	Pulls an image from a registry
push	podman-image-push(1)	Pushes an image to a registry
rm	podman-image-rm(1)	Removes an image
save	podman-image-save(1)	Saves image(s) to an archive
scp	podman-image-scp(1)	Securely copies images to other containers/storage
search	podman-image-search(1)	Searches the registry for an image
sign	podman-image-sign(1)	Signs an image
tag	podman-image-tag(1)	Adds an additional name to a local image
tree	podman-image-tree(1)	Prints the layer hierarchy of an image in a tree format
trust	podman-image-trust(1)	Manages container image trust policy
unmount	podman-image-unmount(1)	Unmounts an image's root filesystem
untag	podman-image-untag(1)	Removes a name from a local image

Summary

- Podman's simple command-line interface makes working with containers easy.
- Podman run, stop, start, ps, inspect, rm, and commit are all commands for working with containers.
- Podman pull, push, login, and rmi are tools for working with images and sharing them via container registries.
- Podman build is a great command for automating the build of container images.
- Podman's command line is based on the Docker CLI and supports it exactly, allowing us to tell people to just alias Docker = Podman.
- Podman has additional commands and options to support more advanced concepts like podman image mount.

Volumes

3

> **This chapter covers**
> - Using volumes to isolate data from the containerized application
> - Sharing content from your host into containers via volumes
> - Using volumes with the user namespace and SELinux
> - Embedding volumes into container images
> - Exploring different types of volumes and the volume commands

Up until now, the containers you have been working with include all their content within the container image. As I described in chapter 1, the only thing required to be shared with traditional containers is the Linux kernel. There are several reasons you need to isolate application data from the application, including the following:

- Avoiding embedding actual data for applications such as databases.
- Using the same container image to run multiple environments.
- Reducing overhead and improving storage read/write performance, since volumes write directly to the filesystem, while containers use the overlay or

fuse-overlayfs filesystem to mount their layers. *Overlay* is a layered filesystem, meaning the kernel needs to copy the previous layer entirely to create a new layer, and fuse-overlayfs switches each read and write from kernel space to user space and back. All of this creates quite an overhead.

- Sharing content available via network storage.

NOTE   bind mounts remount parts of the file hierarchy in a different location on the filesystem. The files and directories in the bind mount are the same as the original (see the mount command man page for an explanation of bind mounts). A bind mount allows the same content to be accessible in two places, without any additional overhead. It is important to understand that bind does not copy the data or create new data.

Supporting volumes also adds complexity, especially concerning security. A lot of the security features of containers prevent the container processes from gaining access to the filesystem outside the container image. In this chapter, you will discover the ways Podman allows you to work around these obstacles.

3.1   *Using volumes with containers*

Let's go back to your containerized application. Up until now, you have simply embedded the web application data into your container filesystem directly. Recall that in section 2.1.8, you used the podman exec command to modify the Hello World index.html data within the container:

```
$ podman exec -i myapp bash -c 'cat > /var/www/html/index.html' << _EOF
<html>
 <head>
 </head>
 <body>
 <h1>Hello World</h1>
 </body>
</html>
_EOF
```

You have made the containerized image more flexible by allowing users to supply their own content for the web service or perhaps to update the web service on the fly. At the same time, while this method is possible, it is error prone and not scalable; it is where volumes come in handy.

Podman allows you to mount host filesystem content into containers using the podman run command via the --volume (-v) option.

The --volume HOST-DIR:CONTAINER-DIR option tells Podman to bind mount HOST-DIR in the host to CONTAINER-DIR in the container. Podman supports other kinds of volumes as well, but in this section, I will focus on bind mount volumes.

It is possible to mount both files or directories in a single option. Changes of the content on the host will be seen inside the container. Similarly, if container processes change the content inside the container, the changes will be seen on the host.

Let's look at an example. Create a directory, html, in your home directory, and then create a new html/index.html file in it:

```
$ mkdir html
$ cat > html/index.html << _EOF
<html>
 <head>
 </head>
 <body>
 <h1>Goodbye World</h1>
 </body>
</html>
_EOF
```

Now launch a container with the option -v ./html:/var/www/html:

```
$ podman run -d -v ./html:/var/www/html:ro,z -p 8080:8080
    quay.io/rhatdan/myimage
94c21a3d8fda740857abc571469aaaa181f4db27a464ceb6743c4a37fb875772
```

Notice the extra :ro,z fields in the --volume option. The ro option tells Podman to mount the volume in read-only mode. The read-only mount means processes within the container cannot modify any content under /var/www/html, while processes on the host are still able to modify the content. Podman defaults all volume mounts to read/write mode. The z option tells Podman to relabel the content to a shared label for use by SELinux (see section 3.1.2).

Now that you have launched the container, open a web browser, and navigate to localhost:8080 to make sure the changes have taken place (see figure 3.1).

```
$ web-browser localhost:8080
```

Figure 3.1   Web browser window connecting to the myimage **Podman container with volume mounted L**

Now you can shut down and remove the container you just created. Removing the container does not affect the content at all. The following command removes the latest (--latest) container, yours. The --force option tells Podman to stop the container and then remove it:

```
$ podman rm --latest --force
```

Finally, remove the content with this command:

```
$ rm -rf html
```

> **NOTE** The `--latest` option is not available on Mac and Windows. You must specify the container name or ID. Remote mode is explained in chapter 9, and Podman on Mac and Windows is explained in appendixes E and F.

3.1.1   *Named volumes*

In the first volume example, you created a directory on disk and then mounted it into the container. Similarly, you can take any existing file or directory and mount it into a container, as long as you have read access to it.

Another mechanism for persisting Podman containers data is named `volume`. You can create one of these with the `podman volume create` command. In the following example you will create a `volume` named `webdata`:

```
$ podman volume create webdata
webdata
```

Podman defaults to creating local-named volumes, with storage allocated in the container storage directories. You can inspect the volume and look for its mount point using the following command:

```
$ podman volume inspect webdata
[
  {
      "Name": "webdata",
      "Driver": "local",
      "Mountpoint":
➡ "/home/dwalsh/.local/share/containers/storage/volumes/webdata/_data",
      "CreatedAt": "2021-10-11T14:10:48.741367132-04:00",
      "Labels": {},
      "Scope": "local",
      "Options": {}
  }
]
```

Podman actually creates a directory in your local container storage, /home/dwalsh/ .local/share/containers/storage/volumes/webdata/_data, to store the content of the volume. You can create content from the host in this directory:

```
$ cat > /home/dwalsh/.local/share/containers/storage/volumes/web-
    data/_data/index.html << _EOL
<html>
 <head>
 </head>
 <body>
 <h1>Goodbye World</h1>
 </body>
</html>
_EOL
```

Now you can run the `myimage` application using this volume:

```
$ podman run -d -v webdata:/var/www/html:ro,z -p 8080:8080
    quay.io/rhatdan/myimage
0c8eb612831f8fe22438d73d801e5bb664ec3b1d524c5c10759ee0049061cb6b
```

Now refresh the web browser to ensure the file created in the host directory is displaying "Goodbye World" (see figure 3.2).

Figure 3.2   Web browser window connecting to the `myimage` Podman container with the named volume mounted

Named volumes can be used for more than one container at a time, and they will stay around even after the container is removed. If you are done with the named volume and container, you can first stop the container without waiting for the processes to finish:

```
$ podman stop -t 0 0c8eb61283
```

Then remove the volume with the `podman volume rm` command. Note the `--force` option, which tells Podman to remove the volume and all containers that rely on the volume:

```
$ podman volume rm --force webdata
```

Now you can make sure the volume is gone by executing the `volume list` command:

```
$ podman volume list
```

If a named volume doesn't exist prior to executing the `podman run` command, it will be created automatically. In the following example, you will specify `webdata1` for the name of the named volume, then list the volumes:

```
$ podman run -d -v webdata1:/var/www/html:ro,z -p 8080:8080\
➥ quay.io/rhatdan/myimage
58ccaf37958496322e34cd933cd4dd5a61ab06c5ba678beb28fdc29cfb81f407

$ podman volume list
DRIVER    VOLUME NAME
local     webdata1
```

Of course, this volume is empty. Remove the `webdata1` volume and container:

```
$ podman volume rm --force webdata1
```

Podman also supports other types of volumes. It uses the concept of volume plugins so third parties can provide volumes; see the `podman-volume-create` man pages for more information.

Podman has other interesting volume features. The `podman volume export` command exports all the content of a volume into an external TAR archive. This archive can be copied to other machines used to recreate the volume on another machine with the `podman volume import` command. Now that you understand the handling of volumes, it is time to dig deeper into volume options.

3.1.2 *Volume mount options*

You have been using volume mount options throughout this chapter. The `ro` option tells Podman to mount the read-only volume, and the lowercase `z` option tells Podman to relabel the content with SELinux labels that will allow multiple containers to read and write in the volume:

```
$ podman run -d -v ./html:/var/www/html:ro,z -p 8080:8080
    quay.io/rhatdan/myimage
```

Podman supports some other interesting volume options.

THE U VOLUME OPTION

Sometimes when you run a rootless container, you need a volume to be owned by the user of the container. Imagine your application needs to allow the web server to write to the volume. In your container, the Apache Web Server process (`httpd`) is run as the apache (`UID==60`) user. The html directory in your home directory is owned by your UID, meaning it is owned by root inside the container. The kernel does not allow a process running as `UID==60` inside the container to make changes to a directory owned by root. You must set the ownership of the volume to `UID==60`.

In rootless containers, the UIDs of the container are offset by the user namespace. My user namespace mapping looks like this:

```
$ podman unshare cat /proc/self/uid_map
      0     3267        1
      1   100000    65536
```

The `UID==0` inside the container is my UID 3267, and UID 1==100000, UID 2==10000 ... UID60==100059, meaning I need to set the ownership of the html directory to 100059.

I can do this fairly simply, using the `podman unshare` command, as follows:

```
$ podman unshare chown 60:60 ./html
```

Now everything works. One problem with this is that I need to do some mental gymnastics to figure out which UID the container will run with.

Many container images exist with the default UID defined in them. The `mariadb` image is another example of this; it runs with the `mysql` user, `UID=999`:

```
$ podman run docker.io/mariadb grep mysql /etc/passwd
mysql:x:999:999::/home/mysql:/bin/sh
```

If you created a volume to be used for the database, you need to figure out what `UID=999` mapped to within the user namespace. On my system this is `UID=100998`.

Podman supplies the `U` command option for this exact situation. The `U` option tells Podman to recursively change ownership (`chown`) the source volume to match the default UID the container executes with.

Try it out by first creating the directory for the database. Notice the directory in the home directory is owned by your user:

```
$ mkdir mariadb
$ ls -ld mariadb/
drwxrwxr-x. 1 dwalsh dwalsh 0 Oct 23 06:55 mariadb/
```

Now run the `mariadb` container with the `--user mysql`, and `bind` mount the ./mariadb directory to /var/lib/mariadb with the `:U` option. Notice that the directory is now owned by the `mysql` user:

```
$ podman run --user mysql -v ./mariadb:/var/lib/mariadb:U \
 docker.io/mariadb ls -ld /var/lib/mariadb
drwxrwxr-x. 1 mysql mysql 0 Oct 23 10:55 /var/lib/mariadb
```

If you look at the mariadb directory on the host again, you will see that it is now owned by `UID 100998` or whatever `UID 999` maps to within your user namespace:

```
$ ls -ld mariadb/
drwxrwxr-x. 1 100998 100998 0 Oct 23 06:55 mariadb/
```

User namespace is not the only security mechanism you need to work around with rootless containers. SELinux, while great for container security, can cause some problems when working with volumes.

THE SELINUX VOLUME OPTIONS

In my opinion, SELinux is the best mechanism for protecting the filesystem from hostile container processes. Over the years, several container escapes have been thwarted by SELinux (see section 10.8 for more information on SELinux).

As I explained previously, volumes leak files from the OS into the container, and from an SELinux point of view, these files and directories must be labeled correctly, or the kernel will block access.

The lowercase z command option you have been using in this chapter tells Podman to recursively relabel all content in the source directory with a label that can be read and written by all containers from an SELinux point of view. If the volume will not be used by more than one container, relabeling with the lowercase z option isn't what you want. If a different hostile container escapes confinement, it might be able to access this data and read/write it. Podman provides an uppercase Z option that tells Podman to recursively relabel the content in such a way that only the processes within the container can read/write the content.

In both previous cases, you relabeled the content of the directory. Relabeling works great if the directory is specified for use by containers. Sometimes you may want to use a container to examine content in a system-specific directory—for example, if you want to run a container that examines all the logs in /var/log or examines all your home directories (/home/dwalsh).

> **NOTE** Using this option on a home directory can have disastrous effects on the system because it recursively relabels all content in the directory as if the data was private to a container. Other confined domains would be prevented from using the mislabeled data.

For these cases, you need to disable SELinux enforcement for container separation to allow the containers to use the volume. Podman provides the command option --security-opt label=disable to disable SELinux support for a single container, basically running the container with an *unconfined* label from an SELinux perspective:

```
$ podman run --security-opt label=disable -v /home/dwalsh:/home/dwalsh -p\
➡ 8080:8080 quay.io/rhatdan/myimage
```

Table 3.1 lists and describes all of the mount options available in Podman.

Table 3.1   Volume mount options

Volume option	Description
nodev	Prevent container processes from using character or block devices on the volume.
noexec	Prevent container processes from direct execution of any binaries on the volume.
nosuid	Prevent SUID applications from changing their privilege on the volume.
O	Mount the directory from the host as a temporary storage using the overlay filesystem. Modifications to the mount point are destroyed when the container finishes executing. This option is useful for sharing the package cache from the host into the container to allow speeding up builds.
[r]shared| [r]slave| [r]private| [r]unbindable	Specify mount propagation mode. Mount propagation controls how changes to mounts are propagated across mount boundaries: ■ private (default)—Any mounts done inside container will not be visible on host and vice versa. ■ shared—Mounts done under that volume inside container will be visible on host and vice versa. ■ slave—Mounts done on host under that volume will be visible inside container but not the other way around. ■ unbindable—An unbindable version of private mode. The prefix r stands for *recursive*, meaning that any mounts underneath the mount point will also be treated the same way.

Table 3.1 Volume mount options *(continued)*

Volume option	Description
`rw|ro`	Mount a volume in read-only (`ro`) or read-write (`rw`) mode. By default, read/write is implied.
`U`	Use the correct host UID and GID based on the UID and GID within the container. Use with caution because this will modify the host filesystem.
`z|Z`	Relabel file objects on the shared volumes. Choose the `z` option to label volume content as shared among multiple containers. Choose the `Z` option to label content as unshared and private.

For more information, see the man pages for `mount` and `mount_namespaces(7)`.

Most of the time, the simple `--volume` option is powerful enough for mounting volumes into containers. Over time, the requests for new mount options grew too complex, so a new option called `--mount` was added.

3.1.3 *podman run --mount command option*

The `podman run --mount` option is a much closer option to the underlying Linux mount command. It allows you to specify all of the mount options that the mount command understands; Podman passes them down directly to the kernel.

The only mount types currently supported are `bind`, `volume`, `image`, `tmpfs`, and `devpts`. (For more information, see the `podman-mount(1)` man page for more information.)

Volumes and mounts are excellent ways to keep data separate from the container image. In most cases, the container image should be treated as read-only, and any data that needs to be written or is not specific to the application should be stored outside of the container image via volumes. In a lot of cases, you will get much better performance keeping your data separate, because reads and writes will not have the overhead of the copy-on-write filesystem. These mounts also make it easier to use the same container images with different data (table 3.2).

Table 3.2 Podman volume commands

Command	Man page	Description
`create`	`podman-volume-create(1)`	Create a new volume.
`exists`	`podman-volume-exists(1)`	Check if a volume exists.
`export`	`podman-volume-export(1)`	Export the contents of a volume into a tar ball.
`import`	`podman-volume-import(1)`	Untar a tarball into a volume.
`inspect`	`podman-volume-inspect(1)`	Display detailed information on a volume.
`list`	`podman-volume-list(1)`	List all of the volumes.
`prune`	`podman-volume-prune(1)`	Remove all unused volumes.
`rm`	`podman-volume-rm(1)`	Remove one or more volumes.

Summary

- Volumes are useful for separating the data used by a container from the application inside an image.
- Volumes mount parts of the filesystem into a container's environment, which means security concerns like SELinux and user namespace need to be modified to allow access.

Pods

Podman is short for *Pod Manager*. A *pod* is a concept popularized by the Kubernetes project; it is a group of one or more containers working together for a common purpose and sharing the same namespaces and cgroups (resource constraints). Additionally, Podman ensures that on SELinux machines, all container processes within a pod share the same SELinux labels. This means they can all work together from an SELinux point of view.

4.1 Running pods

Podman pods (see figure 4.1), just like Kubernetes Pods, always include a container called the *infra* container—sometimes called the *pause* container (not to be confused with the rootless pause container mentioned in section 5.2). The infra container only holds open the namespaces and cgroups from the kernel, allowing containers to come and go within the pod. When Podman adds a container to a pod, it adds the container process to the cgroups and namespaces. Notice that the infra container has a container monitor process, conmon, monitoring it. Every container within a pod has its own conmon.

Conmon is a lightweight C program that monitors the container until it exits, allowing the Podman executable to exit and reconnect to the container. Conmon does the following when monitoring the container:

1 Conmon executes the OCI runtime, handing it the path to the OCI spec file as well as pointing to the container layer mount point in containers/storage. The mount point is called the rootfs.
2 Conmon monitors the container until it exits and reports its exit code back.
3 Conmon handles when the user attaches to the container, providing a socket to stream the container's STDOUT and STDERR.
4 The STDOUT and STDERR are also logged to a file for Podman logs.

NOTE   The infra container (pause container; see figure 4.1) is similar to the rootless pause container; its only purpose is to hold open the namespaces and cgroups, while containers come and go. However, each pod will have a different infra container.

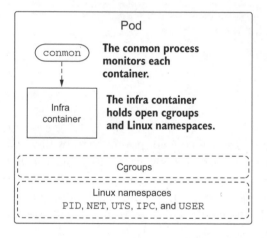

Figure 4.1   **The Podman pod launches conmon with the infra container, which will hold cgroups and Linux namespaces.**

Podman pods also support init containers, as seen in figure 4.2. These containers run before the primary containers in the pods are executed. An example of an init container is a database initialization on a volume. This would allow the primary container to use the database. Podman supports the following two classes of init containers:

- *Once*—Only runs the first time the pod is created
- *Always*—Runs every time the pod is started

The primary container runs the application.

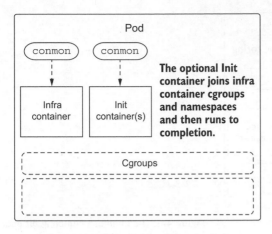

The optional Init container joins infra container cgroups and namespaces and then runs to completion.

Figure 4.2 Podman next launches any init containers with conmon. The init containers examine the infra container and join its cgroups and namespaces.

Pods also support additional containers, which are often called *sidecar* containers (see figure 4.4). Sidecar containers often monitor the primary container, as seen in figure 4.3, or the environment where the primary container runs. The Kubernetes documentation (https://kubernetes.io/docs/concepts/workloads/pods) describes pods with sidecar containers as follows:

> *A Pod can encapsulate an application composed of multiple co-located containers that are tightly coupled and need to share resources. These co-located containers form a single cohesive unit of service—for example, one container serving data stored in a shared volume to the public, while a separate sidecar container refreshes or updates those files. The Pod wraps these containers, storage resources, and an ephemeral network identity together as a single unit.*

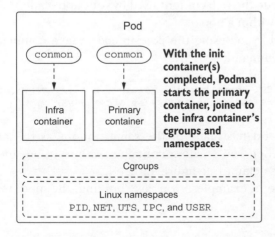

With the init container(s) completed, Podman starts the primary container, joined to the infra container's cgroups and namespaces.

Figure 4.3 Podman waits until the init containers complete before launching the primary containers with their conmon into the pod.

If you want to dive deeper into sidecar containers, there are several good articles on the following website: https://www.magalix.com/blog/the-sidecar-pattern.

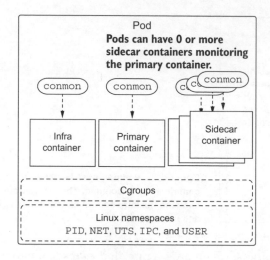

Figure 4.4   **Podman can launch additional containers called sidecar containers.**

NOTE While pods can support more than one sidecar container, I recommend you only use one. There is a real temptation for people to abuse this capability, especially in Kubernetes, but it can use up more resources and become unwieldy.

A big advantage of using pods is that you can manage them as discrete units. Starting a pod starts all of the containers within it, and stopping the pod stops all of the containers.

4.2   *Creating a pod*

In this section, you will create a pod in which you have the myimage application as the primary container within the pod. You will also add a second container to the pod, a sidecar container, which will update the web content used by your application to show two containers working together within a pod.

You can create a pod named `mypod` using the `podman pod create` command, as demonstrated in the following command:

```
$ podman pod create -p 8080:8080 --name mypod --volume ./html:/var/www/html:z
790fefe97b280e5f67c526e3a421e9c9f958cf5a98f3709373ef1afd91965955
```

The `podman pod create` command has many of the same options as the `podman container create` command. When you create a container within a pod, the container inherits these options as its default (see figure 4.5).

Notice that, like the previous examples, you are binding the pod to port `-p 8080:8080`:

```
$ podman pod create -p 8080:8080 --name mypod --volume ./html:/var/www/html:z
```

Because the containers within the pod share the same network namespace, this port binding is shared by all of the containers. The kernel allows only one process to listen

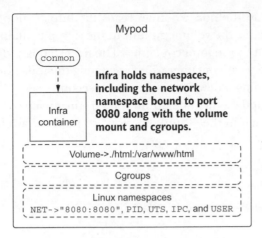

Figure 4.5   Podman creates a network namespace and binds port 8080 within the container to port 8080 on the host. Podman creates the infra container with the /var/www/html directory from the host in the container and joins the cgroups and network namespace.

on port 8080. Lastly, notice that the ./html directory was volume mounted, `--volume ./html:/var/www/html:z`, into the pod:

```
$ podman pod create -p 8080:8080 --name mypod --volume ./html:/var/www/html:z
```

The `:z` parameter causes Podman to relabel the content of the directory. Podman will automatically volume mount this directory into every container that joins the pod. Containers in pods share the same SELinux label, which means they can share the same volumes.

4.3   Adding a container to a pod

You create a container within a pod using the `podman create` command (see figure 4.6). Add the quay.io/rhatdan/myimage container to the pod with the `--pod mypod` option:

```
$ podman create --pod mypod --name myapp quay.io/rhatdan/myimage
Cec045acb1c2be4a6e4e88e21275076fb1de5519a25fb5a55f192da70708a640
```

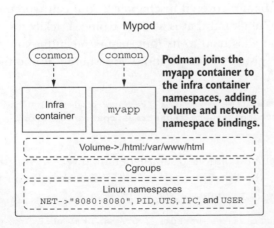

Figure 4.6   Because the pod does not have any init containers, the first `myapp` container is launched into the pod.

When you add the first container to the pod, Podman reads the information associated with the infra container and adds the volume mount to the myapp container and then joins it to the namespaces held by the infra container. The next step is adding the sidecar container to the pod. The sidecar container will be updating the index.html file in the /var/www/html volume, adding a new time stamp every second.

Create a simple Bash script to update the index.html used by the myapp container, called html/time.sh. You can create it in the ./html directory, so it will be available to processes within the pod:

```
$ cat > html/time.sh << _EOL
#!/bin/sh
data() {
  echo "<html><head></head><body><h1>"; date;echo "Hello World</h1></body></html>"
  sleep 1
}
while true; do
   data > index.html
done
_EOL
```

Make sure it is executable. You can do this on Linux with the chmod command:

```
$ chmod +x html/time.sh
```

Now create the second container (--name time), this time using a different image: ubi8. Containers within pods can use totally different images, even images from different distributions. Recall that container images only share the host kernel by default:

```
$ podman create --pod mypod --name time --workdir /var/www/html ubi8 ./time.sh
Resolved "ubi8" as an alias (/etc/containers/registries.conf.d/000-
      shortnames.conf)
Trying to pull registry.access.redhat.com/ubi8:latest…
…
1be0b2fae53029d518e75def71c0d6961b662d0e8b4a1082edea5589d1353af3
```

Remember the concept of short names covered in chapter 2. You can type the long name, registry.access.redhat.com/ubi8, but that is a lot of typing. Luckily for us, the short name, ubi8, already had an alias map to its long name, meaning you do not need to select it from the list of registries. Podman shows you where it found the alias for the long name in the output:

```
$ podman create --pod mypod --name time --workdir /var/www/html ubi8 ./time.sh
Resolved "ubi8" as an alias (/etc/containers/registries.conf.d/000-short-
      names.conf)
```

You also used the --workdir command option to set the default directory for the container to /var/www/html. When the container starts, the ./time.sh will run in the workdir and is actually /var/www/html/time.sh (see figure 4.7):

```
$ podman create --pod mypod --name time --workdir /var/www/html ubi8 ./time.sh
```

Because this container will be run within the mypod pod, it will inherit the
-v ./html:/var/www/html option from the pod, meaning the ./html/time.sh command in the host directory is available to every container within the pod.

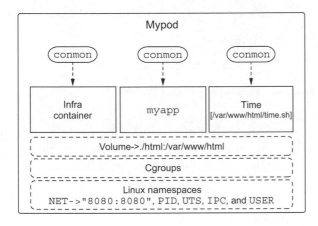

Figure 4.7 **Finally, Podman launches the sidecar container named** time.

Podman examines the infra container, mounts the /var/www/html volume, and joins
the namespaces when it launches the sidecar container. Now it is time to start the pod
and see what happens.

4.4 Starting a pod

You can start the pod with the podman pod start command:

```
$ podman pod start mypod
790fefe97b280e5f67c526e3a421e9c9f958cf5a98f3709373ef1afd91965955
```

Use the podman ps command to see which containers the pod started:

```
$ podman ps
CONTAINER ID  IMAGE                    COMMAND           CREATED     STATUS
    PORTS                NAMES
b9536ea4a8ab  localhost/podman-pause:4.0.3-1648837314                        14
    minutes ago  Up 5 seconds ago  0.0.0.0:8080->8080/tcp  8920b1ccd8b0-
    infra
a978e0005273  quay.io/rhatdan/myimage:latest          /usr/bin/run-http... 14
    minutes ago  Up 5 seconds ago  0.0.0.0:8080->8080/tcp  myapp
be86937986e9  registry.access.redhat.com/ubi8:latest ./time.sh             13
    minutes ago  Up 5 seconds ago  0.0.0.0:8080->8080/tcp  time
```

Notice now that three containers have started. The infra container is based on the
k8s.gcr.io/pause image, your application is based on quay.io/rhatdan/myimage:latest,
and the update container is based on the registry.access.redhat.com/ubi8:latest image.

When the ubi8 sidecar container starts, it begins modifying the index.html via the
time.sh script. Since the myapp container shares the volume mount, /var/www/html,
it can see the changes in the /var/www/html/index.html file. Launch your favorite

web browser, and navigate to http://localhost:8080 to verify the application is working, as seen in figure 4.8.

Figure 4.8   The web browser communicates with `myapp` running in a pod.

A couple of seconds later, press the Refresh button. Notice the date changes, indicating the sidecar container is running and updating the data used by the `myapp` web server running within the primary container, as seen in figure 4.9.

Figure 4.9   The web browser shows that the content in `myapp` has been changed by the second container running in the pod.

Some notable `podman pod start` options include the following:

- `--all`—This tells Podman to start all pods.
- `--latest`—The `-l` tells Podman to start the last pod created. (This is not available on Mac and Windows.)

Now that you have run the application within a pod, you might want to stop the application.

4.5 Stopping a pod

Now that you see the application ran successfully, you can stop the pod with the `podman pod stop` command, as follows:

```
$ podman pod stop mypod
790fefe97b280e5f67c526e3a421e9c9f958cf5a98f3709373ef1afd91965955
```

Use the `podman ps` command to make sure Podman stopped all the containers within the pod:

```
$ podman ps
CONTAINER ID   IMAGE      COMMAND    CREATED    STATUS     PORTS     NAMES
```

Some notable `podman pod stop` options include the following:

- `--all`—This tells Podman to stop all pods.
- `--latest`—The `-l` tells Podman to stop the most recently started pod.
- `--timeout`—The `-t` tells Podman to set the timeout when attempting to stop the containers within a pod.

Now that you have created, run, and stopped the pod, you can start examining it. First, list all the pods on your system.

4.6 Listing pods

You can list pods with the `podman pod list` command:

```
$ podman pod list
POD ID          NAME      STATUS    CREATED          INFRA ID        # OF CONTAINERS
790fefe97b28    mypod     Exited    22 minutes ago   b9536ea4a8ab    3
```

Some notable `podman pod list` options include the following:

- `--ctr*`—This tells Podman to list container information within pods.
- `--format`—This tells Podman to change the output of pods.

Now that you are done with the demonstration, time to clean up the pods and containers.

4.7 Removing pods

In a chapter 8, I discuss how you can generate Kubernetes YAML files to allow you to launch your pod on other systems using Podman or within Kubernetes. But for now, you can remove a pod with the `podman pod rm` command.

Before you do this, list `--all` the containers on the system. Using the `--format` option to show only the ID, image, and pod ID, you will see three containers that make up your pod:

```
$ podman ps --all --format "{{.ID}}  {{.Image}} {{.Pod}}"
b9536ea4a8ab   k8s.gcr.io/pause:3.5 790fefe97b28
a978e0005273   quay.io/rhatdan/myimage:latest 790fefe97b28
be86937986e9   registry.access.redhat.com/ubi8:latest 790fefe97b28
```

Now you can remove the pod with the following command:

```
$ podman pod rm mypod
790fefe97b280e5f67c526e3a421e9c9f958cf5a98f3709373ef1afd91965955
```

Make sure it is gone:

```
$ podman pod ls
POD ID     NAME       STATUS     CREATED    INFRA ID   # OF CONTAINERS
```

Good! It looks like your pod is gone. Verify that Podman removed all of the containers by running the following command:

```
$ podman ps -a --format "{{.ID}} {{.Image}}"
```

The system is fully cleaned up.

Some notable `podman pod rm` options include the following (also see table 4.1):

- `--all`—This tells Podman to remove all the pods.
- `--force`—This tells Podman to first stop all running containers before attempting to remove them. Otherwise, Podman will only remove non-running pods.

Table 4.1 `podman pod` **commands**

Command	Man page	Description
create	podman-pod-create(1)	Create a new pod.
exists	podman-pod-exists(1)	Check if a pod exists.
inspect	podman-pod-inspect(1)	Display detailed information on a pod.
kill	podman-pod-kill(1)	Send a signal to the primary processes of the containers in the pod.
list	podman-pod-list(1)	List all of the pods.
logs	podman-pod-logs(1)	Fetch logs for the pod with one or more containers.
pause	podman-pod-pause(1)	Pause all the containers in a pod.
prune	podman-pod-prune(1)	Remove all stopped pods and their containers.
restart	podman-pod-restart(1)	Restart a pod.
rm	podman-pod-rm(1)	Remove one or more pods.
stats	podman-pod-stats(1)	Display statistics for the containers in a pod.
start	podman-pod-start(1)	Start a pod.
stop	podman-pod-stop(1)	Stop a pod.
top	podman-pod-top(1)	Display running process in the pod.
unpause	podman-pod-unpause(1)	Unpause all the containers in a pod.

Summary

- Pods are a way of grouping containers together into more complex applications, sharing namespaces, and sharing resource constraints.
- Pods share most of the options containers use, and when you add a container to a pod, it shares these options with all containers in the pod.

Part 2

Design

Part 2 of the book covers the underlying design of Podman. Chapter 5 explains all of the different configuration files used with Podman. Podman is developed using multiple different container libraries, each with a distinct method of configuration. You learn how to configure your container storage and where to store your containers as well as images. You also learn how to configure the container registries you use for pulling and pushing container images. Finally, you learn about containers.conf, which allows you to fully customize the way Podman works. Basically, you can change the default values used by the Podman CLI for every container you create.

Chapter 6 then takes a deep dive into how rootless containers work. Rootless containers are a key feature of Podman that allows you to fully work with containers and pods as a normal user, without any additional privileges. This chapter also introduces you to how the user namespace works and allows you to use more than a single UID within a container, without being root. Finally, you will learn some of the problems with rootless containers and how to work around them.

Customization and configuration files

This chapter covers

- Using Podman configuration files based on libraries used
- Configuring the storage.conf file
- Using the registries.conf and policy.json files for configuration
- Using the containers.conf file to configure other defaults
- Using system configuration files to allow non-root users namespace access

Container engines like Podman have dozens of hardcoded defaults built into them. These defaults determine many aspects of the functional and nonfunctional behaviors of Podman, such as network and security settings. Podman developers try to pick the maximum amount of security but still allow most containers to run successfully. Similarly, I want as much isolation from the host as possible.

The security defaults include which Linux capabilities to use, which SELinux labels to set, and the set of syscalls available to the containers. There are defaults for resource constraints, like memory usage and maximum processes allowed within a container. Other defaults include the local path for storing images, the list of container registries, and even system configuration to allow rootless mode to work. The Podman developers wanted to allow users to have ultimate control over these defaults, so the container engine configuration files provide a mechanism for customizing the way Podman and other container engines run.

The problem with defaults is that they are best-guess estimates from developers. While most users run Podman in default configuration, sometimes there is a need to change the configuration. Not every environment has the same configuration, and you might want to default certain machines to different levels of security and different registry configurations. Even rootless users might need different configurations than rootful users. In this chapter, I will show you how to customize different parts of Podman and explain where you can find more information about all of the different knobs available to you.

As you have learned in previous chapters, Podman uses multiple libraries to perform different tasks when working with containers. Table 5.1 describes the different libraries Podman uses.

Table 5.1   Container libraries used by Podman

Library	Description
containers/storage	Defines the storage of container images and other basic storage used by container engines
containers/image	Defines the mechanisms used to move container images from different types of storage; usually used between container registries and local container storage
containers/common	Defines all of the default configuration options for container engines not defined in containers/storage or containers/image
containers/buildah	As explained in chapter 2, it is used for building container images into local storage using rules defined in a Containerfile or Dockerfile; for more information on Buildah, see appendix A.

Each of these libraries has separate configuration files used to set the default settings for the particular library, with the exception of Buildah. The container engines, Podman, and Buildah share the containers/common configuration file containers.conf, described in section 5.3.

NOTE   All of the nonsystem configuration files used by Podman use the TOML format. TOML's syntax consists of name = "value" pairs, [section names], and # comments. The format of TOML can be simplified to the following:

- [table]
- option = value
- [table.subtable1]
- option = value

- `[table.subtable2]`
- `option = value`

See https://toml.io for a more complete explanation of the TOML language. When configuring Podman, usually one of the first concerns is where you are going to store your containers and images.

5.1   Configuration files for storage

Podman uses the github.com/containers/storage library, which provides methods for storing filesystem layers, container images, and containers. Configuration of this library is done using the storage.conf configuration file, which can be stored in multiple different directories.

Linux distributions often provide a /usr/share/containers/storage.conf file, which can be overridden by creating a /etc/containers/storage.conf file. Rootless users can store their configuration in the $XDG_CONFIG_HOME/containers/storage.conf file; if the $XDG_CONFIG_HOME environment variable is not set, the $HOME/.config/containers/storage.conf file is used. Most users will never change the storage.conf file, but in a few situations, advanced users need to do some customizations. The most common reason for changes is relocating the container's storage.

> **NOTE**   When using Podman in remote mode, for example on a Mac or Windows box, the Podman service uses the storage.conf files located in the Linux box. To modify them, you need to enter the VM. When using the Podman machine, execute the `podman machine ssh` command to enter the VM. See appendixes E and F for more information.

Podman reads only one storage.conf and ignores all subsequent ones. Podman first attempts to use the storage.conf from your home directory; next goes the /etc/storage/storage.conf; and finally, if both files do not exist, Podman reads the /usr/share/containers/storage.conf file. You can see the storage.conf file your Podman command is using via the `podman info` command:

```
$ podman info --format '{{ .Store.ConfigFile }}'
/home/dwalsh/.config/containers/storage.conf
```

5.1.1   Storage location

By default rootless Podman is configured to store your images in the $HOME/.local/share/containers/storage directory. The default rootful storage location is /var/lib/containers/storage.

Sometimes you need to change this default location. Perhaps you don't have enough disk space in /var or in the user's home directory, so you want to store your images on a different disk. The storage.conf file calls the storage location the `graphRoot`, and it can be overridden in /etc/containers/storage.conf for rootful containers.

In this section, you will modify the location of the graph driver to /var/mystorage. First, become root and make sure the /etc/containers/storage.conf file exists. If it does not exist, just copy the /usr/share/containers/storage.conf file into it:

```
$ sudo cp /usr/share/containers/storage.conf /etc/containers/storage.conf
```

> **NOTE** Some distributions just ship the /etc/containers/storage.conf.

Now, make a backup, and open /etc/containers/storage.conf file for editing:

```
$ sudo cp /etc/containers/storage.conf /etc/containers/storage.conf.orig
$ sudo vi /etc/containers/storage.conf
```

Set the graphdriver variable graphroot = "/var/lib/containers/storage" to graphroot = "/var/mystorage", and save the file.

Your storage.conf file should include the following:

```
$ grep -B 1 graph /etc/containers/storage.conf
# Primary Read/Write location of container storage
graphroot = "/var/mystorage"
```

Execute podman info to see if the change took place:

```
$ sudo podman info
…
Store:
 configFile: /etc/containers/storage.conf
...
 graphDriverName: overlay
 graphOptions:
  overlay.mountopt: nodev,metacopy=on
 graphRoot: /var/mystorage
...
 volumePath: /var/mystorage/volumes
```

Notice in the storage section that the graphRoot is now /var/mystorage. All images and containers will be stored in this directory.

Now run the podman info command in rootless mode. The storage location will not change; it is still /home/dwalsh/.local/share/containers/storage:

```
$ podman info
store:
 configFile: /home/dwalsh/.config/containers/storage.conf
 containerStore:
  number: 27
  paused: 0
  running: 0
  stopped: 27
 graphDriverName: overlay
 graphOptions: {}
 graphRoot: /home/dwalsh/.local/share/containers/storage
```

You can create a $HOME/.config/containers/storage.conf and change it there, but this does not scale well for systems with multiple users. The key `rootless_storage_` `path` allows you to change the location for all users on your system.

This time, uncomment and modify the `rootless_storage_path` line:

```
$ sudo vi /etc/containers/storage.conf
```

Modify the `rootless_storage_path` line in storage.conf from

```
# rootless_storage_path = "$HOME/.local/share/containers/storage"
```

Change it to

```
rootless_storage_path = "/var/tmp/$UID/var/mystorage"
```

Save the storage.conf file. When you are done, it should look like this:

```
$ grep -B 3 rootless_storage_path /etc/containers/storage.conf
# Storage path for rootless users
#
rootless_storage_path = "/var/tmp/$UID/var/mystorage"
```

Now run `podman info` to see the changes. Notice that the `graphRoot` now points at the /var/tmp/3267/var/mystorage directory:

```
$ podman info
...
store:
 configFile: /home/dwalsh/.config/containers/storage.conf
...
 graphOptions: {}
 graphRoot: /var/tmp/3267/var/mystorage
```

Container/storage supports expanding the `$HOME` and `$UID` environment variables for this path. To revert changes, copy and restore the original storage.conf file:

```
$ sudo cp /etc/containers/storage.conf.orig /etc/containers/storage.conf
```

> **NOTE** If you are running on an SELinux system and change the default location of storage, you need to inform SELinux about it, using the following semanage command. This will tell SELinux to label the new location as if it was in the old location. Next, you will need to change the labeling on disk using the restorecon command. You can do this with the following commands:

```
sudo semanage fcontext -a -e /var/lib/containers/storage /var/mystorage
   sudo restorecon -R -v /var/mystorage
```

In rootless mode you need to do the following:

```
sudo semanage fcontext -a -e $HOME/.local/share/containers/storage/
➥ var/tmp/3267/var/mystorage
sudo restorecon -R -v /var/tmp/3267/var/mystorage
```

Sometimes you might want to change the storage driver or, more likely, the configuration of the storage driver.

5.1.2   Storage drivers

Recall the wedding cake illustration from chapter 2. This illustration shows that images are often made of multiple layers. These layers are stored on disk by the container/storage library, but when you are running a container on them, each layer needs to be mounted on the previous layer (figure 5.1).

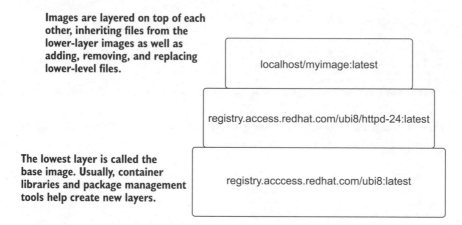

Figure 5.1   Layered images stacked on one another are reassembled and mounted using container/storage.

Container/storage uses a Linux kernel filesystem concept called a *layered filesystem* to do this. Podman, using container/storage, supports multiple different types of layered filesystems. In Linux, these filesystems are called *copy-on-write (CoW)* filesystems. In containers/storage, these different filesystem types are called *drivers*. By default Podman uses the `overlay` storage driver.

> **NOTE** Docker supports two types of overlay drivers: `overlay` and `overlay2`. `overlay2` was an improvement over `overlay`, and the original `overlay` driver is rarely used any more. In contrast, Podman uses the newer `overlay2` driver and just calls it `overlay`. You can select the `overlay` driver in Podman, but this is just an alias for `overlay2`.

Table 5.2 lists all of the storage drivers Podman and containers/storage support. I recommend you just stick to the `overlay` driver, since this is the driver the vast majority of the world uses.

Table 5.2 Container storage drivers

Storage drivers	Description
overlay (overlay2)	This is the default driver, and I strongly recommend its use. It is based on the Linux kernel overlay filesystem. overlay and overlay2 are exactly the same in Podman. It is the most tested driver, which the overwhelming majority of users use.
vfs	This is the simplest driver; it creates full copies of each lower layer up onto the next layer. It works everywhere but is slow and very disk intensive.
devmapper	This driver was heavily used when Docker first became popular—before the overlay driver was available. It reallocates the size of each layer at a maximum size. It is not recommended any longer.
aufs	This driver was never merged into the upstream kernel, so it is only available on a few Linux distributions.
btrfs	This driver allows storage on btrfs snapshots based on the Btrfs filesystem. Some users have had success using this filesystem.
zfs	This driver uses the ZFS filesystem, which is a proprietary filesystem and not available on most distributions.

OVERLAY STORAGE OPTIONS

The overlay driver has some interesting customization options. These options are located in the storage.conf [storage.options.overlay] table.

There are several advanced options available for configuring the overlay driver. I'll quickly mention a few to describe use cases.

The mount_program option allows you to specify an executable to use instead of the kernel overlay driver. Podman usually ships with the fuse-overlayfs executable, which provides a FUSE (userspace) overlay driver. Podman automatically fails over to the fuse-overlayfs mount_program if it is installed on systems where rootless native overlay is not supported. Most kernels support native overlay; however, there are use cases when you might want to configure the mount_program. The fuse-overlayfs has advanced features not currently supported in the native overlay.

Podman is quickly being adopted by the high-performance computing (HPC) community. The HPC community does not allow rootful containers, and in many cases it allows workloads to run only with a single UID. This means some HPC systems do not allow user namespaces with multiple UIDs. Since many images come with multiple UIDs, Podman added an ignore_chown_errors option to containers/storage to allow images with files with different UIDs to be flattened into a single UID. Table 5.3 lists all the current storage options supported by container storage.

> **NOTE** You have examined a few of the storage.conf fields, but there are many more. Use the containers-storage.conf man page to explore all of them:

```
https://github.com/containers/storage/blob/main/docs/containers-
   storage.conf.5.md
$ man containers-storage.conf
```

Table 5.3   Container storage drivers

Storage drivers	Description
ignore_chown_errors	Ignore chowning file UIDs for rootless containers with a single UID. There is no entry in /etc/subuid.
mount_program	Path to a helper program to use for mounting the filesystem instead of using a kernel overlay to mount it. Older kernels did not support rootless overlay.
mountopt	Comma-separated list of mount options to be passed to the kernel. It defaults to "nodev,metacopy=on".
skip_mount_home	Do not create PRIVATE bind mounts on the storage home directory.
inode	Maximum number of inodes in a container image
size	Maximum size of a container image
force_mask	Permissions mask for new files and directories in an image. The values are the following: ■ private—This sets all filesystem objects to 0700. No other users on the system can access the files. ■ shared—This is equivalent to 0755. Everyone on the system can read, access, and execute files in the image. This is useful for sharing container storage with other users. All files within the image are made readable and executable by any user on the system. Even /etc/shadow within your image is now readable by any user. When force_mask is set, the original permission mask is stored in xattrs, and the mount_program, like /usr/bin/fuse-overlayfs, presents the xattr permissions to processes within containers.

Now you know about configuring the container storage! The next configuration you will look at is container registry access.

5.2   *Configuration files for registries*

Podman uses the github.com/containers/image library for pulling and pushing container images, usually from container registries. Podman uses the registries.conf configuration file to specify registries and the policy.json file for signature verification of images. As with the container storage storage.conf, most users never modify these files and just use the distribution defaults.

5.2.1   *registries.conf*

The registries.conf configuration file is a system-wide configuration file for container image registries. Podman uses $HOME/.config/containers/registries.conf if it exists; otherwise, it uses /etc/containers/registries.conf.

> **NOTE**   When using Podman in remote mode, for example on a Mac or Windows box, registries.conf files are stored in the Linux box on the server side. You need to ssh into the Linux box to make the changes. With a Podman

machine, you can execute `podman machine ssh`. See appendixes E and F for more information.

The main key value to use with the registries.conf file is `unqualified-search-registries`. This field specifies an array of `host[:port]` registries to try when pulling via short names, in order. If you specify only one registry in the `unqualified-search-registries` option, Podman will work similarly to Docker and force a single registry on the user.

In this exercise, you will modify the default search registries to be used by Podman. First, you need to make a backup of the /etc/containers/registries.conf file, and then remove docker.io and add example.com:

```
$ sudo cp /etc/containers/registries.conf
    /etc/containers/registries.conf.orig
$ sudo vi /etc/containers/registries.conf
```

Modify the following line:

```
unqualified-search-registries = ["registry.fedoraproject.org",
    "registry.access.redhat.com", "docker.io", "quay.io"]
```

Change the line to

```
unqualified-search-registries = ["registry.fedoraproject.org",
    "registry.access.redhat.com", "example.com", "quay.io"]
```

Save the file, then execute `podman info` to verify the changes:

```
$ podman info
registries:
  search:
  - registry.fedoraproject.org
  - registry.access.redhat.com
  - example.com
  - quay.io
```

Now, if you attempt to pull via an unknown short name, you should see the following prompt:

```
$ podman pull foobar
? Please select an image:
  ▸ registry.fedoraproject.org/foobar:latest
    registry.access.redhat.com/foobar:latest
    example.com/foobar:latest
    quay.io/foobar:latest
```

Copy the original to the registries.conf file:

```
$ sudo cp /etc/containers/registries.conf.orig /etc/containers/registries.conf
```

Table 5.4 describes all of the options available in registries.conf files.

Table 5.4   Container registries.conf global fields

Fields	Description
unqualified-search-registries	An array of host [:port] registries to try when pulling an unqualified image, in order.
short-name-mode	Determines how Podman should handle short names. The values include the following: ■ enforcing—If there is one unqualified search registry, use it. If there are two or more registries defined and you are running Podman in a terminal, prompt the user to select one of the search registries; otherwise, there will be an error. ■ permissive—Behaves as enforcing but does not lead to an error if no terminal: just uses each entry in unqualified search registries until success. ■ disabled—Use all unqualified search registries without prompting.
credential-helpers	An array of default credential helpers is used as external credential stores. Note that containers-auth.json is a reserved value to use auth files as specified in containers-auth.json(5). The credential helpers are set to ["containers-auth.json"] if none are specified.

BLOCKING PULLING FROM CONTAINER REGISTRIES

Another interesting thing you can configure in registries.conf is the ability to block users from pulling from a container registry. In the following example, you will configure registries.conf to block pulls from docker.io. The registries.conf file has a specific [[registry]] table entry that can specify how to handle individual container registries. You can add this table multiple times—once per registry:

```
$ sudo vi /etc/containers/registries.conf
```

Add the following:

```
[[registry]]
Location = "docker.io"
blocked=true
```

Save the file. Examine the settings using podman info:

```
$ podman info
...
registries:
 Docker.io:
   Blocked: true
   Insecure: false
   Location: docker.io
   MirrorByDigestOnly: false
   Mirrors: null
   Prefix: docker.io
```

```
  search:
- registry.fedoraproject.org
- registry.access.redhat.com
- docker.io
- quay.io
```

Now, attempt to pull an image from docker.io:

```
$ podman pull docker.io/ubuntu
Trying to pull docker.io/library/ubuntu:latest…
Error: initializing source docker://ubuntu:latest: registry docker.io is
    blocked in /etc/containers/registries.conf or
    /home/dwalsh/.config/containers/registries.conf.d
```

This demonstrates that administrators have the ability to block content from specific registries. Table 5.5 describes the suboptions available for the [[registry]] table in the registries.conf file.

> **NOTE** Copy the original registries.conf to pull from docker.io for the rest of this book:
>
> ```
> $ sudo cp /etc/containers/registries.conf.orig/
> ➡ etc/containers/registries.conf
> ```

Table 5.5 [[registry]] **table fields**

Fields	Description
location	Name of the registry/repository to apply the filters on
prefix	Select the specified configuration when attempting to pull an image matched by the specific prefix.
insecure	If true, unencrypted HTTP as well as TLS connections with untrusted certificates are allowed.
blocked	If true, pulling images with matching names is forbidden.

Some users work on systems that are fully isolated from the internet but still need to use applications that rely on images from the internet. An example of this situation is if you have an application that expects to use registry.access.redhat.com/ubi8/httpd-24:latest but has no access to registry.access.redhat.com on the internet. You can download the image and put it onto an internal registry and then configure registries.conf with a mirror registry. If you configure an entry in registries.conf, it will look like this:

```
[[registry]]
location="registry.access.redhat.com"
[[registry.mirror]]
location="mirror-1.com"
```

Then your users can use the `podman pull` command:

```
$ podman pull registry.access.redhat.com/ubi8/httpd-24:latest
```

Podman actually pulls mirror-1.com/ubi8/httpd-24:latest, but users will not notice the difference.

> **NOTE** You have examined a few of the registries.conf fields, but there are many more. Use the `containers-registries.conf(5)` man page to explore all of them:

```
$ man containers-registries.conf
https://github.com/containers/image/blob/main/docs/containers-
    registries.conf.5.md
```

Now that you know how to configure storage and registries, it is time to look at how to configure all of the options central to Podman.

5.3   *Configuration files for engines*

Podman and other container engines use the github.com/containers/common library for handling the default settings not related to container storage or container registries. These configuration settings come from the containers.conf file. Podman reads the files in table 5.6 if they exist.

Table 5.6   **containers.conf files read by both rootful and rootless Podman**

File	Description
/usr/share/containers/containers.conf	Usually shipped with the distribution defaults
/etc/containers/containers.conf	System administrator can use this file to set and modify different defaults.
/etc/containers/containers.conf.d/*.conf	Some package tools might drop additional default files into this directory, sorted numerically.

When running in rootless mode, Podman also reads the files in table 5.7 if they exist.

Table 5.7   **containers.conf files read by rootless Podman**

File	Description
$HOME/.config/containers/containers.conf	Users can create this file to override system defaults.
$HOME/.config/containers/contain-ers.conf.d/*.conf	Users can also drop files here if they want, and they will be sorted numerically.

Unlike storage.conf and registries.conf, containers.conf files are merged together, and they do not fully override previous versions. Individual fields can override the same field in the higher-level containers.conf file. Podman does not require any containers.conf file to exist, since it has built-in defaults. Most systems come with only the distribution default overrides in /usr/share/containers/containers.conf.

NOTE Podman supports the CONTAINERS_CONF environment variable, which forces Podman to use the target of the $CONTAINERS_CONF. All other containers.conf files are ignored. This is useful for testing environments or making sure no one has customized the Podman defaults.

containers.conf currently supports five different tables, as shown in table 5.8. You need to be careful that you are in the correct table when you modify options.

Table 5.8 Containers.conf tables

Table	Description
[containers]	Configuration on running individual containers. Examples are the namespaces to stick containers in, whether or not SELinux is enabled, and default environment variables for containers.
[engine]	Default configurations for Podman to use. Examples are the default logging system, paths for OCI runtimes to use, and the location of conmon.
[service_destinations]	Remote connection data for use with podman --remote. Remote service is covered in chapter 9.
[secrets]	Information about the secrets plugin driver to use for containers
[network]	Special configuration for network configuration, including the default network name, location of CNI plugins, and default subnets

Many users of Podman want to change the default ways it launches containers in an environment. I previously explained how the HPC community wants to use Podman to run their workloads, but they are very specific about the volumes that get added to containers, which environment variables are added, and which namespaces are enabled.

Perhaps you want all of your containers to have the same environment variables set. Let's try an example. Run podman to show the default environment in the ubi8 image.

```
$ podman run --rm ubi8 printenv
PATH=/usr/local/sbin:/usr/local/bin:/usr/sbin:/usr/bin:/sbin:/bin
TERM=xterm
container=oci
HOME=/root
HOSTNAME=ba4acf180386
```

NOTE When using Podman in remote mode, for example on a Mac or Windows box, most of the settings of the containers.conf files are used from the Linux box on the server side. A containers.conf file in the user's home directory is used for storing connection data, which is covered in chapter 9. Mac and Windows clients are covered in appendixes E and F.

Now create an env.conf file in the home directory with the env="[foo=bar]" set:

```
$ mkdir -p $HOME/.config/containers/containers.conf.d
$ cat << _EOF > $HOME/.config/containers/containers.conf.d/env.conf
[containers]
env=[ "foo=bar" ]
_EOF
Run any container and you see the foo=bar environment set.
$ podman run --rm ubi8 printenv
PATH=/usr/local/sbin:/usr/local/bin:/usr/sbin:/usr/bin:/sbin:/bin
TERM=xterm
container=oci
foo=bar
HOME=/root
HOSTNAME=406fc182d44b
```

I use containers.conf when configuring Podman to run within a container. Many users want to run Podman within a container for CI/CD systems or for just testing out newer versions of Podman than their distribution enables. Because lots of people were having a hard time running Podman in a container, I decided to try to create a default image, quay.io/podman/stable, to help them. While creating that image, I realized several of the Podman defaults did not work well when running it within a container, so I used containers.conf to change those settings. You can see my containers.conf file at this link: http://mng.bz/o5DM.

You can see the contains.conf by actually running the image:

```
$ podman run quay.io/podman/stable cat /etc/containers/containers.conf
[containers]
netns="host"
userns="host"
ipcns="host"
utsns="host"
cgroupns="host"
cgroups="disabled"
log_driver = "k8s-file"
[engine]
cgroup_manager = "cgroupfs"
events_logger="file"
runtime="crun"
```

Here was what I was thinking while writing this file. First, I decided that since Podman is running inside of a container, I would disable all of the cgroups and namespaces other than the mount and user namespace. If users set cgroups or configured namespaces, then the container run by Podman in a container would follow the parent Podman's rules:

```
[containers]
netns="host"
userns="host"
ipcns="host"
utsns="host"
```

```
cgroupns="host"
cgroups="disabled"
```

The default `log_driver`, event logger, and cgroup manager on many distributions is journald and system, respectively, but inside of the container, systemd and journald are not running, so the container engine needs to use the filesystem:

```
[containers]
log_driver = "k8s-file"
[engine]
cgroup_manager = "cgroupfs"
events_logger="file"
```

Finally, use the OCI runtime `crun` rather than `runc`, mainly because `crun` is a lot smaller than `runc`:

```
[engine]
runtime="crun"
```

Now attempt to run a container within a container. A trick needed to make this work is running the podman/stable image with `--user podman`. This causes the Podman inside the container to run in rootless mode. Since the podman/stable image uses the `fuse-overlay` driver within the container, you also need to add the /dev/fuse device:

```
$ podman run --device /dev/fuse --user podman quay.io/podman/stable podman
➥ run ubi8-micro echo hi
Resolved "ubi8" as an alias (/etc/containers/registries.conf.d/
➥ 000-shortnames.conf
Trying to pull registry.access.redhat.com/ubi8:latest…
Getting image source signatures
Copying blob sha256:5368f457acd16b337e2b150741f727c46f886c69eea
➥ 1a4d56d0114c88029ed87
...
hi
```

> **NOTE** You examined a few of the containers.conf fields, but there are many more. Use the `container.conf(5)` man page to explore all of them:
>
> ```
> $ man containers.conf
> https:/ /github.com/containers/common/blob/main/docs/containers.conf.5.md
> ```

Now you know more about configuration tools specific to container tools like Podman. Next, you'll learn about some other system configuration files Podman needs.

5.4   *System configuration files*

When you run rootless Podman, you are using the /etc/subuid and /etc/subgid files
to specify the UID ranges for your containers. As I explained in section 3.1.2, Podman
reads the /etc/subuid and /etc/subgid files for UID and GID ranges allocated for
your user account. Podman then launches /usr/bin/newuidmap and /usr/bin/new-
gidmap, which verifies the range of UIDs and GIDs Podman specified are actually allocated to you. In certain cases you need to modify these files to add UIDs. Tools like
useradd automatically update the /etc/subuid and /etc/subgid when you add new
users to your system. For example, when I installed my laptop, useradd set up my user
account to use UID 3267 and added the mapping dwalsh:100000:65536 to /etc/sub-
uid and /etc/subgid. Figure 5.2 shows what containers based on this mapping look
like on my system.

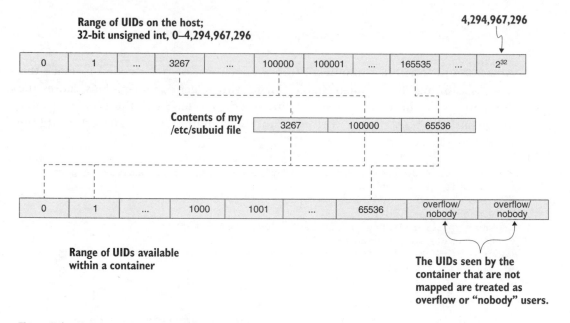

Figure 5.2   User namespace mapping for containers

> **NOTE** You want to keep the ranges of UIDs unique for each user and ensure
> they are not overlapping with any system UIDs. Podman and the system do
> not verify there is no overlap. If two different users had the same UIDs in
> their range, the processes in the containers would be allowed to attack each
> other from the user namespace perspective. Verifying this is a manual pro-
> cess. The useradd tool automatically selects unique ranges.

As the subuid(5) and subgid(5) man pages explain, each line in /etc/subuid and
/etc/subgid contains a username and a range of subordinate user IDs or GIDs,

respectively, that the user is allowed to use. The entry is specified with three fields delimited by colons. These fields are the following:

- Login name or UID
- Numerical subordinate user ID or group ID
- Numerical subordinate user ID or group ID count

Newer versions of the operating system, specifically the packages that ship /usr/bin/ newuidmap and /usr/bin/newgidmap, are gaining the ability to share the contents of these files via the network from an LDAP server. On Fedora, these executables are shipped in the shadow-utils package. Versions 4.9 or later have this feature.

> **TIP** Changes to /etc/subuid and /etc/subgid may not be immediately reflected in the user's account. This is a common problem for users who modify these files after they have already run Podman. But remember: when Podman first runs, it launches the podman pause process in the user namespace, and then all other containers join this Podman process's user namespace. To have a new user namespace take effect, you must execute the podman system migrate command, which stops the podman pause process and re-creates the user namespace.

Summary

- Podman has multiple configuration files based on the libraries it uses.
- Configuration files are shared between rootful and rootless environments.
- The storage.conf file is used to configure containers/storage, including the storage driver as well as the location where containers and their images are to be stored.
- The registries.conf and policy.json files are used to configure the container/ image library—primarily affecting access to container registries, short names, and mirror sights.
- The containers.conf file is used to configure all of the other defaults used within Podman.
- System configuration files /etc/subuid and /etc/subgid are used to configure the user namespace required for running rootless Podman.

Rootless containers

6

This chapter covers

- Why rootless mode is more secure
- How Podman works with the user and mount namespaces
- The architecture of Podman running in rootless mode

In this chapter, you will take a deep dive into what is going on when running Podman in rootless mode. I believe it is helpful to understand what is happening when you run rootless containers and learn about the problems that running in rootless mode can cause. With the introduction of containerized applications over the last few years, certain highly secure environments were not able to take advantage of the new technology.

High performance computing (HPC) systems run the fastest computers in the world. These tend to be at national labs and universities and deal with high-security information. They also handle some of the most secure data in the world and expressly forbid the use of rootful containers. HPC systems deal with huge datasets, including artificial intelligence, nuclear weapons, global weather patterns, and medical research. These systems tend to have thousands of shared computers, and they need to be locked down because of their multi-user shared environments. HPC computing believes running daemons as root is too insecure. If a rogue container process breaks out of confinement and gains root access, it can access highly sensitive data. Administrators of HPC environments couldn't use Open Container Initiative (OCI) containers until Podman came along. The HPC community is now working to move to rootless Podman.

Similarly, large financial company administrators do not allow users and developers access to root on their shared computer systems, out of concern for the financial data involved. The largest financial firms in the world were having difficulty fully adopting OCI containers. Figure 6.1 shows that even though the Docker client can be run as non-root, it connects to a root running daemon, giving full root access to the host OS.

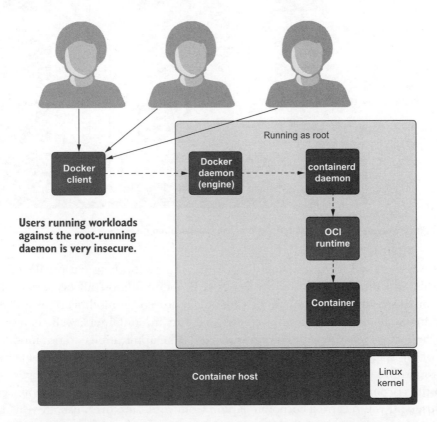

Figure 6.1 Multiple users' workloads sharing the same daemon running as root is inherently insecure.

The bottom line is that allowing users on a shared computing system to run container workloads accessing the same root-running daemon is too insecure. Running each user's containers in rootless mode under different users' accounts is more secure.

Figure 6.2 shows multiple users running Podman independent of each other, without any root access.

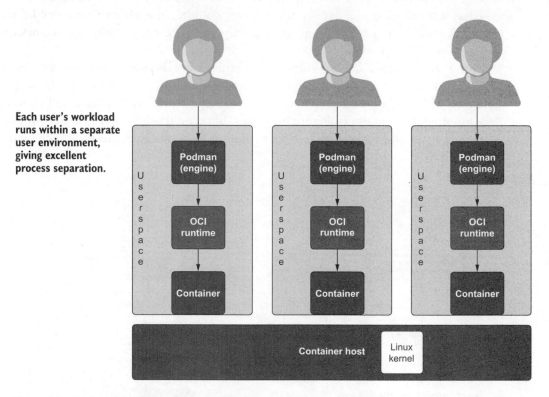

Each user's workload runs within a separate user environment, giving excellent process separation.

Figure 6.2   Each workload running within its unique user space is more secure.

Linux was designed from the ground up with a separation between privileged mode (rootful) and unprivileged mode (rootless). In Linux almost all tasks run without being privileged. Privileged operations are only required for modifications to the core operating system. Almost all applications that run in containers, web servers, databases, and user tools run without requiring root. The applications do not modify core parts of the system. Sadly, most of the images you will find on container registries are built to require root privileges or at least start as root and then drop privileges.

In the corporate world, administrators are very reluctant to give out root access to their users. If you receive a corporate laptop from your employer, usually you are not granted any root access. Administrators need to control what is installed on their systems because of scale, and they need to be able to update hundreds to thousands of machines at the same time, so controlling what is in the OS is critical. If someone else is administering your machine, they need to control who gets root access.

As a security person, I still flinch a little when I see sudo without a password. When I first started working with Docker, I was shocked that it was encouraging the use of the Docker group, giving users full root access on the host, without a password. The holy grail of hackers is to get a root exploit; this means the hackers gain full control over the system.

Bottom line is that if you have a container escape, as bad as that is, you are better off in rootless mode. This is because the hackers have control over only nonprivileged processes, as opposed to a root exploit, where they have full control over the system and all of the data (ignoring other security mechanisms like SELinux). Podman's design goals include the ability to run as many workloads as possible without being root and push the core OS to make it easier for you to run in this more secure mode.

6.1 How does rootless Podman work?

Have you ever wondered what happens behind the scenes of a rootless Podman container? In chapter 2, all of the Podman examples were running in rootless mode. Let's take a look at what happens under the hood of rootless Podman containers. I'll explain each component and then break down all of the steps involved.

> **NOTE** Some of this section is copied and rewritten from the "What Happens behind the Scenes of a Rootless Podman Container?" blog (https://www.redhat .com/sysadmin/behind-scenes-podman), written by myself and coworkers Matthew Heon and Giuseppe Scrivano.

First, let's first clear out all storage, so you can get a fresh environment, and then run a container on quay.io/rhatdan/myimage. (Remember that the `podman rmi --all --force` command removes all images and containers from storage.)

```
$ podman rmi --all --force
Untagged: registry.access.redhat.com/ubi8/httpd-24:latest
Untagged: registry.access.redhat.com/ubi8-init:latest
Untagged: localhost/myimage:latest
Untagged: quay.io/rhatdan/myimage:latest
Deleted: d2244a4379d6f1981189d35154beaf4f9a17666ae3b9fba680ddb014eac72adc
Deleted: 82eb390304938f16dd707f32abaa8464af8d4a25959ab342e25696a540ec56b5
Deleted: 8773554aad01d4b8443d979cdd509e7b8fa88ddbc966987fe91690d05614c961
```

Now that you have a clean system, you need to retrieve the application image, quay.io/ rhatdan/myimage, from the container registry you pushed it to in chapter 2. In the following command, re-create the application on your machine. The command pulls the image back from the container registry and starts the myapp container on your host.

```
$ podman run -d -p 8080:8080 --name myapp quay.io/rhatdan/myimage
Trying to pull quay.io/rhatdan/myimage:latest…
…
2f111737752dcbf1a1c7e15e807fb48f55362b67356fc10c2ade24964e99fa09
```

Now let's dig deep into what just happened when you ran a rootless Podman container. The first thing that happened was Podman needed to set up the user namespace. In the next section, I explain why, and how it works.

6.1.1   *Images contain content owned by multiple user identifiers (UIDs)*

In Linux, user identifiers (UIDs) and group identifiers (GIDs) are assigned to processes and stored on filesystem objects. The filesystem objects also have permission values assigned to them. Linux controls the processes' access to the filesystem based on these UIDs and GIDs. This access is called *discretionary access control* (DAC). When you log in to a Linux machine, your rootless user processes run with a single UID—say, 1000—but container images usually come with multiple different UIDs in their image layers. Let's examine the UIDs needed to run our image. In this example, you examine all the UIDs defined within the container image by running another container.

In the following command, launch a container with the quay.io/rhatdan/myimage image. You need to run the container as root (--user=root) inside the container to examine every file within the image.

```
$ podman run --user=root --rm quay.io/rhatdan/myimage -- bash -c "find /
➥ -mount -printf \"%U=%u\n\" | sort -un" 2>/dev/null
```

Since this is only a temporary container, use the --rm option to make sure the container is removed when it finishes running. The container runs a Bash script, which finds all of the UIDs and users associated with every file/directory in the container. The script pipes the output to show unique entries and redirects stderr to /dev/null to eliminate any errors.

```
$ podman run --user=root --rm quay.io/rhatdan/myimage -- bash -c "find /
➥ -mount -printf \"%U=%u\n\" | sort -un" 2>/dev/null
0=root
48=apache
1001=default
65534=nobody
```

As you can see from the output, our container image uses four different UIDs, shown in table 6.1.

Table 6.1   Unique UIDs required to run the container image

UID	Name	Description
0	root	Owns most of the content within the container image
48	apache	Owns all of the Apache content
1001	default	Default user the container runs as
65634	nobody	Assigned to any UID that is not mapped into the container

For you to pull a container image to your home directory, Podman needs to store at least three different UIDs: 0, 48, and 1001. Since the Linux kernel prevents nonprivileged accounts from using more than a single UID, you are prevented from creating files with different UIDs. You will need to take advantage of the user namespace.

USER NAMESPACE

Linux supports the concept of user namespaces, which is a mapping of UID/GIDs from the host to different UIDs and GIDs inside the namespace. Here is how the man page describes it:

```
$ man user namespaces
...
```

User namespaces isolate security-related identifiers and attributes—in particular, user IDs and group IDs (see credentials(7)), the root directory, keys (see keyrings(7)), and capabilities (see capabilities(7)). A process's user and group IDs can be different inside and outside a user namespace. In particular, a process can have a normal, unprivileged user ID outside a user namespace, while at the same time having a user ID of 0 inside the namespace; in other words, the process has full privileges for operations inside the user namespace but is unprivileged for operations outside the namespace.

Since your container requires more than one UID, the Podman process first creates and enters a user namespace, where it has access to more UIDs. Podman must also mount several filesystems to run a container. These mount commands are not allowed outside a user namespace (along with a mount namespace). Figure 6.3 shows the UIDs used within a user namespace.

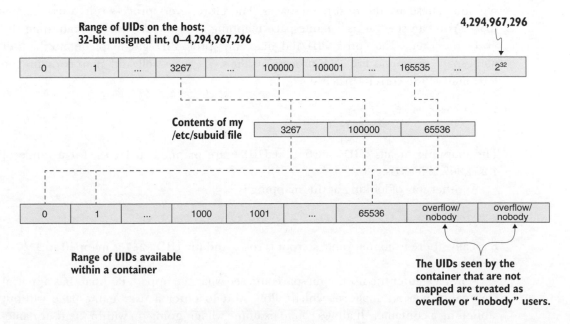

Figure 6.3   User namespace mapping for containers

When I created my system, I used the `useradd` program to create my account. It assigned me `3267` as my UID and GID, defined in /etc/passwd and /etc/group. It also allocated UID `100000-1065535`—additional UIDs and GIDs for me defined in /etc/subuid and /etc/subgid. Let's see the content of these files:

```
$ cat /etc/subuid
dwalsh:100000:65536
Testuser:165536:65536
$ cat /etc/subgid
dwalsh:100000:65536
Testuser:165536:65536
```

You can cat these files on your system, and you'll see something similar. On my system I also have a `testuser` account; `useradd` also added UIDs/GIDs for that user, starting right after my allocation.

Within a user namespace, I have access to UIDs `3267` (my UID) as well as `100000`, `100001`, `100002`, ..., `165535`, for a total of 65,537 UIDs. A root user can modify the /etc/subuid and /etc/subgid files to increase or decrease this number.

The `useradd` command starts at UID `100000` to allow you to have around 99,000 regular users plus 1,000 UIDs reserved for system services on a Linux system. The kernel supports more than 4 billion UIDs (2^{32} = 4,294,967,296). Since `useradd` allocates 65,537 per user, Linux can support more than 60,000 users. The 65,536 (2^{16}) number was picked because up until the Linux kernel 2.4, this was the maximum number of users on a Linux system. Let's look deeper into the user namespace.

Every process on a Linux system is in a namespace, including the init process and systemd. These are the host namespaces. Therefore, every process is in a user namespace. You can see the user namespace mapping for your process by examining the /proc filesystem. The /proc/PID/uid_map and /proc/PID/gid_map contain the user namespace mappings for each process on the OS. /proc/self/uid_map contains the UID map of the current process:

```
$ cat /proc/self/uid_map
     0        0 4294967295
```

The mapping means UIDs starting at UID `0` are mapped to UID `0` for a range of 4,294,967,295 UIDs.

Another way of looking at this mapping is

```
UID 0->0, 1->1,...3267->3267,...,4294967294->4294967294.
```

Basically, there is no mapping, so root is root. And my UID `3267` is mapped to `3267`—itself.

Now let's enter the user namespace and see what is mapped. Podman has a special command, `podman unshare`, which allows you to enter a user namespace without launching a container. It allows you to examine what is going on within the user namespace, while still running as a regular process on your system.

In the following command, I run `podman unshare` to launch the cat /proc/self/
uid_map within the default user namespace for my account:

```
$ podman unshare cat /proc/self/uid_map
        0      3267           1
        1    100000       65536
```

The mappings show that UID 0 is mapped to UID 3267 (my UID) for a range of 1.
Then UID 1 is mapped to UID 100000 for a range of 65536 UIDS.

Any UID not mapped to the user namespace is reported within the user namespace as the nobody user. You saw this earlier when you searched for the UIDs within
the container image:

```
$ podman run --user=root --rm quay.io/rhatdan/myimage -- bash -c "find /
➥ -mount -exec stat -c %u=%U {} \; | sort -un" 2>/dev/null
0=root
48=apache
1001=default
65534=nobody
```

If you look at / on the host, you see it is owned by the real root:

```
$ ls -l -ld /
dr-xr-xr-x. 18 root root 242 Sep 21 22:32 /
```

If you examine the same directory within the user namespace, you see it is owned by
the nobody user:

```
$ podman unshare ls -ld /
dr-xr-xr-x. 18 nobody nobody 242 Sep 21 22:32 /
```

Since the host's UID 0 is not mapped into the user namespace, the kernel reports the
UID as the nobody user. Processes within the user namespace only have access to nobody
files based on only the other or world permissions. In the example that follows, you will
launch a Bash script that shows the user is root within the user namespace but sees
/etc/passwd as owned by the user nobody. You can read the file with the grep command
because /etc/passwd is world readable. But the touch command fails because even root
cannot modify files owned by UIDs not mapped to the user namespace:

```
$ podman unshare bash -c "id ; ls -l /etc/passwd; grep dwalsh
➥ /etc/passwd; touch /etc/passwd"
uid=0(root) gid=0(root) groups=0(root),65534(nobody)
-rw-r--r--. 1 nobody nobody 2942 Sep 28 07:08 /etc/passwd
dwalsh:x:3267:3267:Dan Walsh:/home/dwalsh:/bin/bash
touch: cannot touch '/etc/passwd': Permission denied
```

Looking at your home directory on the host versus inside of the user namespace, you
see that the same files are reported as being owned by your UID:

```
$ ls -ld /home/dwalsh
drwx------. 365 dwalsh dwalsh 24576 Sep 28 07:30 /home/dwalsh
```

Within the user namespace, they are owned by root:

```
$ podman unshare ls -ld /home/dwalsh
drwx------. 365 root root 24576 Sep 28 07:30 /home/dwalsh
```

By default, Podman maps your UID to root within the user namespace. Podman defaults to root because, as I specified at the beginning of this chapter, the majority of container images assume they start with root.

I'll give one last example. Create a directory and a file within the directory while in the user namespace, and use the chown command to change the contents UIDs to 1:1:

```
$ podman unshare bash -c "mkdir test;touch test/testfile; chown -R 1:1 test"
```

Outside the user namespace, you see the test file is owned by UID 100000:

```
$ ls -l test
total 0
-rw-r--r--. 1 100000 100000 0 Sep 28 07:53 testfile
```

When you create the test file and chown it to UID/GID 1:1 within the user namespace, the on-disk owner is actually UID 100000/100000. Remember, within the user namespace, UID 1 is mapped to UID 100000, so when you create a UID 1 file within the user namespace, the OS actually creates UID 100000.

If you attempt to remove the file outside of the user namespace, you get an error:

```
$ rm -rf test
rm: cannot remove 'test/testfile': Permission denied
```

Outside the user namespace, you have access to only your UID; you don't have access to the additional UIDs.

> **NOTE** In section 3.1.2, I showed how user namespace mappings can be problematic with container volumes and discussed ways you can handle them.

Reentering the user namespace, you can remove the file:

```
$ podman unshare rm -rf test
```

Hopefully, you are starting to get a feel for the user namespace; the podman unshare command makes it easy to explore your system within the user namespace and understand what is happening in rootless containers. When running a rootless container, Podman needs more than just to run as root; it also needs access to some of the special powers of root called Linux capabilities.

In Linux, the root processes actually are not all equally powerful. Linux breaks root privileges into a series of Linux capabilities. A root process with all Linux capabilities is all powerful, while a root process without Linux capabilities is not allowed to manipulate a lot of the system. For example, it cannot read non-root files, unless those files have permission flags that allow all UIDs on the system to read (world readable).

Let's see how capabilities work with the user namespace:

```
$ man capabilities
...
DESCRIPTION
For the purpose of performing permission checks, traditional UNIX
implementations distinguish two categories of processes: privileged
processes (whose effective user ID is 0, referred to as superuser or root),
and unprivileged processes (whose effective UID is nonzero). Privileged
processes bypass all kernel permission checks, while unprivileged processes
are subject to full permission checking based on the process's credentials
(usually: effective UID, effective GID, and supplementary group list).
Starting with kernel 2.2, Linux divides the privileges traditionally
associated with superuser into distinct units, known as capabilities, which
can be independently enabled and disabled. Capabilities are a per-thread
attribute.
```

Linux currently has around 40 capabilities. Examples include `CAP_SETUID` and `CAP_SETGID`, which allow processes to change their UIDs and GIDs. `CAP_NET_ADMIN` allows you to manage the network stack.

Another capability called `CAP_CHOWN` allows processes to change the UID/GID of files on disk. In the preceding example, when you chowned the test directory to `1:1`, you used the `CAP_CHOWN` capability within the user namespace:

```
$ podman unshare bash -c "mkdir test;touch test/testfile; chown -R 1:1 test"
```

When you run within a user namespace, you are using namespaced capabilities. The root user within your user namespace has these capabilities beyond the UIDs and GIDs defined within the namespace. Processes with the namespaced capability, `CAP_CHOWN`, are allowed to chown files owned within your user namespace to UIDs that are also within the user namespace. If a process within a user namespace attempts to chown a file not mapped to the user namespace, owned by the `nobody` user, the process is denied permission. Likewise, a process attempting to chown a file with a UID not defined within the user namespace also gets denied. Similarly, the `CAP_SETUID` capability only allows processes to change UIDs to those defined within the user namespace.

When Podman runs a container, it needs to mount several filesystems for the container. In Linux, the `CAP_SYS_ADMIN` capability is required for mounting filesystems. From a security point of view, mounting filesystems can be a dangerous thing to do on Linux. The kernel adds additional controls on which types of filesystems can be mounted and requires your user-namespaced processes to also be in a unique mount namespace. In chapter 10, you will see how Podman limits the number of Linux capabilities available to the namespaced root within a container.

MOUNT NAMESPACE

Mount namespaces allow processes within them to mount filesystems, where the mount points are not seen by processes outside the mount namespace. Inside a mount namespace, you can mount a `tmpfs` on `/tmp`, which blocks the processes within the namespaces view of /tmp. Outside the mount namespace, processes still see the original mount and files within /tmp, but they do not see your mount.

In rootless containers, Podman needs to mount the content in the container images as well as /proc, /sys, devices from /dev, and some `tmpfs` filesystems. For that, Podman needs to create a mount namespace:

```
$ man mount namespaces
...
Mount namespaces provide isolation of the list of mount points seen by the
processes in each namespace instance. Thus, the processes in each of the
mount namespace instances see distinct single-directory hierarchies.
```

When you execute the `podman unshare` command, you are actually entering a different mount namespace as well as a different user namespace.

You can examine a process's namespaces by listing the /proc/self/ns/ directory as follows:

```
$ ls -l /proc/self/ns/user /proc/self/ns/mnt
lrwxrwxrwx. 1 dwalsh dwalsh 0 Sep 28 09:17 /proc/self/ns/mnt ->
➡ 'mnt:[4026531840]'
lrwxrwxrwx. 1 dwalsh dwalsh 0 Sep 28 09:17 /proc/self/ns/user ->
➡ 'user:[4026531837]'
```

Notice that when you enter the user namespace and mount namespace, the identifiers change:

```
$ podman unshare ls -l /proc/self/ns/user /proc/self/ns/mnt
lrwxrwxrwx. 1 root root 0 Sep 28 09:17 /proc/self/ns/mnt ->
➡ 'mnt:[4026533087]'
lrwxrwxrwx. 1 root root 0 Sep 28 09:17 /proc/self/ns/user ->
➡ 'user:[4026533086]'
```

In the following test, you can create a file on /tmp and then attempt to bind mount it onto /etc/shadow. Outside the namespaces, the kernel rightly prevents you from mounting the file, as you can see in the following output:

```
$ echo hello > /tmp/testfile
$ mount --bind /tmp/testfile /etc/shadow
mount: /etc/shadow: must be superuser to use mount.

Once you enter the user namespace and mount namespace, your namespaced
process can successfully mount over the /etc/shadow file. You can see when
you run the following command that /etc/shadow is actually modified:
$ podman unshare bash -c "mount -o bind /tmp/testfile /etc/shadow; cat
/etc/shadow"
hello
```

Once you exit the unshare, everything is back to normal.

USER NAMESPACE AND MOUNT NAMESPACE

As you saw previously, when you over-mount the /etc/shadow file, you might trick some setuid applications, like /bin/su or /bin/sudo, into giving you full root. The reason rootless users are not allowed to mount filesystems is to prevent this type of attack.

As you have seen, the separate mount namespace prevents you from affecting the host's view of the system, and anything you mount is seen only within the mount namespace. Within the user namespace, the container already has a namespaced root. Attacks on your mount points can be escalated to root only within the user namespace—not real root on the host. Containerized processes cannot change their UID (setuid) to real root or any other UID not mapped into the user namespace.

Even with the namespaces, the Linux kernel only allows you to mount certain filesystem types. Many filesystem types are too dangerous to allow for rootless users because they gain access to sensitive parts of the kernel. I work with filesystem kernel engineers to see if there are ways to lock down other filesystem types that could be allowed to be mounted in rootless mode, without affecting the security of the system.

As of kernel 5.13, the kernel engineers added native overlay mounts to the list of allowed mounts. The filesystem types currently allowed are listed in table 6.2.

Table 6.2   Filesystem mounts currently supported in rootless mode

Mount type	Description
bind	Used heavily in rootless containers. Because rootless users are not allowed to create devices, Podman bind mounts /dev on the host into the container. Podman also uses bind mounts to obscure content within the host filesystem from containers. Podman also bind mounts /dev/null over files in /proc and /sys to hide content. Volume mounts, described in chapter 3, also use bind mounts.
binderfs	Filesystem for the Android binder IPC mechanism. It is not supported by Podman.
devpts	Virtual filesystem mounted at /dev/pts. It contains device files used for terminal emulators
cgroupfs	Kernel filesystem used to manipulate cgroups; rootless containers can use cgroupfs to manipulate cgroups in cgroups v2. On v1 this is not supported. This is mounted at /sys/fs/cgroups.
FUSE	Used to mount container images using the fuse-overlayfs in rootless mode. Prior to kernel 5.13, this was the only way to use an overlay filesystem in rootless mode.
procfs	Mounted at /proc within the container. You can examine processes within the container.
mqueue	Implements the POSIX message queues API. Podman mounts this filesystem at /dev/mqueue.
overlayfs	Used for mounting the image. Performs better in the fuse-overlayfs filesystem. In certain use cases, it provides benefits over native overlay, such as NFS home directories.
ramfs	Dynamically resizable, ram-based Linux filesystem, currently not used with Podman.
sysfs	Mounted at /sys.
tmpfs	Used to obscure kernel filesystem directories from containers in /proc and /sys.

6.2   *Rootless Podman under the covers*

Now that you have some understanding of how the user namespace and mount name-space work and why they are needed, let's dig deeper into what Podman does when it runs a container. The first time you run a Podman container after logging in, Podman reads the /etc/subuid and /etc/subgid files, looking for your username or UID. Once Podman finds the entry, it uses the contents as well as your current UID/GID to generate a user namespace for you. Podman then launches the `podman pause` process to hold open the user and mount namespaces (figure 6.4).

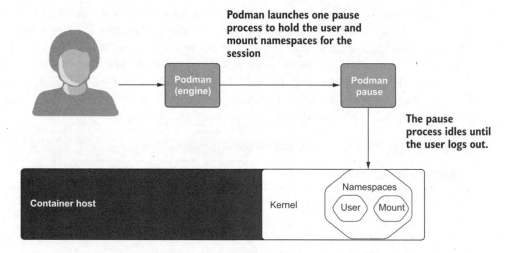

Figure 6.4   Podman launches the pause process to hold open the user and mount namespaces.

Users commonly report that after they run Podman containers, they see a `podman` process still running when they run the following command:

```
$ ps -e | grep podman
  2541 ?     00:00:00 podman pause
```

Subsequent running of the Podman commands joins the namespaces of the `podman pause` process. Podman does this to avoid race conditions when user namespaces are coming up and going down. The `pause` process remains running until you log out. You can also execute the `podman system migrate` command to remove it. The `pause` process's role is keeping the user namespace alive, as all rootless containers must be run in the same user namespace. If they were not, sharing content and other name-spaces (like sharing the network namespace from another container) is impossible.

> **NOTE** I often have users report that when changing the /etc/subuid and /etc/subgid files, their containers don't reflect the changes right away. Since the pause process was launched with the previous user namespace settings, it

needs to be removed. Executing the podman system migrate command restarts the pause process within the user namespace.

You can kill the pause process at any time, but Podman re-creates it on the next run. By default each rootless user has their own user namespace, and all of their containers run within the same user namespace. You can subdivide the user namespace and run containers with different user namespaces, but realize, by default, you only have 65,000 UIDs to work with. Running multiple containers in different user namespaces is much easier to do when running rootful containers. Now that the user namespace and mount namespace are created, Podman creates storage for the container's image and sets up a mount point to start storing the image.

6.2.1 Pulling the image

When pulling the image (figure 6.5), Podman checks if the container image quay.io/rhatdan/myimage exists in local container storage. If it does, Podman sets up the container network (see section 6.2.3). However, if the container image does not exist, Podman uses the containers/image library to pull the image. Following are the steps Podman takes while pulling the image:

1 Resolve the IP address for the registry: quay.io.
2 Connect to the IP address via the HTTPS port (443).
3 Begin pulling the manifest, all layers, and the config of the image using the HTTP protocol.
4 Find the multiple layers or blobs of quay.io/rhatdan/myimage.
5 Copy all layers simultaneously from the container registry to the host.

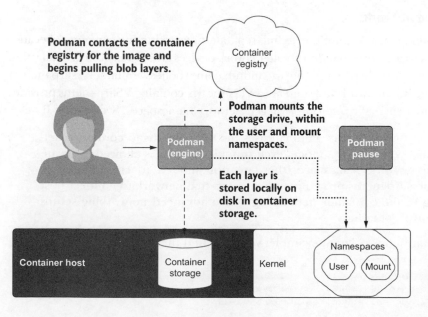

Figure 6.5 Podman pulls an image off a container registry and stores it in the container storage.

As each layer is copied to the host, Podman uses the containers/storage library to reassemble the layers in order, creating an overlay mount point for each of them on top of the previous one in ~/.local/share/containers/storage. If there is no previous layer, it creates the initial layer.

Next, containers/storage untars the contents of the layer into the new storage layer. As the layers are untarred, containers/storage chowns the UID/GIDs of files in the tarball into the home directory. Podman takes advantage of the user namespace CAP_CHOWN, as explained in previous sections. Remember that Podman fails to create content if the UID or GID specified in the TAR file was not mapped into the user namespace.

6.2.2   Creating a container

Once the containers/storage library finishes downloading the image and creating the storage, Podman creates a new container based on the image. Podman adds the container to Podman's internal database. It then tells containers/storage to create writable space on disk and use the default storage driver, usually overlayfs, to mount this space as a new container layer. The new container layer acts as the final read/write layer and is mounted on top of the image.

> **NOTE**   Rootful containers default to using native Linux overlay mounts. In rootless mode, kernel versions newer than 5.13 or with the rootless overlay feature backported (RHEL 8.5 kernels or later also have this feature) use the native overlay mounts. On older kernels, Podman uses the fuse-overlayfs executable to create the layer. In Podman, overlay and overlay2 are the same drivers.

At this point, Podman needs to configure the network inside the network namespace.

6.2.3   Setting up the network

In rootless Podman, you cannot create full, separate networking for containers because rootless processes are not allowed to create network devices and modify the firewall rules. Rootless Podman uses slirp4netns (https://github.com/rootless-containers/slirp4netns) to configure the host network and simulate a VPN for the container. Slirp4netns provides user-mode networking (slirp) for unprivileged network namespaces. See figure 6.6.

> **NOTE**   In rootful containers, Podman uses the CNI plugins to configure networking devices. In rootless mode, even though the user is allowed to create and join a network namespace, they are not allowed to create network devices. The slirp4netns program emulates a virtual network to connect host networking to the container networking. More advanced networking setups require rootful containers.

Remember that in our original example, you specified the 8080:8080 port mapping as follows:

```
$ podman run -d -p 8080:8080 --name myapp
    registry.access.redhat.com/ubi8/httpd-24
```

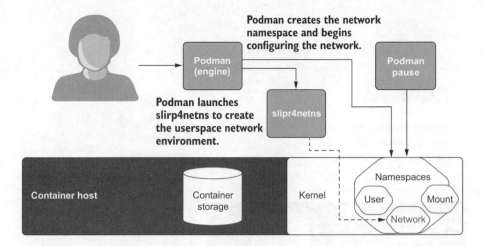

Figure 6.6 Podman creates a network namespace and launches slirp4netns to relay network connections.

Podman configures the slirp4netns program to listen on the host network at port `8080` and allow the container process to bind to port `8080`. The slirp4netns command creates a tap device that is injected inside the new network namespace, where the container lives. Each packet is read back from slirp4netns and emulates a TCP/IP stack in user space. Each connection outside the container network's namespace is converted in a socket operation the unprivileged user can run in the host network's namespace.

> **NOTE** Linux TAP devices create a user space network bridge. In user space, TAP devices can simulate network devices inside of a network namespace. Processes within the namespace interact with the network device. Packets read/written from the network device are routed via the TUN/TAP device to the user space program: slirp4netns.

Now that the storage and network are configured, Podman is ready to finally start the container process.

6.2.4 Starting the container monitor: conmon

Podman now executes conmon (container monitor) for the container, telling it to use its configured OCI runtime, usually `crun` or `runc`. It also executes the `podman container cleanup $CTRID` command when the container exits (see figure 6.7). conmon is described in section 4.1.

6.2.5 Launching the OCI runtime

The OCI runtime reads the OCI spec file and configures the kernel to run the container (see figure 6.8). OCI runtimes do the following:

1 Set up the additional namespaces for the container.
2 Configure cgroups v2 (cgroups v1 is not supported for rootless containers).

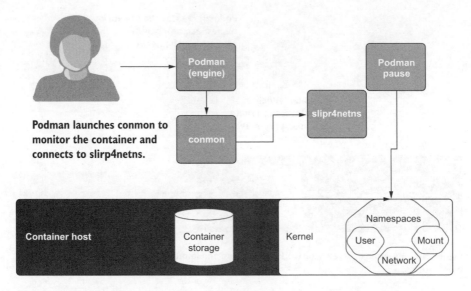

Podman launches conmon to monitor the container and connects to slirp4netns.

Figure 6.7   Podman launches the container monitor, which launches the OCI runtime.

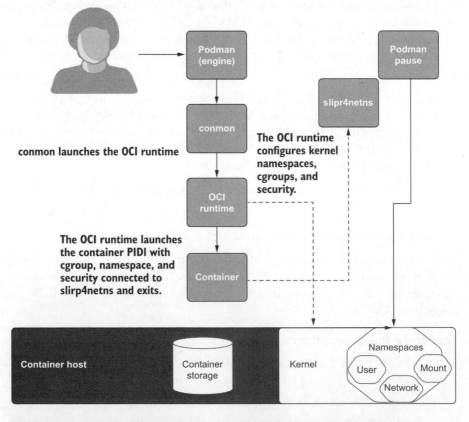

conmon launches the OCI runtime

The OCI runtime configures kernel namespaces, cgroups, and security.

The OCI runtime launches the container PIDI with cgroup, namespace, and security connected to slirp4netns and exits.

Figure 6.8   conmon launches the OCI runtime, which configures the kernel.

3 Set up the SELinux label for running the container.

4 Load the /usr/share/containers/seccomp.json seccomp rules into the kernel.

5 Set the environment variables for the container.

6 Bind mount any volumes onto the paths in the rootfs.

7 Switch the current / to the rootfs /.

8 Fork the container process.

9 Execute any OCI hook programs, passing them the rootfs as well as the container's PID 1.

10 Execute the command specified by the image.

11 Exit the OCI runtime, leaving conmon to monitor the container.

And finally, conmon reports the success back to Podman (see figure 6.9).

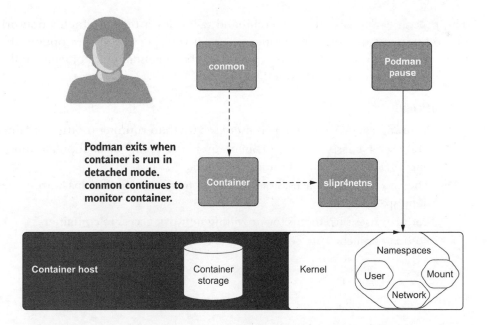

Figure 6.9 Podman and OCI runtime exit, leaving the container running with conmon monitoring it and slirp4netns providing the network.

The Podman command now exits because it ran in --detach (-d) mode.

```
$ podman run -d -p 8080:8080 --name myapp
    registry.access.redhat.com/ubi8/httpd-24
```

NOTE If later you want Podman to interact with the detached container, use the podman attach command, which connects to the conmon socket. conmon allows Podman to interact with the container process through the STDIN, STDOUT, and STDERR file descriptors, which conmon has been monitoring.

6.2.6   *The containerized application runs until completion*

The application process can exit on its own, or you can stop the container by executing the `podman stop` command:

```
$ podman stop myapp
```

When the container process exits, the kernel sends a `SIGCHLD` to the `conmon` process. In turn, conmon does the following:

1 Records the container's exit code
2 Closes the container's logfile
3 Closes the Podman command's `STDOUT`/`STDERR`
4 Executes the `podman container cleanup $CTRID` command
5 Exits itself

The `podman container cleanup` command takes down the slirp4netns network and unmounts all of the container mount points. If you specify the `--rm` option, the container is entirely removed—layers are removed from containers/storage, and the container definition is removed from the DB.

Summary

- Running rootless containers is more secure than running rootful containers.
- The user namespace gives ordinary users the ability to manipulate more than one UID and is key to running containers.
- The mount namespace allows Podman to mount filesystems within the user namespace.
- Podman uses slirp4netns for providing network access to containers.
- Podman launches the `conmon` process to monitor the container.

Part 3

Advanced topics

In part 3 of the book, you learn about advanced ways you can use Podman. This part discusses integrating Podman into your system and how Podman can work with other tools and orchestrators.

In chapter 7, I introduce systemd integration. Podman was developed to fully integrate into the system and takes advantage of the init system: systemd. Systemd can easily be run within Podman containers, and this chapter shows you how. Podman, likewise, can be run within systemd services and provides commands that allow you to automatically create the service configuration files to make this happen.

Chapter 8 shows you how Podman works with Kubernetes. Podman is not a container engine under Kubernetes but can work with Kubernetes YAML files. Because Kubernetes YAML files are used to define applications that run within Kubernetes, Podman makes it easy to move applications to and from a fully orchestrated environment back to a single node. This feature makes it easier for you to develop applications that eventually run under Kubernetes or debug problems that happen under Kubernetes by running these applications locally on your laptop. Kubernetes YAML is a great alternative to docker-compose YAML when running a group of containers on a single node.

Chapter 9 introduces the concept of Podman as a service, which allows tools written to use a RESTful API to generate and manage pods and containers with Podman. Tools like docker-compose and other Python tools built on docker-py can interface with the Podman service, eliminating the need for Docker altogether. The Podman service even allows Podman running on remote systems, such as Windows, macOS, and Linux, to work with Linux Podman containers.

Integration with systemd

This chapter covers

- Running systemd within the container as the primary process
- Generating systemd unit files from existing containers
- Socket-activated containerized services
- Using `sd-notify` containerized services
- The advantages of using journald as a logging driver and events backend
- Using Podman and systemd to manage containerized services' life cycles on edge devices

Systemd is the de facto init system for Linux. Almost every distribution of Linux defaults to systemd as the first process launched after the kernel, which then launches all of the services, including the login sessions for the user. Podman embraces the power of systemd and uses it for starting up lots of its services. When starting containerized services at boot time, Podman encourages users to use systemd unit files with Podman commands. Unit files are what systemd calls its configuration files. Systemd supports a few different types of unit files, including service files in which you can define a service, which you would want systemd to manage. A SystemD.socket is another kind of unit file systemd uses (see section 7.6). The systemd service unit files are a way to share your containerized service with the world. As you see in figure 7.1, Podman's fork/exec model grants systemd the ability to track the processes within a containerized service.

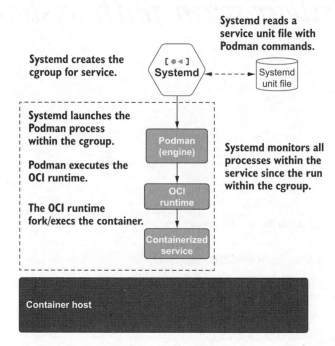

Figure 7.1   Systemd executing a Podman container

Systemd puts all the processes within a unit file service (called a scope) into the same cgroup hierarchy. It then uses the PID cgroup to keep track of all the processes and uses this information to manage the service. Container engines that use client-server methodology prevent systemd from keeping track of the containerized processes.

Podman also takes advantage of other services, as you will see in this chapter, to handle auto-restarting containers, auto-updating, and basic management of containerized services. You will be exposed to many Podman and systemd features in this chapter, but first you will run systemd within a Podman container.

7.1   Running systemd within a container

When containerization was first becoming popular, many evangelists taught the concept of microservices. A *microservice* is defined as one specialized service within a container. This single service runs as the initial PID (PID 1) within the containers and writes its logs directly to stdout and stderr. Kubernetes assumes microservices, and thus gathers logs from the stdin/stderr of the containers it runs. Figure 7.2 shows Podman running microservices.

**Podman launches a separate container for each service,
creating microservices that are only connected via the network.**

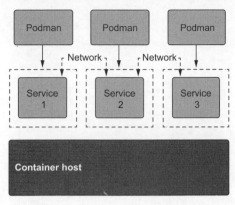

**Figure 7.2 Podman running
three microservices**

An alternative idea was to run systemd as the initial PID within the container and then allow systemd to start one or more services within the container. This school of thought argues that containerized services are to be launched the same way they are launched within a VM. Because service package designers (e.g., RPM and APT) develop systemd unit files as a precise way of launching their services within the OS, container developers should take advantage of these unit files. This approach allows running multiple services within the same container, taking advantage of local communications paths, and speeding up the conversion of large multiservice applications into a container and then, over time, breaking each service into its own microservice.

A final huge advantage of systemd in a container is that the init system handles the cleaning up of a zombie process. In Linux, when a process exits, the kernel sends the signal SIGCHLD to the parent process, and the parent process is supposed to collect the exit status of the exiting process. The kernel removes the process from the system when the parent reads the exit status. If no parent process reads the exit status, the exited process is left in the exited status and is referred to as a *zombie process*. The init system, systemd, reaps most processes on the system. In containers, the initial process running within the container is supposed to reap these processes. Sometimes container processes exit, and if PID1 does not reap them, they just linger and never disappear.

NOTE The podman-run command supports an -init option, which will launch a tiny init program just to reap the zombie processes.

Podman was designed to support both methods—microservices as well as multiservice containers. Figure 7.3 shows systemd running a multiservice application within a container.

Podman examines the cmd option of a container and then launches systemd for init or system. It then automatically launches the container in systemd mode.

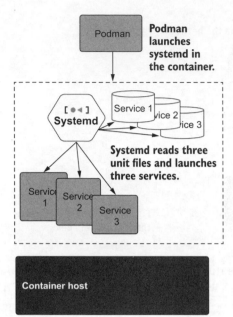

Figure 7.3   **Podman running systemd in a container with three services**

The following list shows all the commands that trigger Podman to run in systemd mode:

- /sbin/init
- /usr/sbin/init
- /usr/local/sbin/init
- /*/systemd (any path ending with the systemd command)

The registry.access.redhat.com/ubi8-init image is an example of an image intended to run in systemd mode.

Pull down the ubi8-init image, and examine the command:

```
$ podman pull ubi8-init
Resolved "ubi8-init" as an alias (/etc/containers/registries.conf.d/
➥ 000-shortnames.conf)
Trying to pull registry.access.redhat.com/ubi8-init:latest…
…
8cb83279f877a4bf3412827bf71c53188c3983194bd4663a1fc1378360844463
$ podman inspect ubi8-init --format '{{ .Config.Cmd }}'
[/sbin/init]
```

Systemd requires the environment to be configured in a certain way; otherwise, systemd attempts to correct the environment. The next section explains how Podman satisfies systemd requirements.

7.1.1 Containerized systemd requirements

Systemd makes some assumptions about the environment it starts in, like /run and /tmp need to have tmpfs mounted on them. When the environment is incorrect, systemd attempts to correct it by mounting tmpfs on /run and /tmp. Mounting requires CAP_SYS_ADMIN privilege within the container, which is not allowed in unprivileged containers. Systemd then blows up.

To fix this problem, after examining the entry point and CMD of a container image to see if they are running systemd, Podman modifies the container environment to match systemd expectations. When systemd sees the mounts, it skips them, allowing systemd to run within a locked-down environment. Table 7.1 describes the requirements systemd needs and Podman provides to successfully run within an unprivileged container.

Table 7.1 Systemd requirements for running within a nonprivileged container

Systemd expectations	Description
/run on a tmpfs	Systemd requires /run to have a tmpfs mounted on it. If /run is not mounted with a tmpfs, systemd will attempt to mount a tmpfs on /run. A default locked-down container is prevented from mounting, so systemd will fail.
/tmp on a tmpfs	Similarly to /run, systemd will attempt to mount a tmpfs on /tmp, if there is not already one mounted there.
/var/log/journald as a tmpfs	Systemd within the container expects to be able to write to /var/log/journald, so Podman mounts a tmpfs to make this possible.
container environment variable	Systemd uses the fact that a container environment variable is set to change some of its default behavior, making it run better within a container.
STOPSIGNAL=SIGRTMIN+3	Unlike most processes on a system, systemd ignores SIGTERM and will only cleanly exit with it when it receives the signal SIGRTMIN+3 (37).

7.1.2 Podman container in systemd mode

You can examine the environment of a systemd-based container with the --systemd =always flag. First, launch a container with systemd mode enabled with the --systemd=always flag. This option runs the container in systemd mode even when not running systemd, making it easier to debug the environment. You can exec systemd at this point and start it as PID1:

```
$ podman create -rm -name SystemD -ti --systemd=always ubi8-init sh
774a50204204768edd73f178b6afdf975cf9353e3b90af9df77273d639f60ac3
```

Use podman inspect to examine the StopSignal for the container; Podman set it to 37 (SIGRTMIN+3):

```
$ podman inspect SystemD --format '{{ .Config.StopSignal}}'
37
```

Now, start up the container, and look at the mounts for /run and /tmp; you will see that both are mounted with a tmpfs. Finally, check to see if the container environment variable is set:

```
$ podman start --attach SystemD
# mount | grep -e /tmp -e /run | head -2
tmpfs on /tmp type tmpfs
➡ (rw,nosuid,nodev,relatime,context="system_u:object_r:container_file_t:s0:
➡ c37,c965",uid=3267,gid=3267,inode64)
tmpfs on /run type tmpfs
➡ (rw,nosuid,nodev,relatime,context="system_u:object_r:container_file_t:s
➡ 0:c37,c965",uid=3267,gid=3267,inode64)
# printenv container
Oci
```

If you just run a container based on ubi8-init, you will see systemd launched:

```
$ podman run -ti ubi8-init
SystemD 239 (239-45.el8_4.3) running in system mode. (+PAM +AUDIT +SELINUX
➡ +IMA -APPARMOR +SMACK +SYSVINIT +UTMP +LIBCRYPTSETUP +GCRYPT +GNUTLS
➡ +ACL +XZ +LZ4 +SECCOMP +BLKID +ELFUTILS +KMOD +IDN2 -IDN +PCRE2
➡ default-hierarchy=legacy)
Detected virtualization container-other.
Detected architecture x86-64.
Welcome to Red Hat Enterprise Linux 8.4 (Ootpa)!
Set hostname to <26bbf9077219>.
Initializing machine ID from random generator.
Failed to read AF_UNIX datagram queue length, ignoring:
➡ No such file or directory
[  OK  ] Listening on initctl Compatibility Named Pipe.
[  OK  ] Reached target Swap.
[  OK  ] Listening on Journal Socket (/dev/log).
[  OK  ] Listening on Journal Socket.
…
```

Here you can notice that systemd ignores SIGTERM by pressing Ctrl-C. So to stop this container you need to go to a different terminal and execute

```
# podman stop -l
```

This causes Podman to send the proper STOPSIGNAL (SIGRTMIN+3) to systemd in the container. Systemd will shut down instantly when it receives this signal.

Now that you understand what systemd requires, it is time to create a service systemd will run. In the following section, you will build a systemd-based Apache service that will run with systemd within the container.

7.1.3   *Running an Apache service within a systemd container*

In this section, you will create a Containerfile that uses ubi8-init as the base image and then install Apache httpd. Finally, you will enable this service and set up the Apache script we have been working with.

Create a Containerfile:

```
$ cat << _EOF > /tmp/Containerfile
FROM ubi8-init
RUN dnf -y install httpd; dnf -y clean all
RUN systemctl enable httpd.service
_EOF
```

Recall that the FROM ubi8-init line will tell Podman to use the ubi8-init image as the base image for your new image:

```
FROM ubi8-init
RUN dnf -y install httpd; dnf -y clean all
RUN systemctl enable httpd.service
```

The RUN dnf -y install httpd; dnf -y clean all line tells Podman to run a container that executes the dnf command and install the httpd package on top of the ubi8-init image. The second dnf command removes excess files and logs dnf created while installing, as there is no reason to include these in the image:

```
FROM ubi8-init
RUN dnf -y install httpd; dnf -y clean all
RUN systemctl enable httpd.service
```

The final RUN systemctl enable httpd.service command tells Podman to launch another build container and execute the systemctl command to enable the httpd .service. When systemd runs on a container created from the newly created image, the httpd service will be started:

```
FROM ubi8-init
RUN dnf -y install httpd; dnf -y clean all
RUN systemctl enable httpd.service
```

Now build the image using podman build, and name the image my-systemd:

```
$ podman build -t my-systemd /tmp
STEP 1/3: FROM ubi8-init
STEP 2/3: RUN dnf -y install httpd; dnf -y clean all
Updating Subscription Management repositories.
Unable to read consumer identity
...
COMMIT my-systemd
--> 104fa99d9a2
Successfully tagged localhost/my-systemd:latest
104fa99d9a2138404039cf15b470ab04784cdaab2226f29bd8343f8e24ec60e2
```

Now run a container on this systemd-based container image with a volume mounted from the host. Since the default Apache package listens on port 80, use --p 8080:80, which, as you learned, maps port 8080 to port 80 within the container. Use an html folder with index.html from section 3.1:

```
$ podman run -d --rm -p 8080:80 -v ./html:/var/www/html:Z my-systemd
71f1678084390925b7488f68ab58cd55e16009d69b717045b8ed5ef14e8599ce
```

You volume mounted (-v ./html/:/var/www/html:Z) in the ./html directory, with the goodbye world index.html file:

```
$ podman run -d --rm -p 8080:80 -v ./html:/var/www/html:Z my-systemd
```

Launch a web browser to check whether the containerized service is working (as seen in figure 7.4):

```
$ web-browser localhost:8080
```

Figure 7.4   Web browser window showing system-based container image running your content

Notice that you did not need to specially handle the HTTPD server processes when designing the image; your container is running HTTPD the same way a VM would. If you need to enable another service within the image, you can easily do this by installing the package and enabling its unit file.

To see one of the shortcomings of this setup, you can run the podman logs command:

```
$ podman logs 71f1678084
```

There is no output. Since systemd is running at the PID1 of the container, it is not writing any output to the logs. You need to exec into the container and use journalctl or read the httpd logs in /var/log/httpd/error_log to see if there were any problems. Now that you have seen how to use systemd within a container, it is time to see how you can use systemd and Podman to take advantage of advanced systemd features.

7.2   *Journald for logging and events*

The systemd journal (journald) is the modern logging system on Linux. It is a system service that collects and stores logging data. A big advantage of using journald is that records are permanently stored, and log rotation is built in. Podman uses journald by default for storing its logging data.

7.2.1 Log driver

Podman defaults to using journald as the log driver on systems running with systemd as the init system. If you run Podman in a container without systemd running, it falls back to using the file driver. One consideration when picking a log driver is whether the log data persists when the container is removed.

A second concern is how large the log file grows. The log records all `stdout` and `stderr` within the container. Containers running for a very long time can create a lot of log content. Only the journald driver has log rotation built into it, provided by systemd. If you use the k8s-file driver there is a risk your system could run out of space. Table 7.2 shows the available log drivers and whether the log data persists and the system supports log rotation.

Table 7.2 Log driver options

Library	Description	Persist logs after container removal	Log rotation
Journald	Use systemd journal to store logging information	✓	✓
k8s-file	Store logging data in Kubernetes format flat file	✗	✗
None	Do not store any logging information	✗	✗

While I recommend you use journald for the log driver, some rootless users are not allowed to use journald, depending on their system configuration. In other cases, like running Podman within a container, journald is not available.

You can see the default log driver on your system by using the following command:

```
$ podman info --format '{{ .Host.LogDriver }}'
k8s-file
```

For some reason, the system settings on your host were set to log to k8s-file. It is simple to override the default log driver for your system using containers.conf. Create a log_driver.conf file in the home directory, $HOME/.config/containers/containers.conf.d, with the log_driver option set:

```
$ mkdir -p $HOME/.config/containers/containers.conf.d
$ cat > $HOME/.config/containers/containers.conf.d/log_driver.conf << _EOF
[containers]
log_driver="journald"
_EOF
$ podman info --format '{{ .Host.LogDriver }}'
journald
```

Great. Next, you will see the benefits of the journald log driver by launching a container with the `--rm` option to remove the container when it exits:

```
$ podman run --rm --name test2 ubi8 echo "Check if logs persist"
Check if logs persist
```

Check that the journal keeps a record of the container being launched:

```
$ journalctl -b | grep "Check if logs persist"
Nov 10 06:19:54 fedora conmon[657915]: Check if logs persist
```

If you had launched with the k8s_file option, Podman would have removed the log file when the container was removed. No log entry would be left behind. Like logs, Podman supports using the systemd journal to store events.

7.2.2   Events

Podman events record different steps in the container life cycle; for example, you can see the start event of the last container you ran:

```
$ podman events --filter event=start --since 1h
2021-11-10 06:35:06.780429582 -0500 EST container start
➥  ecf04c4802bb120f34533560fbfc19ab023bcce63d48945ab0e8ff06cc6eeda1
…
```

Examine the default events logger with the Podman info command:

```
$ podman info --format '{{ .Host.EventLogger }}'
journald
```

You can modify the events logger with the events_logger option in containers.conf similarly to how you did for the log_driver. Table 7.3 shows the available events logging options.

Table 7.3   Events logger options

Library	Description	Persist log data on reboot	Log rotation
Journald	The systemd journal will record all events.	✓	✓
File	Store events in a file, usually on /run.	✗	✗
None	Do not store any events information.	✗	✗

If your system uses the file event logger, the events backend file is stored on $XDG_RUNTIME_DIR for rootless users, which is on a tmpfs by default. The events backend file grows continuously, until you reboot the system when using the file driver. This could cause failures to run containers or the system to run out of space, since the events backend does not roll over unless you are using journald. Also, when you reboot, the events log is lost. Switching to journald preserves the events and handles rotation of the events log. I recommend you keep the log driver and the events driver the same values, either as journald, a flat file, or none, if you don't need the events and logs.

You have examined using systemd within Podman as well as journald to manage log files and events. Now you will look at how to set up your system to automatically run a container when the system comes up using systemd.

7.3   *Starting containers at boot*

As you learned in chapter 1, Podman does not run as a daemon, meaning you cannot rely on a daemon to automatically start containers at boot time. Often you will need to run containerized services via systemd. Systemd can be configured to install, run, and manage containerized applications. Many applications are shipped as container images and will include systemd service unit files for launching. There are many features provided by systemd to improve the way containerized services run on your system.

7.3.1   *Restarting containers*

Podman relies on systemd to start containerized services by launching Podman within systemd unit files. The `podman run` command allows you to choose whether to restart a container (`--restart`) if it is not stopped by a user—for example, if the container crashes or the system reboots. Table 7.4 shows the restart policies available to Podman.

One simple way systemd helps is by starting containers with a restart policy of `always`. If you set the `always` option and the system reboots, Podman uses two systemd services to automatically restart containers marked with `--restart=always`. One service handles rootful containers, and the other handles all rootless containers on the system.

Table 7.4   Restart policy

Option	Description	Restart on boot
`no`	Do not restart containers on exit.	✗
`on-failure[:max_retries]`	Restart containers when they exit with a non-zero exit code, retrying indefinitely or until the optional `max_retries` count is hit.	✗
`always` or `unless-stopped`	Restart containers when they exit, regardless of status, retrying indefinitely.	✓

When your system boots up, systemd runs the following Podman command to start any containers with restart policy set to `always`:

```
/usr/bin/podman start --all --filter restart-policy=always
```

> **NOTE** Podman ships with two systemd service files used to restart services—one for rootful and one for rootless:
>
> /usr/lib/systemd/system/podman-restart.service
> /usr/lib/systemd/user/podman-restart.service

The `--restart=always` works great, but it requires you to create a container on the system and will restart containers even if they fail. Systemd was designed to run services; you will see in the next section that you can easily create a service unit file with Podman to run your containerized service.

7.3.2 *Podman containers as systemd services*

As you have seen, systemd uses unit files to specify how to run a service. Figure 7.5 shows how systemd works with Podman to launch a container.

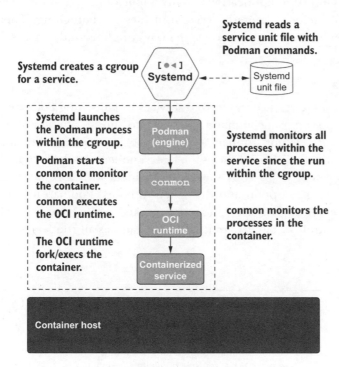

Figure 7.5   Podman fork/exec architecture is ideal for systemd service management.

In figure 7.5, I point out that systemd is able to monitor all the processes running within the systemd unit file. This allows it to easily start and stop the processes. The `conmon` process is also running within the systemd service monitoring the container processes. `conmon` still notices when the container exits, saves its exit code, and cleanly shuts down the container environment. Systemd does not know about the container; it only knows about the processes running within the unit file, including the container processes.

Systemd unit files have many different ways to run and launch processes, and Podman has many different options for running containers. Configuring the unit files can be very complex. Many users have written unit files to run containers, but several have stumbled over problems when doing so. The most common problem is running the `podman run --detach` command within a unit file. When the Podman command detaches and exits, systemd assumes the service is complete and takes it down, even though `conmon` and the container are still running. One of the most common questions I hear from users is the following: "How should I run my container within a systemd unit file?"

Podman has a feature to generate unit files with the best defaults. First, re-create the container from `myimage`, and then use `podman systemd generate` to create a systemd service unit file to manage your container.

Create a container based on the image you created in chapter 2:

```
$ podman create -p 8080:8080 --name myapp quay.io/rhatdan/myimage
...
8879112805e976b4b6d97c07c9426bdde22ee4ffc7ba4daa59965ae25aa08331
```

Now use Podman to generate a unit file off of this container:

```
$ mkdir -p $HOME/.config/systemd/user
$ podman generate systemd myapp > $HOME/.config/systemd/user/myapp.service
```

Notice in the myapp.service script that Podman created an `ExecStart` field. On service start, systemd will execute the `ExecStart` command, which simply starts the container you created:

```
ExecStart=/usr/bin/podman start 8879112805...
```

On service stop, systemd executes the `ExecStop` command added to the unit file:

```
ExecStop=/usr/bin/podman stop -t 10 8879112805...
Let's take a look at the generated service file:
$ cat $HOME/.config/systemd/user/myapp.service
# container-
      8879112805e976b4b6d97c07c9426bdde22ee4ffc7ba4daa59965ae25aa08331.service
# autogenerated by Podman 3.4.1
# Wed Nov 10 08:23:06 EST 2021
[Unit]
Description=Podman container-8879112805...service
Documentation=man:podman-generate-SystemD(1)
Wants=network-online.target
After=network-online.target
RequiresMountsFor=/run/user/3267/containers
[Service]
Environment=PODMAN_SYSTEMD_UNIT=%n
Restart=on-failure
TimeoutStopSec=70
ExecStart=/usr/bin/podman start 8879112805...
ExecStop=/usr/bin/podman stop -t 10 8879112805...
ExecStopPost=/usr/bin/podman stop -t 10 8879112805...
PIDFile=/run/user/3267/containers/overlay-
      containers/8879112805.../userdata/conmon.pid
Type=forking
[Install]
WantedBy=multi-user.target default.target
```

To make this all work, you need to tell systemd to reload its database, so it will notice changes in the unit files:

```
$ systemctl --user daemon-reload
```

Start the service with the following command:

```
$ systemctl --user start myapp
```

Check to see that the service is running:

```
$ systemctl --user status myapp
• myapp.service - Podman container-8879112805....service
  Loaded: loaded (/home/dwalsh/.config/SystemD/user/myapp.service;
➡ disabled; vendor preset: disabled)
  Active: active (running) since Thu 2021-11-11 07:19:08 EST; 3min 9s ago
...
$ podman ps
CONTAINER ID  IMAGE                              COMMAND
➡ CREATED      STATUS        PORTS        NAMES
8879112805e9  quay.io/rhatdan/myimage:latest     /usr/bin/run-http...
➡ 23 hours ago  Up 5 minutes ago  0.0.0.0:8080->8080/tcp  myapp
```

Now you can run the web browser against localhost port 8080 to see it is running (see figure 7.6):

```
$ web-browser localhost:8080
```

Figure 7.6   Web browser window connecting `myapp`

To shut down the service, execute

```
$ systemctl --user stop myapp
```

The ability to generate systemd service files offers a lot of flexibility to users, and it intentionally blurs the difference between a container and any other program or service on the host.

One problem with this unit file is that it's specific to the container you created. You need to first create the container and generate specific service files. You are not able to hand the unit file to another user and have them run your service on their machine.

Luckily, Podman has support for creating a more portable systemd unit file: `podman generate systemd --new`.

7.3.3   *Distributing systemd unit files to manage Podman containers*

As shown previously, the `podman generate systemd` command generated a unit file, which started and stopped an existing container. The `--new` flag instructs Podman to generate units that run, stop, and remove containers. Try it out in the same container:

```
$ podman generate systemd --new myapp > $HOME/.config/systemd/user/
➥ myapp-new.service
```

Notice that with the `--new` option, Podman creates a slightly different unit file. Examine the following `ExecStart` command, and you will see the original `podman create -p 8080:8080 --name myapp quay.io/rhatdan/myimage` command you used to create the container has been changed to use the `podman run` command. Also notice that Podman added additional options to make running under systemd easier (`--cidfile =%t/%n.ctr-id --cgroups=no-conmon --rm --sdnotify=conmon -d --replace`).

Podman now adds the `ExecStop` command (`/usr/bin/podman stop --ignore --cidfile=%t/%n.ctr-id`), which tells systemd how to stop the container when someone executes `systemctl stop` or the system shuts down.

Finally, Podman adds an `ExecStopPost` command (`/usr/bin/podman rm -f --ignore --cidfile=%t/%n.ctr-idType=notify`), which systemd executes once the `ExecStop` command completes. The Podman command removes the container from the system:

```
$ cat $HOME/.config/systemd/user/myapp-new.service
# container-8879112805....service
# autogenerated by Podman 3.4.1
# Thu Nov 11 07:40:34 EST 2021
[Unit]
Description=Podman container-8879112805...service
Documentation=man:podman-generate-SystemD(1)
Wants=network-online.target
After=network-online.target
RequiresMountsFor=%t/containers
[Service]
Environment=PODMAN_SystemD_UNIT=%n
Restart=on-failure
TimeoutStopSec=70
ExecStartPre=/bin/rm -f %t/%n.ctr-id
ExecStart=/usr/bin/podman run --cidfile=%t/%n.ctr-id --cgroups=no-conmon -
➥ rm --sdnotify=conmon -d --replace -p 8080:8080 --name myapp
➥ quay.io/rhatdan/myimage
ExecStop=/usr/bin/podman stop --ignore --cidfile=%t/%n.ctr-id
ExecStopPost=/usr/bin/podman rm -f --ignore --cidfile=%t/%n.ctr-idType=notify
NotifyAccess=all
[Install]
WantedBy=multi-user.target default.target
```

You can remove the container and the image from your system, and when you tell `systemctl` to start the service, Podman will pull the image and create a new container. This means the myapp-new.service unit file can be shared with a different user, and when they run the service, Podman will likewise pull the image and run the container on their systems, without them ever creating the container in the first place. Table 7.5 shows the different commands added to the unit file based on whether you used the `--new` flag.

Table 7.5   Differences between unit files

Option	Commands
With --new	ExecStart=/usr/bin/podman run ...--cidfile=%t/%n.ctr-id --cgroups=no- ➥ conmon --rm --sdnotify=conmon -d --replace -p 8080:8080 --name ➥ myapp quay.io/rhatdan/myimage ExecStop=/usr/bin/podman stop --ignore --cidfile=%t/%n.ctr-id ExecStopPost=/usr/bin/podman rm -f --ignore --cidfile=%t/%n ➥ .ctr-idType=notify
Without --new	ExecStart=/usr/bin/podman start 8879112805... ExecStop=/usr/bin/podman stop -t 10 8879112805... ExecStopPost=/usr/bin/podman stop -t 10 8879112805...

Once you have your containerized service running on many machines, you need to think about maintaining it. Podman has a way to do this without human intervention: auto-update.

7.3.4 *Automatically updating Podman containers*

In chapter 2, we talked about container images aging like stinky cheese. When the container image gets updated with new software or vulnerability fixes, you need to reach out to these machines, pull the updated images, and re-create the containerized services. It is much less labor intensive when machines manage their own updates.

Imagine you configure a service to run on a container image on hundreds of nodes. A few months later, you add new features to the application in the image or, more importantly, a new CVE is found. Now you need to update the image and then recreate the service on all of the nodes.

Podman automates this process with auto-update; each node watches for new images to appear in a container registry. When the image shows up, the node pulls down the image and re-creates the container. No human interaction is involved.

Podman auto-update enables you to use Podman in edge use cases, update workloads once they are connected to the network, and roll back failures to a known good state. In addition, running containers is essential for implementing edge computing in remote data centers or on internet-of-things (IoT) devices. Auto-updates enable you to use Podman in edge use cases, update workloads once they are connected to the network, and reduce maintenance costs.

To implement this behavior, Podman requires containers to have a special label, `--label "io.containers.autoupdate=registry"`, and the container must be run in a systemd unit generated by `podman generate systemd --new`. Table 7.6 describes the auto-update modes available.

Table 7.6 Auto-update modes

`io.containers.autoupdate`	Description
`registry`	Podman connects to the container registry and checks if a different image than the one used to create the container is available; if there is one, Podman will update the container.
`local`	Podman connects to the container registry but compares local images to the one the container was created with; if they are different, Podman updates the container.

First, stop the systemd service if it is running, and remove the existing `myapp` container:

```
$ systemctl --user stop myapp-new
$ podman rm myapp --force -t 0
```

Re-create the myapp container with the special label `"io.containers.autoupdate=registry"`:

```
$ podman create --label "io.containers.autoupdate=registry" -p 8080:8080
➥ --name myapp quay.io/rhatdan/myimage
397ad15601868eb6fd77fe0b67136869cde9e0ffad90ee5095a19de5bb4b999e
```

Re-create the systemd unit file with the `--new` option:

```
$ podman generate systemd myapp --new > $HOME/.config/systemd/user/
➥ myapp-new.service
```

Tell systemd the unit file changed by executing `daemon-reload`, and start the service:

```
$ systemctl --user daemon-reload
$ systemctl --user start myapp-new
```

The myapp-new service is now ready to be automatically updated. When you execute the `podman auto-update` command, Podman examines running containers for the `io.containers.autoupdate` label set to `image`. For each container with that label, Podman reaches out to the container registry and checks if the image has changed since the container was created. If the image has changed, Podman restarts the corresponding systemd unit. Recall that on a systemd restart, the following steps happen:

1 Systemd stops the service by executing the `podman stop` command:

```
ExecStop=/usr/bin/podman stop --ignore --cidfile=%t/%n.ctr-id
```

2 Systemd executes the `ExecStopPost` script. Once the container stops, this script removes the container with `podman rm`:

```
ExecStopPost=/usr/bin/podman rm -f --ignore --cidfile=%t/
➡ %n.ctr-idType=notify
```

3 Systemd restarts the services with the `podman run` command, including the `--label "io.containers.autoupdate=registry"` option:

```
ExecStart=/usr/bin/podman run --cidfile=%t/%n.ctr-id --cgroups=no-conmon --rm
➡ --sdnotify=conmon -d --replace --label
➡ io.containers.autoupdate=registry -p 8080:8080
➡ --name myapp quay.io/rhatdan/myimage
```

The `podman run` command in the third step will reach out to the registry and pull down the updated container image and re-create the containerized application on it. The container, its environment, and all dependencies are restarted.

You can test this by changing your image, pushing it to a registry, and then running the `podman auto-update` command as follows:

```
$ podman exec -i myapp bash -c 'cat > /var/www/html/index.html' << _EOF
<html>
 <head>
 </head>
 <body>
  <h1>Welcome to the new Hello World<h1>
 </body>
</html>
_EOF
```

Now commit the image as `myimage-new`, and push it to the registry with the original name: `myimage`. Finally, remove the image from the local store to simulate that the image was never on your system:

```
$ podman commit myapp quay.io/rhatdan/myimage-new
…
226ec055eef82ac185c53a26de9e98da4e6403640e72c7461a711edcbcaa2422
$ podman push quay.io/rhatdan/myimage-new quay.io/rhatdan/myimage
…
$ podman rmi quay.io/rhatdan/myimage-new
```

Once the new image is at the registry, and you have removed it from local storage, you can run `podman auto-update`, which notices the new image and restarts the service. This triggers Podman to pull the new image and re-create the containerized service:

```
$ podman auto-update
Trying to pull quay.io/rhatdan/myimage…
Getting image source signatures
Copying blob ecfb9899f4ce done
Copying config 37e5619f4a done
Writing manifest to image destination
```

```
Storing signatures
UNIT               CONTAINER          IMAGE
POLICY     UPDATED
myapp-new.service  c8888d1319c4 (myapp)  quay.io/rhatdan/myimage  registry
true
```

Your application has been updated to the latest version of the image.

Some notable `podman auto-update` options include the following:

- `--dry-run`—This option is useful to see if any containers need to be updated, without actually updating them.
- `--roll-back`—This option tells Podman to roll back to the previous image if the update fails, as covered in the next section.

SYSTEMD TIMERS TRIGGER PODMAN UPDATES

Podman ships with two auto-update systemd timer units and two auto-update service units—one each for rootful containers and rootless containers. The timer units triggered by systemd once per day are the following:

- /usr/lib/systemd/system/podman-auto-update.timer
- /usr/lib/systemd/user/podman-auto-update.timer

The timer units tell systemd to execute the appropriate auto-update service unit file:

- /usr/lib/systemd/system/podman-auto-update.service
- /usr/lib/systemd/user/podman-auto-update.service

With this feature, systemd will launch Podman, which looks for containers with the `"io.containers.autoupdate=registry"` label, like you created last section. Once Podman finds a container with the label, it checks if the container's image has been updated on the registry. If the image has changed, Podman starts the update process. This means you can run your systems unattended, and they are updated within 24 hours with the newest version of the container image every time you push an updated image to a registry. If you share the unit file you generated with others, then they also get the auto-updates.

A big concern with auto-update is what happens if the update is broken. In that case, you will have hundreds of nodes updated to a broken service. Systemd has a feature called `sd-notify`, which allows a service to say its initialization is complete and it is ready to be used as a service.

> **NOTE** Some of this section is based on previously written blogs copied and rewritten from the "How to use auto-updates and rollbacks in Podman" blog (http://mng.bz/neDK), written by myself and coworkers Valentin Rothberg and Preethi Thomas.

7.4   Running containers in notify unit files

Unit file services can specify that they wait to start until other services are up and running. For example, you can have a website that relies on a database to be running before the web service accepts connections. Systemd usually considers a service started after it launches the primary process of the service. However, many services take time to initialize and can't accept connections right away. The database in the previous example might take minutes before it is ready for the web service to start receiving connections.

Systemd defines a special service type called notify (or sd-notify) that allows the service process to notify systemd when it is actually fully up and running. Systemd starts the web service only when systemd is notified that the database is ready.

Systemd tells a service that it needs to be notified that the service is ready by passing the NOTIFY_SOCKET environment variable pointing to the systemd socket to be notified. By default, systemd listens on the /run/SystemD/notify socket. When Podman executes within a NOTIFY unit file, it needs to volume mount the socket into the container and pass down the environment variable into the container (figure 7.7).

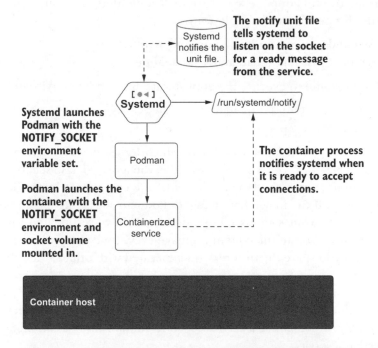

Figure 7.7   Containerized `sd_notify` systemd service launched by Podman

If the service does not notify systemd within the specified time, systemd will mark the service as failed. Podman auto-update checks if the new service is fully up and running, and if the check fails, Podman can automatically roll back to the previous container—again, without human intervention.

7.5 Rolling back failed containers after update

If your defined service supports `sd-notify` and writes to the notify socket within the time limit, the `podman auto-update` command will succeed. However, if it fails, Podman will remove the new container and retag the original image. Finally, it will create the container on the previous image, and your service will come back up in the previous state. You could even set up your system-based containerized service to notify your logging system that the update failed. The rollback gives you time to figure out what went wrong and ship a new image, triggering the auto-update again. As you can see, systemd can be used as the container orchestrator of a single system.

You have now discovered a few nice features systemd provides for running containers without human intervention. One additional feature Podman can take advantage of is socket activation, which allows you to specify a container within a unit file that will not be running until the first packet comes to its socket.

7.6 Socket-activated Podman containers

When systemd was first introduced, it was lauded for speeding up the boot of a system. Before systemd, each service started sequentially, and services that relied on different services to be run needed to wait. To speed up the boot and get better with resource allocation, systemd uses *socket-activated services.* When you set up a socket-activated service, systemd sets up listening IP or UNIX domain sockets on behalf of your service, without starting the service (figure 7.8).

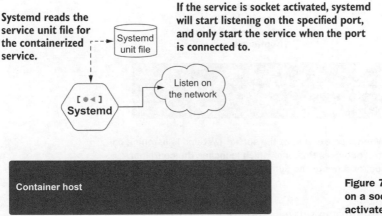

Figure 7.8 Systemd listening on a socket for a socket-activated container

When a connection to the socket arrives, systemd activates the service and hands the connection to it. Afterwards, the service handles connections. The service can at some point in the future idle itself by exiting. If a new connection comes in, systemd accepts the new connection and starts the service again.

Socket activation allows systemd to indicate that a service started instantly, without actually starting or waiting for the service to start, speeding up the boot process. Socket activation allows systemd to run more services on the system, since many services are idle and not using system resources. Basically, your services can be stopped and only run when they are actually needed and not sit idle, waiting for another connection. With containerized services, the main process of the service is Podman, and it needs to pass the connection down to the service running within the container (figure 7.9).

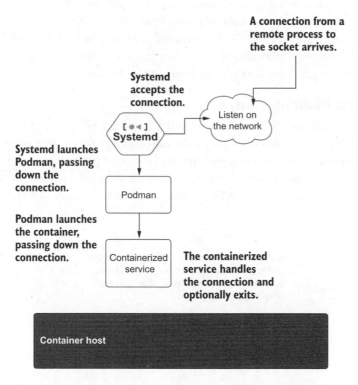

Figure 7.9   When a connection to the socket systemd is listening on arrives, systemd activates Podman, which launches the container, passing the socket down to the container.

Shut down the myapp.service, and create the myapp.socket:

```
$ systemctl --user stop myapp.service
$ cat > $HOME/.config/systemd/user/myapp.socket << _EOF
[Unit]
Description=myapp socket service
PartOf=myapp.service
[Socket]
ListenStream=127.0.0.1:8080
```

```
[Install]
WantedBy=sockets.target
_EOF
```

Now, enable the socket, and make sure no containers are running:

```
$ systemctl --user enable --now myapp.socket
$ podman ps
CONTAINER ID  IMAGE     COMMAND    CREATED    STATUS
➡ PORTS      NAMES
```

Connect a web browser to the socket (see figure 7.10):

```
$ web-browser localhost:8080
```

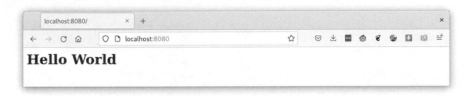

Figure 7.10   A web browser window connecting to the `ubi8/httpd-24` **container running in Podman with updated Hello World HTML.**

Notice that podman.socket started the podman.service, which created a container to handle the connection:

```
$ podman ps
CONTAINER ID  IMAGE                          COMMAND             CREATED
➡ STATUS          PORTS                NAMES
69c34949d632  quay.io/rhatdan/myimage:latest  /usr/bin/run-http...
➡ 2 minutes ago  Up 2 minutes ago  0.0.0.0:8080->8080/tcp  myapp
```

Now if you stop the service, not only will the container be stopped, but it will be removed:

```
$ systemctl --user stop myapp.service
$ podman ps -a
CONTAINER ID  IMAGE     COMMAND    CREATED    STATUS
➡ PORTS      NAMES
```

Socket activation allows you to run the service only when needed, saving system resources. Later, you can take the service down, knowing that if a new connection comes in, systemd and Podman will handle it.

Summary

- Podman enables running systemd as the primary process within a container.
- Journald is recommended for Podman logs and events.
- Systemd can be used to start and restart containers at boot time.
- Podman auto-update is used to manage the life cycle of a container and its image.
- Socket-activated systemd services can be used with Podman-based containers.
- The `podman generate systemd` command makes it easy to generate systemd service files for running your containers.

Working with Kubernetes 8

This chapter covers

- Creating Kubernetes YAML files from existing Podman pods and containers
- Creating Podman containers and pods from a Kubernetes YAML file
- Shutting down and removing pods and containers using the Kubernetes YAML file
- Building container images on the fly before launching pods and containers from a Kubernetes YAML file
- Running Podman inside of a Podman and Kubernetes container

Some readers come to this chapter expecting to see how Podman can be used as the container engine for Kubernetes, similar to how it has used Docker in the past. While there have been some efforts to use Podman as the container engine for Podman (the kind project supports this), I do not generally recommend that you use Podman for this purpose. I recommend you use CRI-O described in appendix A, since it was built specifically to work with Kubernetes and shares the underlying libraries of Podman. Kubernetes is now discouraging users from using the Docker backend and encouraging them to use a CRI-O or containerd as a backend.

This chapter covers using the same structured language with both Kubernetes and Podman as well as how to run Podman containers inside a Kubernetes cluster. You have learned how to create microservices as containers and pods from the command line using Podman. Often software developers and packagers need to take their applications and run them on multiple machines. You might want to take your web application and add a database backend. If the web application becomes popular, you will need to run multiple instances on different nodes. Wiring different microservices together and orchestrating all of them together is not something Podman does. This is where Kubernetes comes in.

In this chapter, you will learn about running these same containers and pods in Kubernetes. The kubernetes.io website says, "Kubernetes, also known as K8s, is an open-source system for automating deployment, scaling, and management of containerized applications." I look at Kubernetes as the tool for running containers on multiple machines at the same time—a way to orchestrate large clusters of containerized microservices.

One problem you may encounter is that most container development happens with tools like Podman and Docker, which use fairly simple command-line interfaces to create containers and pods. But Kubernetes uses a declarative language written in YAML files.

I will not be diving deep into how Kubernetes works in this chapter because there are already many in-depth books on the topic, including *Kubernetes in Action* by Marko Lukša (Manning, 2020) and *Kubernetes for Developers* by William Denniss (Manning, 2020), that describe all the features of Kubernetes. But I will be describing the developer language of Kubernetes: the Kubernetes YAML file.

> **NOTE** The yaml.org website first describes YAML as the "YAML Ain't Markup Language." It further elaborates, "YAML is a human-friendly data serialization language for all programming languages."

Translating command-line options to a structured language like YAML presents a barrier for developers moving from containers on a single node to containers running at scale. How do you specify volumes, the image to be used, the security constraints, the network ports, and so on? In section 8.2, you will learn to use Podman to take your locally created pods and containers to generate Kubernetes YAML files from them.

After writing and deploying your application in a pod using Kubernetes YAML files, users are likely to find problems with your application running within Kubernetes. Testing the application at scale can be difficult, and often you just want to run the application locally on your system, without having to set up and configure a Kubernetes cluster. In section 8.3, you will learn about `podman play kube`. This Podman command allows you to run the Kubernetes YAML file locally, without Kubernetes, so you can test and debug problems.

The final part of this chapter will cover running Podman within containers, including running it within a Kubernetes cluster. Administrators, developers, and quality engineers need to test containers within their continuous integration (CI) systems using Podman. Often these CI systems are built on Kubernetes clusters. Section 8.4 teaches you different ways to run the Podman command within containers launched by Podman and Kubernetes.

8.1   Kubernetes YAML files

The Kubernetes YAML file is the object used to launch pods and containers within Kubernetes. In chapter 5, you learned the configuration files used by Podman are written using TOML, which is very similar to YAML. Both configuration languages are attempting to be human readable. YAML relies on indenting substanzas, which is different syntax than you learned with TOML. You can go to the yaml.org website to learn more about the language.

If you are going to work a lot with Kubernetes YAML files, it is nice to have a text editor or IDE, like Visual Studio and VS Code, that can at least understand YAML; it is even better if it knows the Kubernetes language. Kubernetes YAML is descriptive and powerful. It allows you to model the desired state of your application in a declarative language. As stated in the introduction to this chapter, writing these YAML files is a barrier for developers to get through when moving their containers from a local system to Kubernetes. Most developers just web search an existing Kubernetes YAML file and then begin cutting and pasting their container command, image, and options into the YAML file. While this works, it can lead to unintended consequences—and often unnecessary work.

Scott McCarty, product manager of Podman, tossed out an idea: "What I would really like to do is help users get from Podman to orchestrating their containers with Kubernetes." This led the Podman developers to create a new Podman command: `podman generate kube`.

8.2   Generating Kubernetes YAML files with Podman

Imagine you want to take the containers you generated in the previous chapters and run them within Kubernetes. You need to write the Kubernetes YAML file to make this happen. Where should you start?

In this chapter, you will learn a new command: `podman generate kube`. This Podman command captures the description of local pods and containers and then translates them into Kubernetes YAML. This helps you transition to a more sophisticated orchestration environment like Kubernetes. The generated Kubernetes YAML file can then be used by Kubernetes commands to launch your pods and containers into a Kubernetes cluster.

You can re-create the containers or pods locally using Podman on the command line with the same Podman `run`, `create`, and `stop` commands you have learned in the previous chapters. Using the following commands, re-create the container you have been working with.

First, remove the container if it exists using `podman rm`. You will introduce a new flag, `--ignore`, which tells the `podman rm` command not to report errors when the container does not exist. Then, re-create the container from the command line:

```
$ podman rm -f --ignore myapp
$ podman create -p 8080:8080 --name myapp quay.io/rhatdan/myimage
9305822e6089ca28a1fdbb005c12f57f4a26be273fe5d49a1908eadbcfdcb7d4
```

Now, use the command `podman generate kube myapp` to generate the Kubernetes YAML file. Podman inspects the existing container or pod in its database for all of the fields required to run the container in Kubernetes and then populates them in the Kubernetes YAML file:

```
$ podman generate kube myapp > myapp.yaml
```

Figure 8.1 shows the result of a `podman generate kube` command.

```
$ cat myapp.yaml.
# Save the output of this file and use kubectl create -f to import
# it into Kubernetes.
#
# Created with podman-4.1
apiVersion: v1                                    Kubernetes works with Pods,
kind: Pod  ◄                                      so Podman generates a Pod
metadata:                                         specification.
  creationTimestamp: "2021-11-22T11:57:12Z"
  labels:
    app: myapppod                                 Podman names the pod
  name: myapp_pod  ◄                              myapp_pod based on the
spec:                                             name of the container.
  containers:
  -args:
   -/usr/bin/run-httpd
   image: quay.io/rhatdan/myimage:latest  ◄       The name of the image to
   name: myapp                                    be used by Kubernetes
   ports:
   -containerPort: 8080  ◄                        Ports mappings to expose
     hostPort: 8080                               the container to the internet
   securityContext:
     capabilities:
       drop:                                      Security constraint
       -CAP_MKNOD  ◄                              modifications for your
       -CAP_NET_RAW                               container
       -CAP_AUDIT_WRITE
```

Figure 8.1   Shows the generated `myapp.yaml` file from the `myapp` container

Examine parts of the YAML file. Understand that Kubernetes works with pods, even though you created a container, `podman generate kube`, that creates a pod specification. Podman names the pod `myapp-pod` and the container `myapp` within the specification, based on the name of the original container:

```
metadata:
  creationTimestamp: "2021-11-22T11:57:12Z"
  labels:
    app: myapppod
  name: myapp-pod
spec:
  containers:
  - args:
    - /usr/bin/run-httpd
    image: quay.io/rhatdan/myimage:latest
    name: myapp
```

Notice, in the containers section, that the image name, quay.io/rhatdan/myimage:latest, is recorded, which tells Kubernetes where to download the image for the container from. It also tells Kubernetes the command arguments to start the app within the container, /usr/bin/run-httpd:

```
spec:
  containers:
  - args:
    - /usr/bin/run-httpd
    image: quay.io/rhatdan/myimage:latest
```

In the same container section, you see that the Podman ports are recorded, -p 8080:8080 spec:

```
  containers:
  - args:
    - /usr/bin/run-httpd
    image: quay.io/rhatdan/myimage:latest
    name: myapp
    ports:
    - containerPort: 8080
    hostPort: 8080
```

Finally, at the end of the containers section, you see securityContext, which records that Podman, by default, drops three additional Linux capabilities: CAP_MKNOD, CAP_NET_RAW, and CAP_AUDIT_WRITE:

```
    securityContext:
    capabilities:
    drop:
    - CAP_MKNOD
    - CAP_NET_RAW
    - CAP_AUDIT_WRITE
```

Most containers run fine without these Linux capabilities, but the OCI specification enables these three by default. This tells Kubernetes that this pod can run more securely without these capabilities, and Kubernetes will drop them. You can find out more about Linux capabilities by running the command man capabilities.

At this point, you can just run this Kubernetes YAML file in any Kubernetes cluster, usually running a command like the following:

```
kubectl create -f myapp.yml
```

Often you will have to add sophistication and orchestration to the YAML file and leverage advanced functions of Kubernetes. For example, the generated Kubernetes YAML file will only generate a single instance of your application. If you want to run multiple versions of your applications on different nodes, you could add a `replicas` option to your YAML file, as seen in figure 8.2.

```
# Save the output of this file and use kubectl create -f to import
# it into Kubernetes.
#
# Created with podman-4.1
apiVersion: v1
kind: Pod
metadata:
  creationTimestamp: "2021-11-22T11:57:12Z"
  labels:
    app: myapppod
  name: myapp_pod
spec:
  containers:
  - args:
    - /usr/bin/run-httpd
    image: quay.io/rhatdan/myimage:latest
    name: myapp
    ports:
    - containerPort: 8080
      hostPort: 8080
    securityContext:
      capabilities:
        drop:
        - CAP_MKNOD
        - CAP_NET_RAW
        - CAP_AUDIT_WRITE                  Tells Kubernetes to run two pods
replicas: 2                                with this template
```

Figure 8.2   The modified Kubernetes YAML file ready to run two replicas

The `replicas` flag tells Kubernetes that the myapp.yaml file wants to have two `myapp` pods running on two different nodes at all times. Replicas and other advanced Kubernetes features are out of the scope of Podman. The `podman play kube` command ignores these fields.

Some notable `podman generate kube` options include the following:

- `-f, --filename`—This writes output to the specified path.
- `-s, --service`—This generates YAML for a Kubernetes service object.

Now that you have generated a Kubernetes YAML file, it'd be nice to be able to reverse the process. If you had a Kubernetes YAML file, you may want to generate Podman pods and containers.

8.3   Generating Podman pods and containers from Kubernetes YAML

Imagine you get a Kubernetes YAML file and want to examine it running locally. You could set up a local Kubernetes cluster, but it would be nice if you could just play the pods locally. Podman provides a command for doing this. The podman play kube command creates pods, containers, and volumes based on structured Kubernetes YAML files. The created pods and containers are automatically started. To test this, you can simply remove the container you created and then run the generated myapp.yaml file with the following commands:

```
$ podman rm -f --ignore myapp
$ podman play kube myapp.yaml
Pod:
b70aedd8105a6915428928a2b33fd7ecede632298088ea25d9db74ba9b16201e
Container:
a4d78fdfa5d8f751aafb06f3782e36a3aaf5b3804ca57694385de2ea1e400fe6
```

Kubernetes only runs pods with containers; it does not run just containers by themselves. When the podman play kube command reads the YAML, file it launches the pod along with the container. Notice in figure 8.3 that the play command created a Pod with your container along with the infra containers.

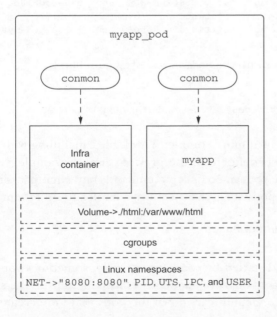

Figure 8.3   The myapp-pod **running with the** myapp **container and the infra container**

The `podman generate kube` command creates the pod named `myapp-pod`, based on the name within the myapp.yaml file. The names of the containers are generated by appending the name of the pod to the name of the container: `myapp-pod-myapp`. If the YAML file defines additional containers, they need to be labeled similarly:

```
$ cat myapp.yaml
…
  name: myapp-pod
spec:
  containers:
  - args:
    name: myapp
```

You can display the pods running on your system with the `podman pod ps` command. Add the `--ctr-names` option to also list the containers running within the pod:

```
$ podman pod ps --ctr-names
POD ID         NAME        STATUS   CREATED    INFRA ID      NAMES
b70aedd8105a  myapp-pod  Running 1 day ago b7a276c62c1d
➥ myapp-pod-myapp,b70aedd8105a-infra
```

Now examine the two containers running with the `podman ps` command, using the following command:

```
$ podman ps
CONTAINER ID  IMAGE                          COMMAND            CREATED
➥ STATUS          PORTS              NAMES
b7a276c62c1d  k8s.gcr.io/pause:3.5
➥ 3 minutes ago  Up 3 minutes ago  0.0.0.0:8080->8080/tcp  b70aedd8105a-infra
a4d78fdfa5d8  quay.io/rhatdan/myimage:latest  /usr/bin/run-http...
➥ 3 minutes ago  Up 3 minutes ago  0.0.0.0:8080->8080/tcp  myapp-pod-myapp
```

Shut down the Pod and container with the `podman pod stop` command:

```
$ podman pod stop myapp-pod
b70aedd8105a6915428928a2b33fd7ecede632298088ea25d9db74ba9b16201e
```

`podman play kube` can execute much more complex YAML files, including with multiple pods, volumes, and containers defined. In the previous simple example, you can just shut down the pod with the `podman pod stop` command, but when `podman play kube` generates multiple unique pods, it gets a little more complex to shut them down.

8.3.1 Shutting down pods and containers based on a Kubernetes YAML file

Although you can stop each pod started by `podman play kube`, sometimes you don't only want to stop the pods and containers but actually remove them from the system. The `podman play kube --down` command tears down the pods that were created by a previous run of `play kube`. The pods are stopped and then removed. Any volumes created are left intact. Shut down the myapp.yaml pod created in the previous example:

```
$ podman play kube myapp.yaml --down
Pods stopped:
B70aedd8105a6915428928a2b33fd7ecede632298088ea25d9db74ba9b16201e
Pods removed:
b70aedd8105a6915428928a2b33fd7ecede632298088ea25d9db74ba9b16201e
```

Notice that Podman not only stopped the pod but also removed it. You can verify the pod is gone with the `podman pod ps` command:

```
$ podman pod ps
POD ID      NAME        STATUS      CREATED     INFRA ID    # OF CONTAINERS
```

This leaves you back in a state where you can run `podman play kube` again, which will create fresh pods and containers:

```
$ podman play kube myapp.yaml
Pod:
302b1d2c0048a49ea32c2e6ffa0e0549af199ab2bc32de285eef5da628efe28c
Container:
b9f080dc6e13b4a4c37fa66a9b727dbeb2af30f0c3824044aba8a46eebfe15c5
```

This mimics what happens with Kubernetes running pods and containers. Kubernetes always creates pods and containers fresh and tears them down when it completes. The ability to generate all of the pods and containers from the YAML file and then remove them with the `--down` flag is similar to the workflow of `docker-compose`. Podman has the big advantage of using the same YAML file for running the pods and containers as in a multinode, orchestrated environment with Kubernetes. One other feature `docker-compose` has is the ability to build the images defined within the YAML file, which the Podman developers also added to `podman play kube`.

8.3.2 Building images using Podman and Kubernetes YAML files

Users who were using `podman play kube` as a replacement for `docker-compose` requested Podman to add a feature to build images, rather than always pull them from a container registry. While Kubernetes does not support such a feature, Podman developers decided to add the `--build` flag to `podman play kube`. Because `podman build` can process Containerfiles or Dockerfiles, enhancing `podman play kube` was simple.

The idea is to create a containerized application via a container image that is produced on demand. Normal Kubernetes workflow requires developers to build the image using `podman build` and push it to a container registry using `podman push`, as you learned in chapter 2. Then you can retrieve the image from the registry using `podman play kube`. The `podman play kube --build` option allows it to execute `podman build` internally and generate the image on demand, rather than forcing you to use a container registry.

NOTE The --build option is not available with the remote Podman client, so you can't use it on Mac or Windows.

In this example, you are going to re-create the Containerfile used in section 6.1.3:

```
$ cat > ./Containerfile << _EOF
FROM ubi8-init
RUN dnf -y install httpd; dnf -y clean all
RUN systemctl enable httpd.service
_EOF
```

Recall that this Containerfile builds a container image with systemd running as the init system and the HTTPD service running and listening on port 80. First, remove all pods and containers:

```
$ podman pod rm --all --force
$ podman rm --all --force
```

Now rebuild the my-systemd image:

```
$ podman build -t mysystemd.
STEP 1/3: FROM ubi8-init
STEP 2/3: RUN dnf -y install httpd; dnf -y clean all
Updating Subscription Management repositories.
Unable to read consumer identity
...
Successfully tagged localhost/mysystemd:latest
bb1634ce1457f2eb70f84af33599d211eae64cb5f951e40e91481b6e58b747bf
```

Now re-create a container on the image with the ./html directory (using a code example from section 3.1) mounted into the container:

```
$ podman create --rm -p 8080:80 --name myapp -v ./html:/var/www/
➡ html:Z mysystemd
fec6de5716ac246613723a4cc26407005e0bc315affdc62b56883bd94acd795e
```

Now generate the Kubernetes YAML file using podman generate kube:

```
$ podman generate kube myapp > myapp2.yaml
```

Notice that this time Podman generated the YAML file with a volumes section for html:

```
$ cat myapp2.yaml
...
spec:
  containers:
  - image: localhost/mysystemd:latest
    ...
    volumeMounts:
    - mountPath: /var/www/html
      name: home-dwalsh-podman-html-host-0
```

```
    volumes:
  - hostPath:
      path: /home/dwalsh/podman/html
      type: Directory
      name: home-dwalsh-podman-html-host-0
```

Get back to a fresh environment by removing all of the pods with the podman pod rm
--all --force command. Remove all containers and images using the podman rm and
podman rmi commands, so you can start with a clean slate:

```
$ podman pod rm --all --force
$ podman rm --all --force
fec6de5716ac246613723a4cc26407005e0bc315affdc62b56883bd94acd795e
$ podman rmi mysystemd
Untagged: localhost/mysystemd:latest
Deleted: bb1634ce1457f2eb70f84af33599d211eae64cb5f951e40e91481b6e58b747bf
Deleted: 70e0c1a7580089420267b5928210ad59fdd555603e647b462159ea94f97946f9
```

The podman play kube --build command requires subdirectories matching the image
names to exist for images to be built. Podman examines the Kubernetes YAML file for
all images and then looks for the matching subdirectory. Each directory is treated as a
context directory and should contain a Containerfile or a Dockerfile. Podman then
executes podman build on each subdirectory. Since the YAML file needs the mysystemd image, you need to create a mysystemd directory and place the Containerfile in
the directory:

```
$ mkdir mysystemd
$ mv Containerfile mysystemd/
```

You can now run podman play kube --build, and it will rebuild the container image
and launch the Pod and containers for your application:

```
$ podman play kube myapp2.yaml --build
STEP 1/3: FROM ubi8-init
STEP 2/3: RUN dnf -y install httpd; dnf -y clean all
Updating Subscription Management repositories.
…
--> 305bb9b8da1
Successfully tagged localhost/mysystemd:latest
305bb9b8da12db682b0eae93ad492e632d2ba43e03f6a6b68467d7429a8a2664
a container exists with the same name ("myapp") as the pod in your YAML file;
➥ changing podname to myapp-pod
Pod:
30739dd554acfeab66a9767301127bab0fe994461686f45a3a89b137c3954840
Container:
ce633ac4e7a1e4d08e0428a8401fcfc4ac75fbcca4be07bc167add6093a44afa
```

Podman rebuilt the mysystemd image based on the mysystemd/Containerfile and then
generated the myapp-pod pod and the myapp container for your application, without
even reaching out to a container registry.

You can share this YAML file and the mysystemd directory with other users, and they can build and launch your application all with Podman. Remember, though, if they wanted to launch it inside of Kubernetes, you need to push the built image to a container registry, and then edit the YAML file to point the image to the registry image. Now that you have been exposed to the integration of Podman with Kubernetes, I want to explore one last idea: running Podman within Podman and Kubernetes containers.

8.4 *Running Podman within a container*

Running Podman within a container, or within a Kubernetes cluster, is a common problem. Users want to be able to test container images and tools within CI/CD systems using containers. Often, they want to build container images with `podman build`. Sometimes, they just want to test a newer version of Podman than has been released within their distribution.

One challenge with Podman is that it can be configured in so many different ways that users were looking for best practices for running Podman within a container. Because of this I, along with some of my colleagues, decided to create a container image, quay.io/podman/stable, which makes it easier to run Podman within a container. As you understand, Podman can run in two different modes: rootful and rootless. By default, Podman containers start as the container root within their user namespace. To help you understand running Podman within a container, you will first experiment with running Podman within Podman. Table 8.1 describes the different ways you can run a container within a container and the capabilities required to allow the internal Podman to execute a container.

Table 8.1 Requirements for running Podman within a container

Host mode	Container mode	Capabilities	Explanation
Rootful	Rootful	`CAP_SYS_ADMIN`	Has full access to the host user's namespace
Rootful	Rootless	`CAP_SETUID` `CAP_SETGID`	Runs in a separate user's namespace based on /etc/subuid and /etc/subgid inside the container
Rootless	Rootful	Namespaced `CAP_SYS_ADMIN`	Has full access to the user's user namespace
Rootless	Rootless	Namespaced `CAP_SETUID`, `CAP_SETGID`	Runs in a separate user namespace based on /etc/subuid and /etc/subgid inside the container. The user namespace must be a subset of the user namespace in which you are running the Podman command.

8.4.1 Running Podman within a Podman container

In the first example, you will run a rootful Podman within a rootless container. You need to use the `--privileged` command because, to run successfully, Podman needs to be able to mount filesystems. When Podman is run as root, mounting requires the `CAP_SYS_ADMIN` capability, which is given by the `--privileged` option. Try it out by executing the following command:

```
$ podman run --privileged quay.io/podman/stable podman version
Trying to pull quay.io/podman/stable:latest…
Getting image source signatures
Copying blob b1f89b7294d7 done
…
Version:      4.1.0
API Version:     4.1.0
Go Version:      go1.18.2
Built:        Mon May 30 12:03:28 2022
OS/Arch:      linux/amd64
```

The quay.io/podman/stable image is also configured to run a rootless Podman within a Podman container. You can activate this behavior by adding running as the Podman user with the `--user podman` option. In this mode, Podman within the container needs `CAP_SETUID` and `CAP_SETGID` to set up the user namespace. Luckily, Podman gives this access to containers by default:

```
$ podman run --user podman quay.io/podman/stable podman version
```

If you really want to lock the container down, you can drop all capabilities other than `CAP_SETUID` and `CAP_SETGID`, using the `--cap-drop=all --cap-add CAP_SETUID,CAP_SETGID` options:

```
$ podman run --cap-drop=all --cap-add CAP_SETUID,CAP_SETGID
➥ --user podman quay.io/podman/stable podman version
Version:      4.1.0
API Version:     4.1.0
Go Version:      go1.18.2
Built:        Mon May 30 12:03:28 2022
OS/Arch:      linux/amd64
```

These examples, which show how you can run Podman within a Podman container, can also easily be done with Docker running Podman within a container.

Note that Docker runs with a seccomp filter, which blocks the unshare and mount system calls. You need to either disable seccomp filtering in Docker—

```
docker run -security-opt seccomp=unconfined …
```

—or run Docker with Podman's seccomp filters:

```
docker run -security-opt seccomp=/usr/share/containers/seccomp.json … .
```

In this section, you learned about Podman integration with Kubernetes. In the next section, you will learn how to configure Podman to run within a Kubernetes pod or container.

8.4.2   *Running Podman within a Kubernetes pod*

A common use case for CI/CD systems is using Podman to run containers within Kubernetes. As you learned, running Podman within a container requires either `CAP_SYS_ADMIN` for rootful containers or `CAP_SETUID` and `CAP_SETGID` to run in rootless mode. Understand that Podman containers almost always require more than one UID to run, especially when running `podman build`. Lots of Podman problems have been raised by users of Kubernetes attempting to run Podman in a locked-down Kubernetes container, with only one UID and without Linux capabilities. These containers are the default for OpenShift and lots of the cloud-based Kubernetes environments. Running a container engine like Podman in environments without some Linux capabilities and access to more than one UID is impossible.

The equivalent version of running rootful Podman using the quay.io/podman/stable image within a `privileged` Kubernetes container can be launched with this Kubernetes YAML file:

```
apiVersion: v1
kind: Pod
metadata:
 name: podman-priv
spec:
 containers:
   - name: priv
     image: quay.io/podman/stable
     args:
       - podman
       - version
     securityContext:
       privileged: true
```

Similarly, you can launch a rootless Podman within a Kubernetes container by using the following YAML file. Note that you specify the `runAsUser: 1000` as the UID, not the `podman` user. Kubernetes does not support translating usernames within containers to UIDs:

```
apiVersion: v1
kind: Pod
metadata:
  name: podman-rootless
spec:
  containers:
  - name: rootless
    image: quay.io/podman/stable
    args:
      - podman
      - version
```

```
securityContext:
  capabilities:
    add:
      - "SETUID"
      - "SETGID"
  runAsUser: 1000
```

NOTE See the following articles written by me along with my colleague, Urvashi Mohnani, that offer many more examples on running Podman within containers:

- "How to Use Podman inside of a Container" (http://mng.bz/vXDM)
- "How to Use Podman inside of Kubernetes" (http://mng.bz/49EV)

As you can see, it is fairly easy to run Podman containers within Kubernetes, as long as you understand the Podman requirements. There is ongoing work within the Kubernetes community to take advantage of user namespaces, making it easier to run Podman containers within Kubernetes containers and making them more secure.

Summary

- The `podman generate kube` command easily allows you to move locally running pods and containers into a Kubernetes YAML file suitable for running within a Kubernetes cluster.
- These YAML files can also be used to generate local pods and containers via the `podman play kube` command.
- The `--down` option allows `podman play kube` to shut down all pods and containers launched by a previous `podman play kube` command.
- The `--build` option allows `podman play kube` to generate the container image defined within the Kubernetes YAML file based on a Containerfile/Dockerfile, eliminating the need to push the image to a container registry.
- `podman play kube` is a suitable replacement for `docker-compose` because it shares the same YAML format as Kubernetes.
- Running Podman within Podman and Kubernetes containers is possible as long as you understand the Podman requirements for running in a locked-down environment.

Podman as a service

This chapter covers

- Running Podman as a service
- Podman service support for two REST APIs
- Python libraries podman-py and docker-py for managing Podman containers
- Support for `docker-compose`
- Remote command-line communication with the Podman service
- Managing SSH communications with remote Podman instances

In previous chapters, you learned about the Podman command line. The problem with this is sometimes you want to work with containers from a remote system. Similarly, you might want to write code in a scripting language to interact with containers. Docker, being written as a client-server application, supports a popular remote API, which led to the creation of libraries written in Python and JavaScript to access the daemon. Docker-py is a popular Python library used to interact with the Docker daemon.

Many CI/CD, GUI, and remote management systems have been built to manage Docker containers. Code editors like Visual Studio even have built-in plug-ins that talk directly to the Docker API. Advanced tools like `docker-compose` led to a new programming language that is used to orchestrate multiple containers on a host by interacting with the Docker daemon.

Podman provides similar features and can be run as a service. Podman supports running the Podman service in rootless as well as rootful mode. In this chapter, you will learn about the service and how to interact with it. You will write a simple program in Python that uses the docker-py and newer podman-py libraries to interact with the Podman service. You will learn how to set up remote Docker-based tools, including `docker-compose`, to actually use the Podman service, with no Docker daemon available.

> **NOTE**   The Podman service is only supported on Linux. Because the Podman service launches Linux containers, it only runs on Linux machines. Windows and Mac versions of Podman communicate with the Podman service over the REST API to launch containers. For more information on Podman on Mac, see appendix E, and for Windows, see appendix F.

The Podman command has a `--remote` option that allows you to interact with the Podman service, either on the local machine or, most often, on a remote machine. You will learn to set up the Podman connections to make interacting with remote services easy and secure. But first you need to know how to enable the Podman service.

9.1   *Introducing the Podman service*

The Podman project supports a REST (or RESTful) API. The `podman system service` command creates a listening service that answers API calls for Podman. The service can be run in rootful or rootless mode. This command offers an optional argument to specify a URI on which the Podman service will listen. For example, the unix:///tmp/podman.sock URI tells Podman to listen on the /tmp/podman.sock UNIX domain socket. The tcp:localhost:10000 URI socket tells Podman to listen on TCP socket, port `10000`. By default, Podman listens on a UNIX domain socket under the /run directory (table 9.1).

> **NOTE**   If you are not familiar with REST API or remote APIs in general, I recommend that you read "What is a REST API?" by Red Hat: https://www.redhat.com/en/topics/api/what-is-a-rest-api.

Podman running as a service in this case is different from having a centralized daemon, like Docker does, in multiple ways. The biggest difference is that the Podman command can run without the service and interacts with containers and images created by the service. Other container tools can interact with the storage and containers without going through the service. The service also exits when there are no connections to it. You could even run multiple services at the same time on the same datastore (although I would not recommend this). The Docker daemon forces all interaction with containers and images to go through the daemon. Table 9.1 shows the default locations where the Podman service listens for incoming connections.

Table 9.1   Default locations for the podman.socket

Mode	Default location
Rootful	unix:///run/podman/podman.sock
Rootless	unix://$XDG_RUNTIME_DIR/podman/podman.sock example unix:///run/user/1000/podman/podman.sock)

Although the Podman service can be set up to run on a TCP socket as well, I caution you to be very careful because there is no authorization or additional security built into the service to prevent hackers from gaining access. The service relies on the SSH service to gain remote access to the Podman service, and this approach is recommended.

The Podman service was designed to run as an on-demand service, exiting 5 seconds after the last connection. This time limit avoids a long-running daemon that uses system resources even when the service is not being used. While the Podman service could launch a separate process for each connection, this could become a bottleneck. Try this out by running the following command; after 5 seconds you will see the command exit. If you had active connections to the service, it would continue to run:

```
$ podman system service
```

You can specify the timeout for this exit in seconds with the `--time` option. Specifying `--time 0` causes the podman system service command to run until you stop it. Most users never interact directly with the Podman system service to activate the service but rely on systemd services to manage it.

9.1.1   Systemd services

Podman provides multiple systemd unit files for running Podman as a service. Because Podman was not designed as a daemon, and the developers did not want to always have a long-running daemon, they decided to take advantage of systemd socket activation. This allows the Podman service to be launched as an on-demand service. Figure 9.1 shows how systemd listens on the Podman socket and then launches the Podman service when it receives a connection.

The Podman package provides two podman.socket unit files: one for rootful Podman and the other for rootless Podman. Table 9.2 defines the location of the systemd socket files to be used in rootful and rootless mode.

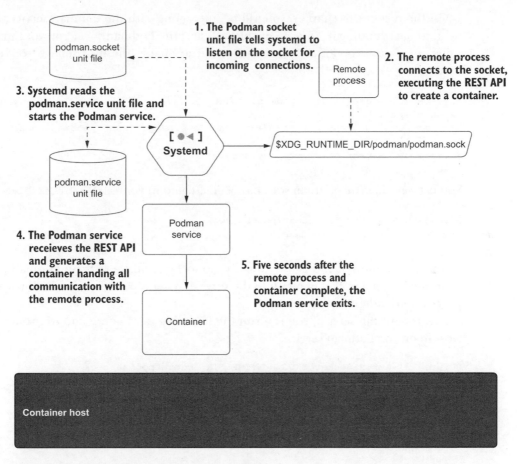

1. The Podman socket unit file tells systemd to listen on the socket for incoming connections.

2. The remote process connects to the socket, executing the REST API to create a container.

3. Systemd reads the podman.service unit file and starts the Podman service.

4. The Podman service receieves the REST API and generates a container handing all communication with the remote process.

5. Five seconds after the remote process and container complete, the Podman service exits.

Figure 9.1   **Podman service running under systemd**

Table 9.2   **Podman socket unit files**

Mode	Systemd socket file
Rootful	/usr/lib/systemd/system/podman.socket
Rootless	/usr/lib/systemd/user/podman.socket

These two socket activation services tell systemd to listen on the default UNIX domain socket listed in table 9.1. When a process connects to the socket, systemd launches the matching service, which runs the `podman system service` command. Systemd then hands the socket off to the service. After the Podman service completes the API request, it waits for another connection. If no connection happens for 5 seconds, Podman exits, freeing up the resources it was using. If a new connection comes in, systemd repeats the process and launches a new instance of the Podman service.

In the rest of this chapter, you will be interacting with the Podman service, so you need to start running it. You can enable and start the Podman socket on your machine using the `--user` option, which tells systemd to enable the user service (or rootless mode service):

```
$ systemctl --user enable podman.socket
Created symlink
➥ /home/dwalsh/.config/systemd/user/sockets.target.wants/podman.socket ?
➥ /usr/lib/systemd/user/podman.socket.
$ systemctl --user start podman.socket
```

You can see that the podman.sock has been created in your XDG_RUNTIME_DIR:

```
$ ls $XDG_RUNTIME_DIR/podman/podman.sock
/run/user/3267/podman/podman.sock
```

At this point, the systemd is listening on the socket, and there is no Podman process running. When a packet comes into the service, systemd launches the Podman service process to handle the connection.

To try out the service, you can run the following `curl` command to probe for the version on the Podman service:

```
$ curl -s --unix-socket $XDG_RUNTIME_DIR/podman/podman.sock
➥ http://d/v1.0.0/libpod/version | jq
{
  "Platform": {
  "Name": "linux/amd64/fedora-35"
  },
  "Components": [
  {
    "Name": "Podman Engine",
    "Version": "4.0.0-dev",
    "Details": {
        "APIVersion": "4.0.0-dev",
         "Arch": "amd64",
         "BuildTime": "2022-01-04T13:42:14-05:00",
         "Experimental": "false",
        "GitCommit": "66ffbc845d1f0fd5c29611ac3f09daa24749dc1e-dirty",
        "GoVersion": "go1.16.12",
        "KernelVersion": "5.15.10-200.fc35.x86_64",
        "MinAPIVersion": "3.1.0",
        "Os": "linux"
      }
  },
  {
      "Name": "Conmon",
      "Version": "conmon version 2.0.30, commit: ",
      "Details": {
        "Package": "conmon-2.0.30-2.fc35.x86_64"
      }
  },
```

```
{
    "Name": "OCI Runtime (crun)",
    "Version": "crun version 1.4\ncommit:
3daded072ef008ef0840e8eccb0b52a7efbd165d\nspec: 1.0.0\n+SYSTEMD
➥ +SELINUX +APPARMOR +CAP +SECCOMP +EBPF +CRIU +YAJL",
    "Details": {
       "Package": "crun-1.4-1.fc35.x86_64"
    }
  }
],
"Version": "4.0.0-dev",
"ApiVersion": "1.40",
"MinAPIVersion": "1.24",
"GitCommit": "66ffbc845d1f0fd5c29611ac3f09daa24749dc1e-dirty",
"GoVersion": "go1.16.12",
"Os": "linux",
"Arch": "amd64",
"KernelVersion": "5.15.10-200.fc35.x86_64",
"BuildTime": "2022-01-04T13:42:14-05:00"
}
```

Now that you have the service running, it's time to investigate the APIs.

9.2   Podman-supported APIs

The Podman service provides two APIs over the same socket (table 9.1). The compatibility API targets the latest released version of the Docker API, implementing all endpoints, except the Swarm APIs. The Podman team treats any problem concerning a difference with the Docker API as a bug. If the API works against the Docker daemon, it must work against the Podman service.

The Podman Libpod API provides support for Podman's unique features, such as pods. While it would be great for all projects to support the native Libpod API, it takes time to transition, and it may be impossible for older, no-longer-maintained projects based on the Docker API.

I recommend that all new users of Podman work with the Libpod API, but if you are using legacy code or want to develop code that will work with both Podman and Docker, then you should use the compatibility API. Table 9.3 lists the two different REST APIs provided by Podman.

Table 9.3   Podman-supported APIs

Mode	Description	Documentation
Compatibility	A compatibility layer offering support for the Docker v1.40 API	https://docs.docker.com/engine/api/
Libpod	A Podman-native Libpod layer	https://docs.podman.io/en/latest/_static/api.html

The easiest way to interact with the remote API is via the `curl` command. Examine the list of images available with the `curl` command and the `jq` command to pretty-print the JSON code. Also notice the `libpod` field in the URL. This field tells Podman to use its native API.

> **Listing 9.1   The default output when connecting `curl` to the Podman socket**

```
$ curl -s --unix-socket $XDG_RUNTIME_DIR/podman/podman.sock
➥ http://d/v1.0.0/libpod/images/json | jq
[
  {
   "Id":
"Sha256:2c7e43d880382561ebae3fa06c7a1442d0da2912786d09ea9baaef87f73c29ae",
   "ParentId": "",
   "RepoTags": [
     "quay.io/rhatdan/myimage:latest"        ◁─┐  The image you have
   ],                                            been working on
…
  }
]
```

You can also run the Docker API by eliminating the `libpod` field. For this command, you get the same output because the APIs have the same output:

```
$ curl -s --unix-socket $XDG_RUNTIME_DIR/podman/podman.sock
➥ http://d/v1.0.0/images/json | jq
[
  {
   "Id":
"Sha256:2c7e43d880382561ebae3fa06c7a1442d0da2912786d09ea9baaef87f73c29ae",
   "ParentId": "",
   "RepoTags": [
     "quay.io/rhatdan/myimage:latest"
   ],
…
  }
]
```

An example in which the APIs differ is listing pods, since Docker does not support the concept of a pod, the `compat` API does not have interfaces for it.

First, create a pod for the test by running the following command:

```
$ podman pod create --name mypod
116291543d5691c597132ec73a428f29f2c1f71a65fdfbaca17eb5440a5d47f6
```

Now, use the Libpod pods or JSON API to see JSON related to the pod you just created:

```
$ curl -s --unix-socket $XDG_RUNTIME_DIR/podman/podman.sock
➥ http://d/v1.0.0/libpod/pods/json | jq
[
  {
    "Cgroup": "user.slice",
    "Containers": [
      {
       "Id": "8eeceeb4fd6aa3897e05b5361b5c27c6e98bc29707484f95994f49437536599e",
       "Names": "4b10a21c5b8c-infra",
```

```
    "Status": "running"
     }
  ],
  "Created": "2022-01-05T06:51:52.604528462-05:00",
  "Id": "4b10a21c5b8c2b4f8a598de1eace7b94918d813055891276c2472df856a7fbc1",
  "InfraId":
➡ "8eeceeb4fd6aa3897e05b5361b5c27c6e98bc29707484f95994f49437536599e",
  "Name": "test_pod",
  "Namespace": "",
  "Networks": [],
  "Status": "Running",
  "Labels": {}
},
{
  "Cgroup": "user.slice",
  "Containers": [
     {
     "Id": "7a7405a31917da7bde01a6000809e0ee12f40b69fc76963d87a8ae254b34d8c7",
     "Names": "e10eb9303705-infra",
     "Status": "configured"
     }
  ],
  "Created": "2022-01-05T09:18:01.648324833-05:00",
  "Id": "e10eb930370592834fc168a7460fabe9b3e0e20a54b48a2bf3236cecd75f8138",
  "InfraId":
➡ "7a7405a31917da7bde01a6000809e0ee12f40b69fc76963d87a8ae254b34d8c7",
  "Name": "mypod",
  "Namespace": "",
  "Networks": [],
  "Status": "Created",
  "Labels": {}
  }
]
```

If you try the same query against the Docker API endpoint, it fails with a Not Found error.

```
$ curl -s --unix-socket $XDG_RUNTIME_DIR/podman/podman.sock
➡ http://d/v1.0.0/pods/json
Not Found
```

This is because the Docker API and Docker itself do not understand pods. While you can do a lot of testing with the API directly with tools like curl, it is better to have higher-level languages to interact with the API, such as Python.

9.3 Python libraries for interacting with Podman

Python is arguably the most popular scripting language on Linux platforms. Almost every Linux system has Python installed by default. Just like the API, there are two very similar Python libraries available: the docker-py library, which works with the compatibility library, and podman-py, which supports the newer Libpod API. This section uses some Python commands and might require a limited knowledge of Python but is easy enough for you to follow along if you have limited experience.

9.3.1   *Using docker-py with the Podman API*

The most popular Python package for interacting with containers is docker-py (https://github.com/docker/docker-py). Docker-py is a Python bindings library used originally to communicate with the Docker daemon. It can also communicate with the Podman compatibility service. The Docker-py library allows you to run the same containers as the Podman command, except you can do it from Python.

Thousands of tools and examples built on docker-py exist and are running in production. These tools have been used for CI/CD systems as well as GUIs, management tools, and debugging tools. For these commands, you can use the Podman `compat` API, which works fine with docker-py.

Usually, you can install docker-py with `apt-get` or `dnf install`. It is also available via PyPI. Consult the install commands for your Linux platform. On RPM-based systems, the package is called `python-docker`.

On my Red Hat-based system, I install it using the following `dnf` command:

```
$ sudo dnf install -y python-docker
```

After docker-py is installed, you can start using it to interact with the Podman service. Imagine you want to build a Python script to interact with the Podman service to list the currently available images. Notice I have to reset the `DockerClient` URL to point at the Podman socket. You might have to modify the location of podman.sock on your system:

```
$ cat > images.py << _EOF
import docker
client=docker.DockerClient(base_url='unix:/run/user/1000/podman/podman.sock')
print(client.images.list(all=True))
_EOF
```

Run the images.py script, and see the images installed on your box:

```
$ python images.py
[<Image: 'quay.io/rhatdan/myimage:latest'>, <Image: 'k8s.gcr.io/pause:3.5'>]
```

It is inconvenient to have to fully specify the path to the Podman socket inside the Python script, but luckily, Docker tools support a special environment variable called `DOCKER_HOST`. You can set `DOCKER_HOST` to point at the socket that implements the Docker API.

First, set the `DOCKER_HOST` environment variable to point at podman.sock:

```
$ export DOCKER_HOST=unix://$XDG_RUNTIME_DIR/podman/podman.sock
```

Now, change the script to use the `docker.from_env()` function:

```
$ cat > images.py << _EOF
import docker
```

```
client=docker.from_env()
print(client.images.list(all=True))
_EOF
```

Run the new script, and you see that it uses the DOCKER_HOST environment variable to discover the Podman service socket:

```
$ python images.py
[<Image: 'quay.io/rhatdan/myimage:latest'>, <Image: 'k8s.gcr.io/pause:3.5'>]
```

> **NOTE** On many Linux distributions, the podman-docker package is available locally. When you install this package, it installs a Docker script that redirects Docker commands to run Podman commands. It also links all of the Docker man pages to Podman man pages. Finally, it sets up a symbolic link between the docker.sock and the podman.sock for rootful containers, allowing Docker tools to use /var/run/podman/podman.sock, with no environment modifications.

The great thing is that this DOCKER_HOST trick can be used with most docker-py scripts that have been written over the years, and you can easily switch your scripts from using the Docker daemon to using the Podman service. If you want to use more advanced Podman features, you need to use the podman-py package.

9.3.2 *Using podman-py with the Podman API*

Podman-py (https://github.com/containers/podman-py), like docker-py, is a Python bindings library used to communicate with the Podman service. The podman-py library is newer than the docker-py library and supports all of the advanced features of Podman using the Libpod API.

The Podman Python library uses the default locations of the podman.sock and connects to it automatically. When run as non-root, the library connects to the root-less socket located in /run/user/$UID/podman/podman.sock. Running Python with the Podman library as root connects automatically to /run/podman/podman.sock.

Similarly to docker-py, on my system I can install the podman-py library via the python-podman package:

```
$ sudo dnf install -y python-podman
Last metadata expiration check: 0:27:40 ago on Sun 19 Jun 2022 02:14:49 PM EDT.
Dependencies resolved.
…
Installed:
  python3-podman-3:4.0.0-1.fc36.noarch
Complete!
```

Now build a functionally similar script, podman-images.py, using the podman-py library. This time you don't need to worry about the location of the Podman socket. The podman-py library connects to the default location:

```
$ cat > podman-images.py << _EOF
import podman
client=podman.PodmanClient()
print(client.images.list())
_EOF
```

Run the script, and you will see the same results as the docker-py example, but this library uses the Libpod API:

```
$ python podman-images.py
[<Image: 'quay.io/rhatdan/myimage:latest'>, <Image: 'k8s.gcr.io/pause:3.5'>]
```

If you want to show advanced features, like information on all the pods in the Podman database, call the `pod.lists()` function, and iterate through each pod:

```
$ cat >> podman-images.py << _EOF
for i in client.pods.list():
    print(i.attrs)
_EOF
Now the script shows the images as well as information on the pods.
$ python podman-images.py
[<Image: 'quay.io/rhatdan/myimage:latest'>, <Image: 'k8s.gcr.io/pause:3.5'>]
{'Cgroup': 'user.slice', 'Containers': [{'Id':
➥ 'f8679839c25729eb422d38e505ae3a4b7ffe18942e2f77a997bd388e0f52313e',
➥ 'Names': '116291543d56-infra', 'Status': 'configured'}], 'Created':
➥ '2021-12-14T06:44:04.56055485-05:00', 'Id':
    '116291543d5691c597132ec73a428f29f2c1f71a65fdfbaca17eb5440a5d47f6',
➥ 'InfraId':
    'f8679839c25729eb422d38e505ae3a4b7ffe18942e2f77a997bd388e0f52313e',
➥ 'Name': 'mypod', 'Namespace': '', 'Networks': None, 'Status':
➥ 'Created', 'Labels': {}}
```

As you can see with the Python bindings, you could begin to build a Python version of Podman, which can communicate with the remote socket.

9.3.3   *Which Python library should you use?*

The developers of the podman-py library based their design on the docker-py library to make it easier for developers to transition. If you want to build an application that works with Podman and Docker, the only choice is docker-py because podman-py does not work with Docker. If you want to take advantage of advanced features of Podman, you have to use podman-py. Podman-py is under heavy development, but docker-py has a huge installed base. Podman-py works out of the box with rootful and rootless Podman service, while if you use docker-py you have to set the DOCKER_ HOST environment variable to point at the podman.socket. Table 9.4 compares the features of the podman-py and docker-py libraries to help you understand when to use a particular library.

Table 9.4   Podman-py vs. docker-py

Support	Podman-py	Docker-py
Podman service	✓	✓
Docker daemon	✗	✓
Supports pods	✓	✗
Advanced Podman features	✓	✗

Using the low-level Python libraries docker-py and podman-py for communicating with container engine daemons and services, engineers developed higher-level tools to orchestrate and manage containers. The most popular of these is `docker-compose`.

9.4   *Using docker-compose with the Podman service*

In the previous chapters, you have seen how to manage containers with the Podman command line as well as how to manage multiple containers using Kubernetes YAML launched with `podman play kube`. You were introduced to launching containers with Kubernetes. In this section, you will work with yet another orchestration tool, `docker-compose` (https://docs.docker.com/compose), often referred to as just `compose`.

`compose` is one of the most popular tools for launching containers. The `compose` tool predates Kubernetes and concentrates on orchestrating multiple containers on a single node, whereas Kubernetes orchestrates multiple containers on multiple nodes. `compose`, like Kubernetes, uses a YAML file for its container definitions. One of the reasons `compose` was created was that building complex command lines to run multiple containers can be complicated. Using a structured language like YAML makes it easier to support running complex applications with multiple containers on a single node.

`compose` has a huge user base, and it is likely you might want to run a `compose` YAML file in your infrastructure. If you don't believe this will happen, you can skip this section.

The `compose` tool was written using docker-py and launches containers by using the Docker REST API. Since Podman now supports the `compat` REST API, it also supports using `docker-compose` to launch Podman containers. Because Podman works in rootless as well as rootful mode, you can even use `docker-compose` to launch rootless Podman containers.

In the rest of this section, you will create a `compose` YAML file just to get a feel for how the `compose` command works with the Podman service. You first need to install `docker-compose`. On my Fedora system, I can do this with the following command:

```
$ sudo dnf -y install docker-compose
```

Make sure the Podman systemd socket-activated service is running by running the following command:

```
$ systemctl –user start podman.socket
```

Verify the system service is running by hitting the ping endpoint, and see if you get a response. This step needs to be successful before you can proceed further.

```
$ curl -H "Content-Type: application/json" --unix-socket
➥ $XDG_RUNTIME_DIR/podman/podman.sock http://localhost/_ping
OK
```

Since `docker-compose` supports the `DOCKER_HOST` environment variable, make sure it is set using this command:

```
$ export DOCKER_HOST=unix://$XDG_RUNTIME_DIR/podman/podman.sock
```

As was stated earlier in this section, `compose` supports its own YAML file, which is different than the Kubernetes YAML described in chapter 8.

First, create a directory called example, and then navigate into it. Move the html directory you have been using into the example directory:

```
$ mkdir example
$ mv ./html example
$ cd example
```

You need to create the docker-compose.yaml file in the example directory you have been working in. The YAML file will create a container called myapp based on quay.io/rhatdan/myimage:latest. Set up the container to use volumes from the host ./html directory as well as a built-in volume, myapp_vol, used just for the example:

```
cat > docker-compose.yaml << _EOF
version: "3.7"
services:
  myapp:
    image: quay.io/rhatdan/myimage:latest
    volumes:
      - ./html:/var/www/html
      - myapp_vol:/vol
    ports:
      - 8080:80
volumes:
  myapp_vol: {}
_EOF
```

Now clean up the images and containers you have on your system to make sure you are starting from a clean slate. Run the following commands to do that:

```
$ podman pod rm --all --force
$ podman rm --all --force
$ podman rmi --all --force
$ podman volume rm --all --force
```

To show how `compose` interacts with the Podman service, launch the container with the `compose` command. Notice that `compose` tells Podman to pull down the image. Then `compose` tells Podman to create a container named `example_myapp_1` along with a volume named `example_myapp_vol`, which will be volume mounted into the container along with the ./html directory.

Listing 9.2 The output of executing `docker-compose` against the Podman socket

```
$ docker-compose up
Pulling myapp (quay.io/rhatdan/myimage:latest)...         ◁──┐ Pulling the
59bf1c3509f3: Download complete                               │ myimage image
c059bfaa849c: Download complete
Creating example_myapp_1 ... done         ◁──┐ Creating the example_
Attaching to example_myapp_1                 │ myapp_1 container
```

In a different terminal, run the `podman ps` command:

```
$ podman ps --format "{{.ID}} {{.Image}} {{.Ports}} {{.Names}}"
230fce823ff6  quay.io/rhatdan/myimage:latest  0.0.0.0:8080->80/tcp
➥ example_myapp_1
```

Now check to see if Podman created a volume:

```
$ podman volume ls
DRIVER     VOLUME NAME
local      example_myapp_vol
```

Go back to the original window, and enter Ctrl-C to stop `docker-compose`:

```
^CGracefully stopping... (press Ctrl+C again to force)
Stopping example_myapp_1   ... done
```

This will shut down the container:

```
$ podman ps --format "{{.ID}} {{.Image}} {{.Ports}} {{.Names}}"
```

If you execute the `podman ps -a` command, you will see that the container still exists but is not running:

```
$ podman ps -a --format "{{.ID}} {{.Image}} {{.Ports}} {{.Names}}"
230fce823ff6  docker.io/library/alpine:latest  0.0.0.0:8080->80/tcp
➥ example_myapp_1
```

Now, if you run `docker-compose down`, it will tell Podman to remove the container from the system:

```
$ docker-compose down
Removing example_myapp_1 ... done
Removing network example_default
```

Verify all containers are gone with the `podman ps -a` command again:

```
$ podman ps -a --format "{{.ID}}  {{.Image}}  {{.Ports}}  {{.Names}}"
```

As you can see, Podman works nicely with `docker-compose` to orchestrate containers.

> **TIP** While `docker-compose` works nicely with the Podman service, I think if you are starting a fresh project, it is better to work with Kubernetes YAML and `podman play kube` because this allows you to more easily move your containers into Kubernetes.

As you have seen, the Podman service is useful for allowing remote processes to manipulate your pods and containers. Even the Podman command can be used as a client and communicate with the Podman service.

9.5   *podman --remote*

As you scale out applications, you probably want to run your containerized applications on multiple machines. You could `ssh` into each box and run Podman commands locally to manage the environment, or you could write code to use the Python library described in section 9.4. The Podman developers also built client support into the Podman command. You can use the `podman` command to directly connect to these remote Podman services and manage the container environment on the remote machines.

The Podman command has a special option, `--remote`, allowing it to communicate with the socket-activated Podman service. Instead of executing the commands and containers as a child of the Podman process, it communicates with the service over the REST API.

Because Podman is a tool for running Linux containers, the `complete podman` command can only be run on Linux. The Podman developers wanted to support other operating systems, at least in client mode. To support running Podman on non-Linux machines, Podman can be built in two different ways. Up until now, you have been working with the fully fledged Podman, which has the `--remote` option. The Podman executable can be compiled with only support for communicating with the Podman service. Podman built this way is often called `podman-remote`. The `podman-remote` command is the command that is shipped on some operating systems, like Mac and Windows (covered more fully in appendixes E and F). If you have been testing Podman on a Mac or Windows machine while reading this book, then you have already been using `podman-remote`, which transparently communicates with the Podman service running in a VM or on a different machine.

9.5.1   *Local connections*

As previously mentioned, the `podman --remote` command connects, by default, to the local podman.socket, referred to as a local connection (figure 9.2). Try out `podman --remote` with the Podman system service you enabled in section 9.1.1. Notice how

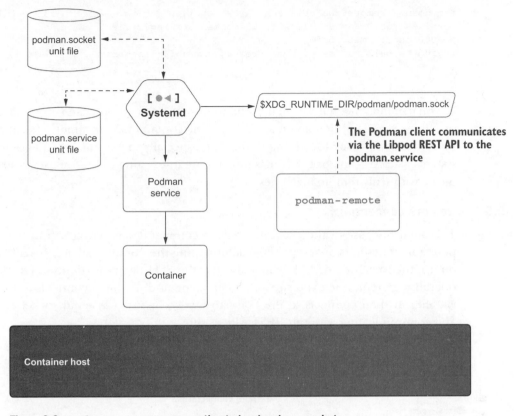

Figure 9.2 `podman --remote` **connecting to local podman.socket**

the `podman --remote` version shows you the version of the Podman client as well as the Podman server; in this case, they are the same executable.

Listing 9.3   The output of `podman --remote` **executing the version API**

```
$ podman --remote version
Client:                          Client version
Version:      4.1.0              of Podman
API Version:  4.1.0
Go Version:   go1.18.2
Built:        Sun Jun 19 07:35:42 2022
OS/Arch:      linux/amd64
Server:                          Server version
Version:      4.1.0              of Podman
API Version:  4.1.0
Go Version:   go1.18.2
Git Commit:   a2b78b627f0a9deef83a5b5e4ecffc9cdb5a72b1-dirty
Built:        Sun Jun 19 07:35:42 2022
OS/Arch:      linux/amd64
```

You can use the exact same commands to start the container:

```
$ podman --remote run ubi8 echo hi
Resolved "ubi8" as an alias (/etc/containers/registries.conf.d/
➡ 000-shortnames.conf)
Trying to pull registry.access.redhat.com/ubi8:latest…
..
hi
```

As you can imagine, it is not that useful in this mode, since you can run Podman without the --remote option and manage the same container environment. Local connections are mainly used for testing of the API, especially in continuous integration (CI) systems. podman --remote becomes much more interesting when you use it to communicate with truly remote machines.

9.5.2   *Remote connections*

The main purpose of the podman --remote command is allowing you to manipulate pods and containers on a separate machine using the Podman service. Install Podman on a Linux machine or VM, which also has the SSH daemon running. On the local operating system, when you run a Podman command, Podman connects to the server via SSH. It then connects to the Podman service by using systemd socket activation and communicating with our REST API, as shown in figure 9.3.

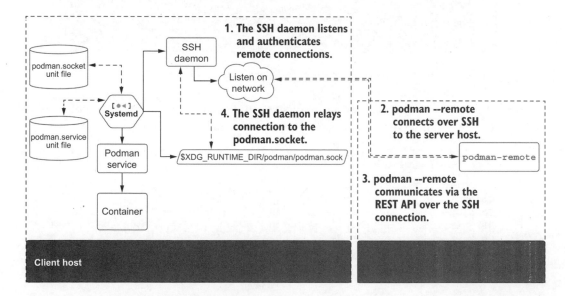

Figure 9.3   podman --remote connecting over SSH to the server machine

The command-line interface of Podman with the --remote option is exactly the same as the regular Podman commands. When you run the Podman commands, it feels like you are running the containers locally; however, the container processes are running on the remote machine. There are a few options that are not supported in remote mode, listed in table 9.5.

Table 9.5 Options not supported by the `podman --remote` command

Options	Explanation
`--env-host`	The environment on two different machines makes little sense to share; in some cases these can be two different operating systems, like Windows and Macs talking to a Linux Podman service.
`--group-add=keep-groups`	The `--group-add` option works in `--remote` mode, but the `keep-groups` special flag does not. The `keep-groups` flag tells Podman to leak the groups that the current process has access to into the container. Since this is a client-server procedure, the leaking is impossible.
`--http-proxy`	The `--http-proxy` option tells Podman to use the HTTP proxy environment variables off of the client machine and leak them into the server. Since the proxy is normally set up on the server, the `--http-proxy` option is not allowed with the `--remote` option.
`--preserve-fds`	The `--preserve-fds` option leaks file descriptors from the calling process into the container; since this is a remote connection, there is no way to leak the file descriptors.
`--volume`	This is supported, except that the source volume will come from the remote machine, not necessarily the one that is running the `podman` command (unless they are on the same machine). If you are using a VM, you need to mount the directory on the host machine into the VM first; then Podman inside of the VM sees the mount and mounts it into the container.
`--latest, -l`	Since there are potentially multiple different users talking to the same server at the same time, the concept of `--latest` was too racy, so it is not supported.

Podman commands are executed on the server. From the client's point of view, it seems like Podman runs locally. Now you need to complete the configuration of the Podman service on the remote server.

ENABLING SSHD CONNECTIONS

For the Podman client to communicate with the server, you need to enable and start the SSH daemon on your Linux machine, if it is not already enabled:

```
$ sudo systemctl enable --now -s sshd
```

Now that the SSHD daemon is running, you need to enable the Podman service on the remote machine.

ENABLING THE PODMAN SERVICE ON THE SERVER MACHINE

Before performing any Podman client commands, you must enable the podman.sock systemd service on the Linux server or VM. In these examples, you are running Podman as a normal, unprivileged user. For rootless Podman on a server to run properly, enable this socket permanently using the following command:

```
$ systemctl --user enable --now podman.socket
```

Normally, when you log out of a system, systemd stops all processes on the system. You need to tell systemd to allow the remote users processes to linger for rootless mode:

```
$ sudo loginctl enable-linger $USER
```

This also tells systemd to start listening on this socket at boot time. Once you have the service running on one system, you can verify the socket is listening with a Podman command:

```
$ podman --remote info
Host:
  arch: amd64
  buildahVersion: 1.16.0-dev
...
```

> **NOTE** You can enable the rootful podman service with the following command:
>
> ```
> $ sudo systemctl enable --now podman.socket
> ```

The previous enable-linger command is only for rootless mode. Now that you have the remote service enabled and running along with the SSHD daemon, you can go back to the client machine.

9.5.3 *Setting up SSH on the client machine*

Remote Podman uses SSH to communicate between the client and server when they are on separate machines. By default, SSH will ask you to provide the usernames and passwords on each command, unless you set up SSH keys. To set up your SSH connection, you need to generate an SSH key pair from your client machine. If you have existing SSH keys, you can just use them; it's even better if you already have shared keys with the server. On my Linux system, I can generate SSH keys with a command like the following:

```
$ ssh-keygen -t ed25519
Generating public/private ed25519 key pair.
Enter file in which to save the key (/home/myuser/.ssh/id_ed25519):
```

Once you have finished generating your keys, you can set up trust between the client and server machine with the ssh-copy-id command or some similar command. The public key, by default, will be in your home directory under $HOME/.ssh/id_ed25519 .pub. You need to copy the contents of id_ed25519.pub and append it into ~/.ssh/ authorized_keys on the Linux server. See https://red.ht/3HuxPT6 for more information on configuring your SSH environment:

```
$ ssh-copy-id myuser@192.168.122.1
passwd:
```

If you do not wish to use SSH keys, you will be prompted with each Podman command for your login password. Now that you have shared your SSH keys with the server, the next step is configuring the connection with Podman.

9.5.4   *Configuring a connection*

The `podman system connection` command allows you to manage SSH connections to be used by the `podman --remote` command. You can add a connection by using the `podman system connection add` command; name the connection `server1`. The default identity file will be chosen, or you can use the `--identity` option to specify the SSH key to use. Finally, you need to specify the full SSH URL for the Podman socket. This includes the user account, `myuser`, and IP address, as well as the path to the Podman socket for the user account:

```
$ podman system connection add server1 --identity ~/.ssh/id_ed25519
➡ ssh://myuser@192.168.122.1/run/user/1000/podman/podman.sock
```

This Podman command adds a remote connection to Podman. Since this was the first connection added, Podman marks the connection as the default.

List the available connections with the `podman system connection list` command. Notice that the * after the connection name indicates it is the default connection:

```
$ podman system connection list
Name      Identity          URI
system1*    id_ed25519
➡ ssh://myuser@192.168.122.1/run/user/1000/podman/podman.sock
```

Now you can test the connection with `podman info`:

```
$ podman --remote info
host:
  arch: amd64
  buildahVersion: 1.23.1
  cgroupControllers:
...
```

> **NOTE** You can use the `--connection (-c)` if you have more than one connection and want to choose the non-default `man podman-system-connection` for all possible options.

You can use the `podman` option or the `podman-remote` clients to manage containers running on Linux servers or VMs. The communication between client and server relies heavily on SSH connections, and the use of SSH keys is encouraged. Once you have Podman installed on your remote server, you need to set up a connection using `podman system connection add`, which can then be used by subsequent Podman commands. Table 9.6 lists the available Podman system commands.

Table 9.6   Podman system commands

Command	Man page	Description
connection	podman-system-connection(1)	Manages remote SSH destinations
df	podman-system-df(1)	Shows Podman's disk usage
info	podman-system-info(1)	Displays Podman system information
migrate	podman-system-migrate(1)	Migrates containers to a new user namespace
prune	podman-system-prune(1)	Removes unused pod, container, volume, and image data
renumber	podman-system-renumber(1)	Migrates lock numbers
reset	podman-system-reset(1)	Resets Podman storage
service	podman-system-service(1)	Runs the API service

Summary

- Podman can be run as a REST API service.
- Podman supports two REST API endpoints.
- The Podman socket supports two APIs.
- Compatibility mode or Docker mode allows Docker client tools to work with Podman.
- Podman mode allows remote clients to take advantage of advanced Podman features.
- Podman-py is a Python bindings library used to communicate with the Podman service.
- Docker-py is a Python bindings library used to communicate with the Podman compatibility service.
- Podman supports running `docker-compose` with the compatibility service to orchestrate `compose` containers on a single node.
- The `podman --remote` command communicates with the Podman service over SSH to manage containers.
- The `podman system connect` command manages SSH connections to remote Podman services, making it easier to manage containers in your environment.

Part 4

Container security

In the final part of the book, part 4, I divulge all I know about container security. This part is very technical, but you learn some key concepts that will help you understand when a container gets permission denied. It also explains the benefits of running applications within a container from a security point of view. Containerizing applications adds tremendous protection from potential hacks to your host system.

In chapter 10, I explain all of the features of the kernel that Podman uses to isolate containers from each other as well as the host system. I explain SELinux, seccomp, Linux capabilities, read-only mount points, and many other features.

Chapter 11 digs into security considerations. You learn the security best practices for running your containers in production, how you should design your application, and how you should run your containerized application in production.

10 Security container isolation

This chapter covers

- All Linux security features used to keep containers isolated from each other
- Read-only access to kernel filesystems needed for processes within a container but which must be blocked from write access
- Masking of kernel filesystems to hide information from the host system
- Linux capabilities limiting the power of root
- The PID, IPC and network namespaces, which hide most of the operating system from processes within containers
- The mount namespace, which along with SELinux limit the container processes' access to only the designated image and volumes
- The user namespace, which allows you to write root processes inside of a container that are not root outside of a container

In this chapter and chapter 11, I review and demonstrate some additional security considerations when using Podman to run containers. Some of the content was covered in other chapters, but I think it is useful to concentrate on these features from a security perspective.

One of the most frequent problems I see with people running containers is that when the container process is denied some access, the user's first reaction is to run the container in --privileged mode, which turns off all security separation for your container. Understanding how to deal with the security features discussed in this chapter helps you avoid needing to do this.

When I look at containers from a security point of view, I examine how to protect the host kernel and filesystem from the processes inside the container. I wrote a coloring book, *The Container Coloring Book* (https://red.ht/3gfVlHF), illustrated by Máirín Duffy (@marin), describing the security features of containers based on the three pigs (figure 10.1).

Figure 10.1
The Container Coloring Book
(https://red.ht/3gfVlHF)

The analogy I use in the book is that the three pigs are applications. I then discuss where they live and their choices of housing compared to computer systems.

The single-family house is equivalent to one application on a single isolated node. Living in a duplex is equivalent to running each application in a separate VM. Living in a hotel or apartment building is similar to containers, where you get your own apartment, but you rely on the security of the front desk to control the access to your living space. If the front desk is compromised, then your apartment is going to be compromised. Containers are similar to this in that they rely on the security of the kernel. If one container can take over the host kernel, then it can take over all of the container applications running on the system. Also, if they escape to the underlying filesystem, they might be able to read and write all of the data of the containers on the system.

From this perspective, I see the number-one goal of the host as being to protect the host kernel and filesystems from the container processes. The rest of this chapter describes the tools used to protect the host kernel and filesystem from container processes.

Protecting the kernel from potentially hostile containers is the primary goal of container security. If the kernel is vulnerable, then the rest of the system and all containers are vulnerable. In many cases, the only exposure to the host system for a container is the host kernel itself.

Processes within a container can interact with the kernel in many different ways. This section examines these communications and the operating system features used to secure the container processes.

The Linux kernel provides filesystems that allow processes to communicate and configure the kernel. Protecting these filesystems from confined container processes is the first security feature you will examine.

10.1 Read-only Linux kernel pseudo filesystems

These Linux kernel pseudo filesystems are generally mounted under /proc and /sys. Table 10.1 lists some of the Linux kernel pseudo filesystems mounted on my machine.

Table 10.1 Filesystems mounted as read only

Filesystem mount point	Pseudo filesystem description
/sys	The sysfs filesystem allows viewing and manipulating objects from user-space, which are created and destroyed by kernel space.
/sys/kernel/security	The security pseudo filesystem is used to read and configure general security modules. An example is the Integrity Measurement Architecture (IMA) model.
/sys/fs/cgroup	The cgroup filesystem is used to manage control groups.
/sys/fs/pstore	The pstore filesystem stores nonvolatile information useful for diagnosing the cause of a system crash.
/sys/fs/bpf	The Berkeley Packet Filter (BPF) filesystem is a mechanism to instrument the Linux kernel with user programs that reveal kernel information and control the way processes run on a system.
/sys/fs/selinux	The SELinux filesystem is used to configure SELinux in the kernel (see section 10.2.7).
/sys/kernel/config	The configfs filesystem is for creating, managing, and destroying kernel objects from user-space.

Most processes require read access to these pseudo kernel filesystems to succeed, but only administrator processes require write access. Normally, the kernel relies on the separation of root from non-root or possession of the CAP_SYS_ADMIN capability (see section 10.2.2) to modify these filesystems.

Often containers need to run as root, requiring container security to use other means to prevent the writing of these kernel filesystems by the root process. Podman does not mount most of these advanced kernel pseudo filesystems. It does mount /sys, /sys/fs/cgroup, and /sys/fs/selinux as read only. When you are in a PID namespace, the /proc filesystem changes, meaning the /proc inside a container is not the host's /proc. Processes within the container can only affect other processes within the container.

The /sys filesystems and the namespaced /proc filesystem sometimes leak host information into the container. Because of this, Podman mounts /dev/null over files and mounts read-only tmpfs filesystems over directories to prevent container access. Podman also bind mounts certain subdirectories as read only over themselves to prevent the container process from writing to them. See table 10.2 for a complete list of files and directories that Podman masks over for security purposes.

Table 10.2 Filesystem fields masked over with Podman

Type of masking	Paths
Read-only tmpfs mounted over the directory	/proc/acpi, /proc/kcore, /proc/keys, /proc/latency_stats, /proc/timer_list, /proc/timer_stats, /proc/sched_debug, /proc/scsi, /sys/firmware, /sys/fs/selinux, /sys/dev/block
Read-only bind mount over the directory	/proc/asound, /proc/bus, /proc/fs, /proc/irq, /proc/sys, /proc/sysrq-trigger

I have found that almost all container images run fine with this additional security. Sometimes a containerized application may need additional access to one of these masked-over directories.

10.1.1 Unmasking the masked paths

Rather than force the container to run --privileged mode, you can tell Podman to unmask a directory. In the following example, you run a container and see there are no files or directories under /proc/scsi because it is mounted over with a tmpfs:

```
$ podman run --rm ubi8 ls /proc/scsi
```

You can use the --security-opt unmask=/proc/scsi flag to remove the mount point and expose the underlying files and directories:

```
$ podman run --rm --security-opt unmask=/proc/scsi ubi8 ls /proc/scsi
device_info
scsi
sg
```

You can even use a * to unmount all directories under a certain path:

```
$ podman run --rm --security-opt unmask=/proc/* ubi8 ls /proc/scsi
device_info
scsi
sg
```

Unmasking makes your container slightly less secure, but it is much better than going all the way to --privileged and turning off all of the security. In certain situations, you might want to make the system more secure by masking over parts of the pseudo filesystems. The podman run man pages list the masked filesystems:

```
$ man podman run
...
     • unmask=ALL or /path/1:/path/2, or shell expanded paths (/proc/*):
Paths to unmask separated by a colon. If set to ALL, it will unmask all the
paths that are masked or made read only by default. The default masked
     paths are /proc/acpi, /proc/kcore, /proc/keys, /proc/latency_stats,
/proc/sched_debug, /proc/scsi, /proc/timer_list, /proc/timer_stats,
/sys/firmware, and /sys/fs/selinux.
     The default paths that are read only are /proc/asound, /proc/bus,
/proc/fs, /proc/irq, /proc/sys, /proc/sysrq-trigger, /sys/fs/cgroup.
```

10.1.2 *Masking additional paths*

If you are very security conscious or have a container you don't trust with certain access provided to containers, you can add additional masked paths with the --security-opt mask flag. For example, if you want to prevent a container process from seeing the devices in /proc/sys/dev, run the following:

```
$ podman run --rm ubi8 ls /proc/sys/dev
cdrom
hpet
i915
mac_hid
raid
scsi
tty
```

You can mask over it with the --security-opt mask=/proc/sys/dev flag:

```
$ podman run --rm --security-opt mask=/proc/sys/dev ubi8 ls /proc/sys/dev
```

You saw how Podman prevents root processes from reading and, more importantly, writing to pseudo filesystems. The container processes can actually see what is mounted over within the container by looking at /proc/self/mountinfo.

Listing 10.1   **The mount table within a Podman container**

```
$ podman run -rm ubi8 cat /proc/self/mountinfo
...
```

```
1628 1610 0:5 /null /proc/kcore rw,nosuid -
⇨ devtmpfs devtmpfs rw,seclabel,size=4096k,
⇨ nr_inodes=1048576,mode=755,inode64
...
1620 1595 0:86 / /sys/firmware ro,relatime - tmpfs tmpfs
rw,context="system_u:object_r:container_file_t:s0:c406,c915",size=0k,uid=32
⇨ 67,gid=3267,inode64
...
```

**Shows /dev/null mounted
over /proc/kcore**

**Shows a tmpfs mounted
read-only over /sys/firmware**

You might be asking yourself, "If the container knows what has been mounted, what prevents the root user within the container from removing the mounts or remounting filesystems' read/write and then attacking the host kernel?

10.2 *Linux capabilities*

Most Linux people understand Linux has two types of users: root (privileged process) and everyone else (nonprivileged processes). Root is all powerful, and non-root has much more limited powers, specifically when configuring and modifying the kernel. Sometimes a non-privileged process needs privileges to execute a certain command-line ping or sudo. Linux supports a way to mark these files as setuid, and when a non-privileged process executes them, the new process gains the privilege.

The binary difference between privileged and unprivileged processes ended in Linux around 2000. Kernel engineers broke down the power of root into a group of different privileged capabilities. Currently, on my system, the Linux kernel supports 41. You can see the complete list of capabilities using the capsh program. Execute the capsh program to see the list of capabilities on your system. You will see the current set of capabilities for your processes as being empty. The Bounding set of capabilities is the set of capabilities your process can get from executing a setuid program.

Listing 10.2   `capsh –print` showing the capabilities available to your user's process

**The Current set of capabilities
shows no capabilities.**

**The Bounding set of capabilities
shows all (41) capabilities.**

```
$ capsh --print
Current: =
Bounding set =
cap_chown,cap_dac_override,cap_dac_read_search,cap_fowner,cap_fsetid,cap_kill,
⇨ cap_setgid,cap_setuid,cap_setpcap,cap_linux_immutable,cap_net_bind_service,
⇨ cap_net_broadcast,cap_net_admin,cap_net_raw,cap_ipc_lock,cap_ipc_owner,
⇨ cap_sys_module,cap_sys_rawio,cap_sys_chroot,cap_sys_ptrace,cap_sys_pacct,
⇨ cap_sys_admin,cap_sys_boot,cap_sys_nice,cap_sys_resource,cap_sys_time,
⇨ cap_sys_tty_config,cap_mknod,cap_lease,cap_audit_write,cap_audit_control,
⇨ cap_setfcap,cap_mac_override,cap_mac_admin,cap_syslog,cap_wake_alarm,
⇨ cap_block_suspend,cap_audit_read,cap_perfmon,cap_bpf,cap_checkpoint_restore
Ambient set =
...
uid=3267(dwalsh) euid=3267(dwalsh)
gid=3267(dwalsh)
```

**Because you ran the capsh command
as a normal user, you see your UID
and GID listed.**

This means your user process can execute the sudo command and get the full set of capabilities as root. You can read information about what each capability does in the capabilities man page by executing man capabilities. Over the years, the community has figured out that almost all containers do not require the full list of capabilities because they seldom modify the kernel.

10.2.1 Dropped Linux capabilities

Because container-confined processes are not supposed to manipulate the operating system, and specifically the kernel, Podman can run root within its containers with far fewer capabilities. You can examine the default list of capabilities available within a Podman container by executing the same capsh program.

> **Listing 10.3 The default list of capabilities available within a Podman container**

The Current set of capabilities shows just 11 capabilities, since the container process is running as root.

The Bounding set of capabilities shows the same (11) capabilities.

```
$ podman run --rm ubi8 capsh --print
Current: =
cap_chown,cap_dac_override,cap_fowner,cap_fsetid,cap_kill,cap_setgid,
   cap_setuid,cap_setpcap,cap_net_bind_service,cap_sys_chroot,
   cap_setfcap+eip
Bounding set =
cap_chown,cap_dac_override,cap_fowner,cap_fsetid,cap_kill,cap_setgid,
   cap_setuid,cap_setpcap,cap_net_bind_service,cap_sys_chroot,cap_setfcap
...
uid=0(root)
gid=0(root)
groups=
```

Because containers default to running as root, you see the UID and GID as root.

As you observe, Podman, by default, dropped 30 capabilities—from 41 down to 11—when running a container. Even though the container has root privileges, it is far less powerful than root on the system.

> **NOTE** Docker also drops capabilities but leaves 14 capabilities. Podman runs with tighter security by dropping the following additional capabilities: CAP_MKNOD, CAP_AUDIT_WRITE, and CAP_NET_RAW.

The list of capabilities still allowed within a container mainly concern controlling multiple processes; for example, CAP_SETUID and CAP_SETGID allow processes inside the container to change to different UIDs. An example of where this is important is running your web application as UID=60, but when the container process started, it needed to run as root for a short time before changing its UID to 60. If Podman dropped CAP_SETUID, then the root process within the container is not allowed to change to the web services UID.

Another interesting capability Podman allows is CAP_NET_BIND_SERVICE, which enables a process to bind to a network port less than 1024—for example, port 80. Recall from chapter 2 that you cannot bind port 80 on your host to port 80 within the container. User processes do not have `CAP_NET_BIND_SERVICE`, so they cannot bind to port 80. Table 10.3 lists the default capabilities available to root running within a container with Podman. This list can be modified in the containers.conf file using the `default_capabilities` field under the containers table.

Table 10.3   Default list of capabilities allowed root processes in a container

Option	Description
CAP_CHOWN	Make arbitrary changes to file UIDs and GIDs.
CAP_DAC_OVERRIDE	Bypass file read, write, and execute permission checks.
CAP_FOWNER	Bypass permission checks on operations on the filesystem UID.
CAP_SETFSID	Don't clear `set-user-ID` and `set-group-ID` mode bits when modifying a file.
CAP_KILL	Bypass permission checks for sending signals.
CAP_NET_BIND_SERVICE	Bind a socket to internet domain privileged ports (port numbers less than `1024`).
CAP_SETFCAP	Set arbitrary capabilities on a file.
CAP_SETGID	Change a process's group ID (GID) or supplementary GID list.
SET_SETPCAP	Add and drop any capability from the calling thread's bounding set.
CAP_SETUID	Make arbitrary manipulations of the process user ID (UID).
CAP_SYS_CHROOT	Allow `chroot`, and change mount namespaces.

I introduced section 10.2 by asking what prevents the root process from unmounting or remounting the read-only filesystems. The answer is Podman dropping the `CAP_SYS_ADMIN` capability.

10.2.2 *Dropped CAP_SYS_ADMIN*

The most powerful Linux capability is `CAP_SYS_ADMIN`. I describe this capability in the following way: Imagine you are a kernel engineer adding a new feature into the kernel, and this feature requires privilege access. You look to see the list of capabilities, and you don't find a capability that is a great match for the access. Kernel engineers can go through the hassle of creating a new capability; or, say this is something a system administrator needs to do and there is a `CAP_SYS_ADMIN`. I might as well require that capability. If you look at the man capabilities information, you see multiple pages of features the `CAP_SYS_ADMIN` capability blocks.

One feature `CAP_SYS_ADMIN` controls is the ability to mount and unmount filesystems. Because this capability is dropped by default, root processes in Podman containers cannot unmount or remount the read-only mount points.

As you learned previously, 11 capabilities are still allowed. In most cases, your containerized process does not even need those capabilities, meaning you can drop additional ones.

10.2.3 Dropping capabilities

I recommend people run their applications with the least privileges possible. One way of increasing the security of the system is dropping additional capabilities.

Imagine your containerized process does not need to bind to ports < 1024. You can execute Podman with the `--cap-drop=CAP_NET_BIND_SERVICE` flag and drop that capability from your container.

Listing 10.4 Capabilities inside a container when you drop `CAP_NET_BIND_SERVICE`

Notice the list of Current capabilities no longer includes CAP_NET_BIND_SERVICE.

```
$ podman run --cap-drop CAP_NET_BIND_SERVICE ubi8 capsh --print
Current: =
cap_chown,cap_dac_override,cap_fowner,cap_fsetid,cap_kill,cap_setgid,
➥  cap_setuid,cap_setpcap,cap_sys_chroot,cap_setfcap+eip
Bounding set =
cap_chown,cap_dac_override,cap_fowner,cap_fsetid,cap_kill,cap_setgid,
➥  cap_setuid,cap_setpcap,cap_sys_chroot,cap_setfcap
...
```

Notice that the list of Bounding capabilities no longer includes CAP_NET_BIND_SERVICE.

You can even drop all capabilities using the `--cap-drop=all` flag:

```
$ podman run --cap-drop all ubi8 capsh --print
Current: =
Bounding set =
```

Even though your container is running as root, it has no capabilities to modify the kernel. Sometimes your container fails to run with the limited list of capabilities provided by Podman; in this case, you can add required capabilities.

10.2.4 Adding capabilities

In some situations, your container might fail because it does not have a certain capability. You can simply run `--privileged` and turn off all security in these cases, but a better solution is just adding required capabilities.

Imagine you have a container that wants to create a raw IP packet on its namespaced network, which requires `CAP_NET_RAW`. Podman, by default, does not allow this. Rather than running the container as `--privileged`, you can use the `--cap-add CAP_NET_RAW` flag:

```
$ podman run --cap-add CAP_NET_RAW ubi8 capsh --print
Current: = cap_chown,cap_dac_override,cap_fowner,cap_fsetid,cap_kill,
➥  cap_setgid,cap_setuid,cap_setpcap,cap_net_bind_service,cap_net_raw,cap_
➥  sys_chroot,cap_setfcap+eip
Bounding set =cap_chown,cap_dac_override,cap_fowner,cap_fsetid,cap_kill,
➥  cap_setgid,cap_setuid,cap_setpcap,cap_net_bind_service,cap_net_raw,cap_
➥  sys_chroot,cap_setfcap
...
```

If this is the only capability needed by your container, you can both drop all capabilities and just add back in this CAP_NET_RAW by using the --cap-drop and --cap-add flags at the same time:

```
$ podman run --cap-drop=all --cap-add CAP_NET_RAW ubi8 capsh --print
Current: = cap_net_raw+eip
Bounding set =cap_net_raw
...
```

10.2.5 *No new privileges*

Podman has an option, --security-opt no-new-privileges, which disables the ability for container processes to gain additional privileges. Basically, it locks the processes into the group of Linux capabilities they have when they are started. Even if they can execute a setuid program, the kernel denies it from gaining additional capabilities. The no-new-privileges option also affects SELinux and prevents SELinux label transitions. Even if SELinux had a bug in its rules database, the container process would not be allowed to change its label.

10.2.6 *Root with no capabilities is still dangerous*

Dropping capabilities means your container is running much more securely, but running all of your containers without any Linux capabilities is much more secure. Another problem to consider when running a container as root, even if you drop all capabilities, is that the process is still running as root. The root process is allowed to modify all files on the system that are owned by root. The root process can modify a system file and trick a privileged administrator into executing it. Also, some client-server applications trust the client side of the connection simply if it is running as root (e.g., Docker). Podman can solve both of these problems by using the user namespace.

10.3 *UID isolation: User namespace*

Back in section 6.1.1, I introduced the concept of the user namespace. Recall that UIDs were allocated via the /etc/subuid and /etc/subgid files for a rootless user. For my accounts, the range of UIDs from 100000–165535 was allocated along with my UID 3265 and was used by Podman when launching containers. See figure 10.2 for a description of the user namespace mapping.

This user namespace allows my account to have root access within the container that is not root on the host. Running containers in a user namespace eliminates the problem of having processes running as the root user, and the inherent trust is built into some daemons.

One problem with rootless users is that, by default, all of the containers run with the same user namespace. Theoretically, from a user namespace point of view, one container can attack another container, since they run with duplicate UIDs. Also, if the container processes break out, they can read/write content in your home directory, since the root processes within the containers are running with your UID.

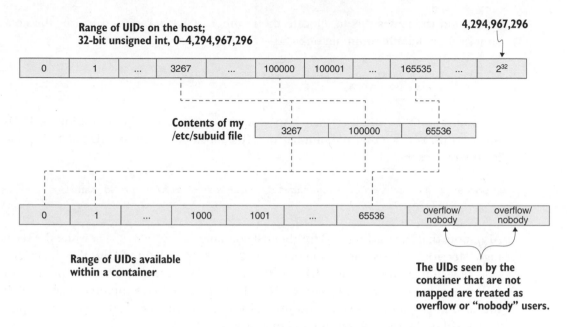

Figure 10.2   The mapping of UIDs used by rootless Podman for my account

10.3.1   Isolating containers using the --userns=auto flag

Podman has a feature for allocating unique ranges of UIDs for every container it launches. Since there are limited UIDs allocated for each user account, this feature works best when launched by the root user.

To launch multiple containers within their own user namespace, you need to first allocate the UIDs and GIDs to be used for these containers. On a Linux system, there are 4 billion UIDs available. Podman recommends that you allocate the highest 2 billion UIDs for your containers. You can do this by adding the following containers line to your /etc/subuid and /etc/subgid file.

Listing 10.5   The contents of the /etc/subuid and /etc/subgid files

```
# cat /etc/subuid
dwalsh:100000:65536
containers:2147483647:2147483648      ◁    Allocates the top 2 billion UIDs to the
# cat /etc/subgid                           container user used by Podman. Adding
dwalsh:100000:65536                          this line tells other tools on your system,
containers:2147483647:2147483648      ◁    like useradd, to avoid allocating UIDs and
                                             GIDs within this range.
```

You can launch a container within a unique user namespace using the --userns=auto option. Podman allocates the UIDs for the container starting with UID 2147483647, which you specified in the /etc/subuid file. Podman then examines the container image for all UIDs defined within it as well as the /etc/passwd file if it exists in the image and then uses this to allocate the number of UIDs required to run the container with a default minimum of 1024:

```
# podman run --userns=auto ubi8 cat /proc/self/uid_map
    0 2147483647   1024
```

If I run a second container with a specific user 2000, then the allocation of UIDs reflects this. You see that the number of UIDs allocated is 2001—UID 2000 plus one for the root user:

```
# podman run --user=2000 --userns=auto ubi8 cat /proc/self/uid_map
    0 2147484671   2001
```

Also, note that the starting UID for the first container was 2147483647, while the starting UID for the second container was 2147484671. Subtracting the first UID 2147483647 from the second UID 2147484671 gives you 1024, which is the number of UIDs allocated for the first container. No UID within the first container overlaps with the second container, meaning no process within the first container can attack processes within the second container, and vice versa.

You can override the default size of the user namespace used within the container with a size option if Podman does not allocate enough UIDs or GIDs for your container. In this example, you tell Podman to allocate 5000 UIDs for the container with --userns=auto:size=5000:

```
# podman run --userns=auto:size=5000 ubi8 cat /proc/self/uid_map
    0 2147486672   5000
```

When containers are removed, Podman reclaims the UIDs used for the deleted containers and uses those UIDs for the next container created with the --userns=auto flag. You see this when you launch back-to-back containers with the --rm option. Notice that they start with the same UID. In the following example, both containers start with UID 2147491672:

```
# podman run --rm --userns=auto ubi8 cat /proc/self/uid_map
    0 2147491672   1024
# podman run --rm --userns=auto ubi8 cat /proc/self/uid_map
    0 2147491672 1024
```

The name used in /etc/subuid and the minimum and maximum number of UIDs used for user namespaces is defined in the storage.conf file described in table 10.4.

Table 10.4   The fields used within storage.conf files to override the user namespace auto settings

Option	Description
`root-auto-userns-user`	Defines the username used to look up one or more UID/GID ranges in the /etc/subuid and /etc/subgid file. These ranges are partitioned into containers configured to create a user namespace automatically. Containers configured to automatically create a user namespace can still overlap with containers with an explicit mapping set. The `root-auto-userns-user` setting is ignored by rootless users. It defaults to `containers`.
`auto-userns-min-size`	Defines the minimum size for a user namespace created automatically. It defaults to `1024`.
`auto-userns-max-size`	Defines the maximum size for a user namespace created automatically. It defaults to `65536`.

10.3.2   User-namespaced Linux capabilities

In section 10.2 you learned about Linux capabilities and how they are used to break up the power of root. When a container is launched within a user namespace, it can have Linux capabilities. These capabilities can only affect the UIDs and GIDs mapped into the user namespace. Capabilities that do not involve UIDs and GIDs are limited. Usually, they only affect the other namespaces that are mapped with the user namespace.

For example, CAP_NET_ADMIN is the capability that allows you to manipulate the network stack. It allows a process to set up firewall rules and network routing tables. A process with a namespaced CAP_NET_ADMIN is only allowed to modify the namespaced network assigned to the user namespace, not the host's network namespace.

In the following example, the list of capabilities within a user-namespaced container is the same as when you launch one without a user namespace. In the second command using the --userns=auto flag, the capabilities are namespaced capabilities:

```
# podman run --rm ubi8 capsh --print | grep Current
Current: = cap_chown,cap_dac_override,cap_fowner,cap_fsetid,cap_kill,
➥ cap_setgid,cap_setuid,cap_setpcap,cap_net_bind_service,cap_sys_chroot,
➥ cap_setfcap+eip
# podman run --rm --userns=auto ubi8 capsh --print | grep Current
Current: = cap_chown,cap_dac_override,cap_fowner,cap_fsetid,cap_kill,
➥ cap_setgid,cap_setuid,cap_setpcap,cap_net_bind_service,cap_sys_chroot,
➥ cap_setfcap+eip
```

To prove this, attempt to chown a file within a container to a nonexistent UID. It fails because the CAP_CHOWN capability only allows the root process inside a container to chown files to any UID as long as the UID is mapped to the user namespace:

```
# podman run --rm --userns=auto:size=5000 ubi8 chown 6000 /etc/motd
chown: changing ownership of '/etc/motd': Invalid argument
```

It succeeds if you chown to a UID mapped within the user namespace:

```
# podman run --rm --userns=auto:size=5000 ubi8 chown 4000 /etc/motd
```

Suppose you launch all of your system containers with the `--userns=auto` flag. In that case, you get the benefit of running the container within its unique user namespace isolated from all other containers and UIDs on the host system. You also get root privileges with limited capabilities, and these processes outside the container have no capabilities on the host system.

10.3.3 *Rootless Podman with the --userns=auto flag*

The `--userns=auto` works with rootless containers, based on the number of UIDs available to the user. But this number is very limited. You can run the previous examples and see that the user namespaces start at UID 1. UID 1 is relative to the user namespace of the rootless user:

```
$ podman run --userns=auto ubi8 cat /proc/self/uid_map
    0   1       1024
$ podman run --userns=auto ubi8 cat /proc/self/uid_map
    0   1025   1024
```

If you examine your user namespace, you'll see that UID 1 in your user namespace is 100000:

```
$ podman run --rm ubi8 cat /proc/self/uid_map
    0   3267    1
    1   100000   65536
```

This means the first rootless user-namespace container is running UID 0 mapped to UID 1 in the rootless user namespace. UID 1 is the rootless UID 100000 on the host system. A couple of problems with rootless users of `--userns=auto` is that since the default user only gets 65,536 UIDS, at max, you can launch 64 containers, and you cannot run any containers that require more than 65,536 UIDs.

> **NOTE** If you launch a container without using the `--userns=auto` flag, the UIDs mapped to the user namespace can and probably do overlap with the UIDs in the user-namespaced isolated containers. You need to be careful that none of the UIDs used within such containers use those UIDs because those UIDs are vulnerable to attack from a UID perspective. To avoid overlaps, I suggest using a high range of UIDs.

10.3.4 *User volumes with the --userns=auto flag*

When using the user namespace, it is difficult to determine which user's UID needs to own the volume you're mounting into a container to allow access. In the following example, you first create a directory and then volume mount it into the container and attempt to create a file in it.

Listing 10.6   Drawbacks of using volumes within a user namespace

```
# mkdir /mnt/test
# ls -ld /mnt/test
drwxr-xr-x. 2 root root 6 Feb 8 16:23 /mnt/test       ◁
# podman run --rm -v /mnt/test:/mnt/test --userns=auto ubi8 ls -ld /mnt/test
drwxr-xr-x. 2 nobody nobody 6 Feb 8 21:23 /mnt/test                      ◁
# podman run --rm -v /mnt/test:/mnt/test:Z --userns=auto ubi8 touch /mnt/test
touch: setting times of '/mnt/test':
⇒  Permission denied
```

The directory is owned by root on the host.

The directory is listed as the user nobody, since the root UID=0 is not mapped into the user namespace. All files and directories owned by UIDs not mapped to the container are treated as the nobody user. The :Z tells Podman to relabel for SELinux.

Even root is not allowed to write into a directory of an unmapped user, unless the directory is world writable.

Podman supports a special option on the --volume flag U, which tells Podman to chown all files or directories in the source directory to match the UID of the container's primary process:

```
# ls -ld /mnt/test
drwxr-xr-x. 2 root root 6 Feb 8 16:38 /mnt/test
# podman run --rm -v /mnt/test:/mnt/test:Z,U
⇒  --userns=auto ubi8 touch /mnt/test/test1         ◁
# ls -ld /mnt/test
drwxr-xr-x. 2 2147503960 2147503960
⇒  19 Feb 8 16:38 /mnt/test                          ◁
```

After adding the U option, processes within the container can write to the volume.

Podman chowned the source volume to 2147503960 to match the root user mapping in the container.

A new, advanced feature of the Linux kernel is called idmapped mounts. It allows users to remap the UIDs inside a source volume to match the user namespace without actually chowning the files on disk. In the next example, you will recreate the /mnt/test directory and, this time, mount it with the idmap option. When the ID-mapped volume shows up inside the container, the files appear to be owned by the root of the user namespace, and you are allowed to read and write the files based on standard permissions. When you finish writing the files, they are mapped back correctly into the user namespace, unlike the U option, which writes them back based on the real UID of the container process:

```
# chown -R root:root /mnt/test                       ◁
# podman run --rm -v /mnt/test:/mnt/test:idmap,Z
⇒  --userns=auto ubi8 ls -ld /mnt/test              ◁
drwxr-xr-x. 2 root root 31 Feb 9 11:56 /mnt/test
# podman run --rm -v /mnt/test:/mnt/test:idmap,Z
⇒  --userns=auto ubi8 touch /mnt/test/test          ◁
# ls -l /mnt/test
total 0
-rw-r--r--. 1 root root 0 Feb 9 06:57 test
-rw-r--r--. 1 root root 0 Feb 8 17:02 test1
```

Reset the source volume to root ownership.

Mount the source volume /mnt/test into the container with the idmap option. Notice the path is owned by root within the container.

Create a file within the source directory to prove the container can write to the directory.

Notice on the host system that the newly created file is owned by the real root.

NOTE   The `idmap` features are brand new as of writing and are not available on all filesystems. It is only supported in privileged mode at this time, but hopefully, this changes soon. Currently, the OCI runtime that supports this feature is `crun`.

Understanding the security benefits of running containers with user namespaces is very important. Next, I'll show you some security benefits in the other namespaces.

10.4   *Process isolation: PID namespace*

I often say that namespaces were not intended as a security mechanism, but in reality, they do provide additional security via isolation and information masking. The PID namespace hides the fact that there are other processes running on a system. Being aware that a particular application is running on a system can be valuable to someone hacking a container. When you run a container within its own PID namespace, it is only able to see the other processes running within the container. By default, Podman runs containers within their own PID namespaces.

Some applications shipped as container images require additional access to the system. If you have such an application that needs to monitor the processes on the host, you'll need to turn off the PID namespace to expose all the processes on the system. Turning off the PID namespace with Podman is simple: just add the `--pid=host` flag. In the next couple of examples, you see that with the PID namespace, you only see the container process within the container. The second command exposes all processes within the system to the container.

> Listing 10.7   The differences between using the `pid` namespace and disabling it

```
$ podman run --rm ubi8 find /proc -maxdepth 1
  -type d -regex ".*/[0-9]*"
/proc/1
$ podman run --rm --pid=host ubi8 find
  /proc -maxdepth 1 -type d -regex ".*/[0-9]*"
/proc/1
/proc/2
/proc/3
/proc/4
...
```

Running the find command looking for all processes within the container, you see only one process.

Running the find command in a --pid=host container, you see all of the processes on the system.

NOTE   On an SELinux system, exposing the host's processes via the `--pid=host` option also has a side effect of disabling SELinux separation. SELinux blocks access to the host's processes and causes problems when processes within the container interact with these processes. Other security mechanisms, like dropped capabilities and user namespaces, are not dropped and can block access to the processes.

10.5 *Network isolation: Network namespace*

The network namespace sets up isolation from the host network. It allows Podman to set up virtual private networks to control which containers can talk to other containers. Podman has the ability to create multiple networks and then assign containers within those networks. By default, all containers run within the host network. But it is simple to set up additional networks using the podman network create command. In the next example, you will create two networks—net1 and net2:

```
$ podman network create net1
net1
$ podman network create net2
net2
```

When you create new containers, you can assign them to a specific network with the --network net1 option:

```
$ podman run -d --network net1 --name          Start a background
  cnet1 ubi8 sleep 1000                          container in network net1.
74ce5b2396f77fce8c499b121aeb8731f1e1b22e363a6a72d243487cf93a5897
$ podman run --network net1 alpine
  ping -c 1 cnet1                                Make sure the container
PING cnet1 (10.89.0.4): 56 data bytes           is reachable from another
64 bytes from 10.89.0.4: seq=0 ttl=42 time=0.077 ms   container within the network.
```

If you attempt to ping the network from the default network namespace via the container name, or even the IP address, it fails:

```
$ podman run --rm alpine ping -c 1 cnet1
ping: bad address 'cnet1'                       Make sure the cnet1
$ podman run alpine ping -c 1 10.89.0.4         container is still available
PING 10.89.0.4 (10.89.0.4): 56 data bytes       by the IP address.
64 bytes from 10.89.0.4: seq=0 ttl=42 time=0.073 ms
```

Similarly, if you attempt to ping it from a different network, --network net2, it also fails:

```
$ podman run --rm --network net2 alpine ping -c 1 cnet1
ping: bad address 'cnet1'
```

Creating private networks for your containers allows you to isolate them from each other, even over the network, using the network namespace.

> **NOTE** For these examples, I used the alpine image because it comes with the ping package installed, while the ubi8 image does not include it. You can easily add the ping executable to ubi8 via a Containerfile and podman build.

You can expose your host network to the container using the --net=host option, allowing a container to bind to ports on the host. In certain situations, you can get better performance when you eliminate the network namespace.

10.6   IPC isolation: IPC namespace

The inter-process communication (IPC) namespace isolates certain IPC resources, namely, System V IPC objects and POSIX message queues. It also isolates the /dev/shm tmpfs from the host and other containers. The IPC namespace allows containers to create named IPCs with the same name as other containers on the same system, without causing a conflict.

Thus, IPC isolation prevents one container from attacking another via an IPC or /dev/shm. You can join two IPC-namespaced containers together using the --ipc=container:NAME or run them within a pod. They share the same IPC namespace. They can use IPC together but are still isolated from the host.

Listing 10.8   IPC namespace keeping /dev/shm private to each container

```
$ podman run -d --rm --name ipc1 ubi8 bash        Create a container named ipc1, touch
➥  -c "touch /dev/shm/ipc1; sleep 1000"          /dev/shm/ipc1, and then go to sleep.
93df44264dd4b87d24f59dfffb92a6a0b6359bc5bcf94213d5e38499a10d3f3e
$ podman run --rm ubi8 ls /dev/shm
$ podman run --rm --ipc=container:ipc1 ubi8 ls /dev/shm
ipc1
```

Run a second container to see that the /dev/shm/ipc does not exist because the container is running in a separate IPC namespace.

Run a container with a shared IPC namespace, and you will see that the /dev/shm is shared and the IPC file exists.

You can share the host's IPC namespace with your container by executing the --ipc=host option.

NOTE   On SELinux systems, Podman modifies all containers that share the same IPC namespace to share the same SELinux label. Otherwise, SELinux blocks the IPC communications between containers when the labels do not match. Using the --ipc=host option causes SELinux separation to be disabled; otherwise, SELinux blocks access to the host's IPC.

10.7   Filesystem isolation: Mount namespace

The next, and perhaps most important, namespace isolation is the mount namespace. The mount namespace hides the entire host filesystem from the container processes. The container processes only see the filesystem content defined to be in the mount namespace. Podman creates the filesystem mount point rootfs and bind mounts all volumes onto it. Podman then executes the OCI runtime, which then executes the pivot_root syscall, which in turn changes the root mount in the mount namespace of the calling process. It moves the root mount to the rootfs directory. Thus, all of the content of the host operating system disappears, and the container processes only see the provided content. By dropping the CAP_SYS_ADMIN capability, the processes inside the container have no ability to affect the mounts of the rootfs to expose the underlying filesystems.

NOTE Read the `pivot_root(2)` man page to find out more about the `pivot_root` system call: `man 2 pivot_root`.

While the mount namespace and the lack of `CAP_SYS_ADMIN` provide excellent isolation, there have been some container escapes to the underlying filesystem, which is where SELinux steps in. One example of this was a flaw in the OCI runtime `runc` (CVE-2019-5736), which allowed container processes to overwrite the `runc` executable in rootful containers. This exploit allowed containers to escape their containment and take over users' systems. This exploit affected all container engines, including Podman, Docker, CRI-O, and containerd. The good news is that well-configured SELinux can stop it. Podman is mainly run in rootless mode, and rootless Podman is protected in two ways: SELinux and not running as root. I wrote about this exploit in this "Latest container exploit (runc) can be blocked by SELinux" blog post, available on Red Hat's website (http://mng.bz/Qn6j).

10.8 Filesystem isolation: SELinux

SELinux is a labeling system, where every process and filesystem object gets labeled. Then rules are written to the kernel about how the process labels interact with the filesystem labels as well as other process labels. SELinux supports multiple different security mechanisms; containers take advantage of two of these. The first is called *type enforcement*, with which SELinux controls what processes can do based on their type. The second is called *MCS enforcement*, and it additionally uses categories assigned to processes.

SELinux is not supported on all distributions. Fedora, RHEL, and other Red Hat distributions support SELinux, while Debian-based distributions, like Ubuntu, often do not. If your Linux distribution does not support SELinux, you might want to skip this section.

10.8.1 SELinux type enforcement

The SELinux labels have four components: the SELinux user, role, type, and MCS level (see table 10.5).

Table 10.5 SELinux label type examples

Object	User	Role	Type	MCS level
Container process	`system_u`	`system_r`	`container_t`	`s0:c1,c2`
Container process	`system_u`	`system_r`	`container_t`	`s0:c361,c871`
Container file	`system_u`	`object_r`	`container_file_t`	`s0:c1,c2`
Container file	`system_u`	`object_r`	`container_file_t`	`s0:s361,c871`
/etc/shadow label	`system_u`	`object_r`	`shadow_t`	`s0`
Container process	`system_u`	`system_r`	`spc_t`	`s0`
User process	`unconfined_u`	`unconfined_r`	`unconfined_t`	`s0-s0:c0.c1023`

In this section, you will concentrate on the SELinux type. I wrote *The SELinux Coloring Book* to explain the labeling, using the analogy of cats and dogs (figure 10.3).

Figure 10.3   *The SELinux Coloring Book* (http://mng.bz/Xay6)

As the coloring book explains, imagine you have a group of processes labeled as cat types and another group of processes labeled as dog types. Imagine you also have objects on the filesystem labeled as dog food type and cat food type. Finally, imagine you write rules to the kernel saying that cat types are allowed to eat cat food types, and dog types can eat dog food types. With SELinux, anything that is not explicitly allowed is denied. The cat processes can eat the cat food, and the dog processes can eat the dog food, but if a dog type attempts to eat cat food, the Linux kernel steps in and blocks the access.

    Containers work the same way. Podman labels each container process with the container_t type. All the files within the container are labeled as a container_file_t type. Rules are written into the kernel, saying the `container_t` processes are allowed to read, write, and execute files labeled with the `container_file_t` type.

> **NOTE**   SELinux does not care about ownerships and permissions, so you can, for example, define a process type that has access to all filesystem types and is not confined by SELinux, often called an *unconfined type*. You can see a couple of unconfined types running on your Linux system. The `id -Z` command shows your user processes are running with the `unconfined_t` type and a privileged container runs with the `spc_t` type.

When Podman constructs the rootfs for the container, it labels all of the files in the rootfs as `container_file_t`. This means the container process can read, write, and execute all of the files within the container's rootfs, but if they escape to the host filesystem, the SELinux kernel blocks access to the host filesystem objects. In the next few examples, you can examine what is happening in containers with SELinux. In this first example, you can see the label of the containerized process; notice the type is `container_t`. But when you run with the `--privileged` flag, Podman changes the label to `spc_t`, an unconfined domain:

```
$ podman run --rm ubi8 cat /proc/self/attr/current
system_u:system_r:container_t:s0:c694,c944
$ podman run --rm --privileged ubi8 cat /proc/self/attr/current
unconfined_u:system_r:spc_t:s0
```

Examine the files within the container, using the `ls -Z` command. You see the files are all labeled as `container_file_t`:

```
$ podman run --rm ubi8 ls -Z /
system_u:object_r:container_file_t:s0:c88,c191 bin
system_u:object_r:container_file_t:s0:c88,c191 boot
system_u:object_r:container_file_t:s0:c88,c191 dev
system_u:object_r:container_file_t:s0:c88,c191 etc
system_u:object_r:container_file_t:s0:c88,c191 home
system_u:object_r:container_file_t:s0:c88,c191 lib
...
```

Because Podman configured the SELinux environment properly, container processes have full access to all of the objects within the container's rootfs, and SELinux pretty much stays out of the way, unless something else breaks down and somehow the container process escapes out of the rootfs into the host operating system. At that point, SELinux starts blocking access. Imagine the container process you are running on your system broke out of the container and attempted to read the SSH keys in your home directory. Let's look at the labels on those files. You see that those files are labeled with the `ssh_home_t` type:

```
$ ls -1Z $HOME/.ssh/
unconfined_u:object_r:ssh_home_t:s0 authorized_keys
unconfined_u:object_r:ssh_home_t:s0 authorized_keys2
```

```
unconfined_u:object_r:ssh_home_t:s0 config
...
```

Because there is no rule in SELinux policy allowing a `container_t` process to read an `ssh_home_t` file, the SELinux kernel blocks access. You can demonstrate this by volume mounting the .ssh directory into a container. When you attempt to list the directory, the container process gets `Permission denied`:

```
$ podman run -v $HOME/.ssh:/.ssh ubi8 ls /.ssh
ls: cannot open directory '/.ssh': Permission denied
```

As you learned in section 3.1.2, Podman has SELinux volume options z and Z, which tell SELinux to relabel the content of the source volume to make it usable inside of the container. This is not a good idea to do with the .ssh directory.

Instead, let's create a temporary file and show the SELinux labels in action. First, create a temporary file in your home directory named foo. Label it `user_home_t`. Volume mount it into the container, and see that the container process is denied access.

Listing 10.9   How SELinux works with volumes inside Podman containers

```
$ mkdir foo                              Files created in your home directory
$ ls -Zd foo          ◁──────────────── default to the user_home_t type.
unconfined_u:object_r:user_home_t:s0 foo                             By default, container
$ podman run -v ./foo:/foo ubi8 touch /foo/bar      ◁────            processes are not allowed to
touch: cannot touch '/foo/bar': Permission denied                   write to content in the user's
$ podman run --privileged -v ./foo:/foo ubi8 touch                  home directory. Podman
➥ /foo/bar                                                          does not change the labels
$ ls -Z foo                                      ◁──                on volumes by default.
unconfined_u:object_r:user_home_t:s0 bar
$ rm foo/bar                                          The file created by the privileged
$ podman run -v ./foo:/foo:Z ubi8 touch /foo/bar     container has the label of the user
$ ls -Z ./foo                                 ◁──    home directory (user_home_t).
system_u:object_r:container_file_t:s0:c454,c510 bar
                                                     The labels of the newly
The :Z option on the volume mount tells Podman to    created file match the label
relabel the content of the directory to match the    within the container.
labels of files within the rootfs (container_file_t).
```

The --privileged flag causes SELinux separation to be disabled, running
the container with an unconfined type (spc_t). The command simulates a
container escape, showing that without SELinux, an escaped container is
allowed to write to the filesystem.

SELinux type enforcement has shown itself to be invaluable in blocking container escape when no other mechanism was available. Table 10.6 shows a list of container escapes that have been blocked by SELinux.

SELinux type enforcement does a great job protecting the host operating system from container processes. The problem is that `type enforcement` does not protect you from one container attacking another.

Table 10.6   Major container exploits blocked by SELinux

Common vulnerabilities and exposures	Description
CVE-2019-5736	Execution of malicious containers allows for container escape and access to the host filesystem.
CVE-2015-3627	Insecure opening of file-descriptor 1, leading to privilege escalation
CVE-2015-3630	Read/write proc paths allow host modification and information disclosure.
CVE-2015-3631	Volume mounts allow Linux Security Modules (LSM) profile escalation.
CVE-2016-9962	`runc` exec vulnerability

10.8.2   SELinux Multi-Category Security separation

SELinux does not block processes of one type from attacking other processes of the same type. One way to think about this is going back to the cats and dogs analogy. Type enforcement prevents the `dog` from eating the `cat food`, but it does not prevent `cat-A` from eating `cat-B`'s `cat food`.

Recall when I introduced this section, I said there were two types of SELinux security Podman takes advantage of. SELinux has a mechanism to enforce process separation based on the Multi-Category Security (MCS) level field. SELinux defines 1,024 categories, which can be combined together to give a level to each container. Podman allocates two categories for each container and then makes sure the process label level matches the filesystem label levels. Then the SELinux kernel enforces the MCS levels matching, or the access is denied.

> **NOTE** MCS Separation is actually about dominance. Each category must dominate the MCS level. A level of `S0:C1,C2` can write to levels `S0:C1,C2`, `S0:C1`, `S0:C2`, and `S0`. But the `S0:C1,C2` is not allowed to write to `S0:C1,C3`, since the original label does not include the `C3`. In practice, Podman only uses two categories or no categories. When you use the `:z` option on a volume, Podman relabels the source directory with the level `s0`—no categories. The `s0` allows processes from any container to read and write filesystem objects with this level, from an SELinux perspective.

Revisit table 10.4, but this time concentrate on the MCS level field (table 10.7).

Table 10.7   Container process labels, with MCS level highlighted

Object	User	Role	Type	MCS level
Container process	`system_u`	`system_r`	`container_t`	`s0:c1,c2`
Container process	`system_u`	`system_r`	`container_t`	`s0:c361,c871`
Container file	`system_u`	`object_r`	`container_file_t`	`s0:c1,c2`
Container file	`system_u`	`object_r`	`container_file_t`	`s0:s361,c871`

Table 10.7   Container process labels, with MCS level highlighted (continued)

Object	User	Role	Type	MCS level
/etc/shadow label	system_u	object_r	shadow_t	s0
Container process	system_u	system_r	spc_t	s0
User process	unconfined_u	unconfined_r	unconfined_t	s0-s0:c0.c1023

Now look at how MCS leveling works with Podman. If you run containers back to back and examine the SELinux label, you notice that each container's MCS level is unique:

```
$ podman run --rm ubi8 cat /proc/self/attr/current
System_u:system_r:container_t:s0:c648,c1009
$ podman run --rm ubi8 cat /proc/self/attr/current
system_u:system_r:container_t:s0:c393,c834
```

This MCS level prevents the processes from attacking each other. Recall that in section 10.2.8, you created the foo/bar file with a container private label. If you volume mount this file into another container and then try to write to the file, you get permission denied.

Listing 10.10   SELinux preventing different containers from sharing a volume

The file foo/bar has a private MCS level, which Podman does not give to another container.

Other containers are not allowed to access the foo/bar file based on having a different MCS level.

```
$ ls -Z ./foo
system_u:object_r:container_file_t:s0:c454,c510 bar
$ podman run -v ./foo:/foo ubi8 touch /foo/bar
touch: cannot touch '/foo/bar': Permission denied
$ podman run --security-opt label=level:s0:c454,c510
➥ -v ./foo:/foo ubi8 touch /foo/bar
```

If you force the container MCS level to match the previous container's label, SELinux allows the access.

Recall that the Z volume option tells Podman to label the container private to the container, while the z volume option tells Podman to label the container shared for all containers. You can use this option if you have a directory you want to allow multiple containers to use.

Listing 10.11   Volume option z causing Podman to relabel volumes with a shared label

```
$ podman run -v ./foo:/foo:z ubi8 touch /foo/bar
$ ls -Z foo/
system_u:object_r:container_file_t:s0 bar
$ podman run --rm -v ./foo:/foo ubi8 touch /foo/bar
```

The -v ./foo:/foo:z tells Podman to label the volume as shared.

Other containers with different MCS levels can successfully modify the content.

Podman uses the :s0 MCS level because all containers are allowed to write to it.

NOTE   SELinux has 1,024 categories, and Podman chooses two categories for each container. Level `s0:c1,c1` is not allowed. These categories must not match, and the order is not important. Level `s0:c1,c2` is the same as `s0:c2,c1`. There are 1024 x 1024 ÷ 2 − 1024 = ~500,000 unique combinations available, meaning you can create half a million unique containers on your system.

Sometimes it is necessary to disable SELinux container separation for your container. For example, you might want to share your home directory within a container. It is a bad idea to relabel your home directory with the `Z` or `z` options. Recall that when relabeling volumes, they need to be private to the container. Relabeling the home directory can cause other SELinux problems with other confined domains. You can run the container with the `--privileged` flag, but you probably want the other security mechanisms to still be enforced. To achieve this, you can use the `--security-opt label:disable` flag:

```
$ podman run --rm --security-opt label=disable ubi8 cat
➥ /proc/self/attr/current
unconfined_u:system_r:spc_t:s0
$ podman run --rm -v $HOME/.ssh:/ssh --security-opt label=disable ubi8 ls /ssh
authorized_keys
authorized_keys2
config
fedora_rsa
fedora_rsa.pub
...
```

NOTE   The udica project's (https://github.com/containers/udica) goal is to generate SELinux policies for containers. Basically, Udica examines a container you have created via `podman inspect` and then writes a policy type that allows access to the volumes you want to mount into the container.

SELinux is a very powerful tool for protecting the host operating system from the containers. It is easy to deal with for containers as long as you understand how to handle volumes. Understanding how to protect the filesystem, it is time now to look at protecting the Linux kernel from potentially vulnerable system calls.

10.9   System call isolation seccomp

A *system call*, often called a *syscall*, is how a computer program requests a service from the kernel of the operating system on which it is executed. Common syscalls are `open`, `read`, `write`, `fork`, and `exec`. In Linux, there are over 700 system calls.

Recall from the beginning of this chapter that the Linux kernel is the single point of failure hostile containers can attack to escape confinement. If a bug exists in the Linux kernel that can be attacked via a system call, the container processes might escape. The Linux kernel feature seccomp allows processes to voluntarily limit the number of system calls they and their children can make. Podman, by default, eliminates hundreds of the system calls using this feature. Suppose the Linux kernel has a flaw in one of its system calls, which a container process can use to escape, but Podman eliminated it from the table of system calls available to the container. In that case, the container is blocked from using it.

Podman's seccomp filters are stored as a JSON file in the /usr/share/containers/seccomp.json file. Podman also modifies the list of seccomp filters based on the capabilities you allow to the container. When you add a capability, Podman adds the system calls required for that capability. Capabilities and seccomp are both enforced separately; Podman just tries to make it easier for the user. If the user provides their own seccomp JSON file, it needs to be similar to the default one for the capability modifications to work.

You can modify the seccomp filter by editing this file. In the following example, you remove the mkdir syscall from seccomp.json, and then run a container in which you try to make a directory. The seccomp filter blocks the syscall, and your container fails.

> **Listing 10.12   How seccomp filters can block syscalls within a Podman container**

```
$ sed '/mkdir/d' /usr/share/containers
➥ /seccomp.json > /tmp/seccomp.json
$ diff /usr/share/containers/seccomp.json/
➥ tmp/seccomp.json
249,250d248
<        "mkdir",
<        "mkdirat",
$ podman run --rm --security-opt seccomp=/
➥ tmp/seccomp.json ubi8 mkdir /foo
mkdir: cannot create directory '/foo': Function not implemented
$ podman run --rm ubi8 mkdir /foo
```

Use the sed command to delete all entries that make mkdir and create /tmp/seccomp.json.

Use the diff command to show the removed mkdir entries.

Use the --security-opt seccomp= /tmp/seccomp.json flag to use an alternative seccomp filter; the mkdir command fails because the mkdir system call is not available.

Run the same command again with a default filter to show the mkdir succeeds.

NOTE   Not many people modify the seccomp filters because it is difficult to figure out the number of system calls required by a container. There are tools to generate this list of system calls using the Berkeley Packet Filter (BPF). The package at the following webpage is a hook that monitors a container and automatically generates a seccomp.json file to use later to lock down the container: https://github.com/containers/oci-seccomp-bpf-hook/.

Sometimes the default container seccomp.json file is too tight. Your container might not work because it needs a system call that is not available. In this case, you can disable seccomp filtering by using the --security-opt seccomp=unconfined flag.

As you see, system call filtering is powerful and can really limit the container processes' access to the host kernel. The next level is to use KVM isolation.

10.10 *Virtual machine isolation*

At the beginning of this chapter, I compared process isolation based on where the three pigs chose to live. They could live in separate houses, a duplex, or a condominium.

Each one was getting slightly less secure. Container security, by default, is living in a condo. But you can use VM isolation, which basically puts your container into a VM, to get better isolation.

In appendix B, I cover how different OCI runtimes, Kata and libkrun, take advantage of Kernel-based Virtual Machine (KVM) to run their containers within a lightweight virtual machine. These virtual machines run their own kernel and initialization tools to launch the container. By doing this, almost all of the host kernels' system calls are eliminated, making it much more difficult to escape confinement.

The problem with this isolation is that it comes at a cost. As with a duplex, you end up sharing fewer services between your containers. Memory management, CPU, and other resources are harder to share. Sharing volumes into a container is also going to perform worse.

Now you've finished examining Podman security features used for container isolation. Next let's look at other security features.

Summary

- Container security is all about protecting the Linux kernel and host filesystem from hostile container processes.
- Defense in depth means your container tooling takes advantage of as many security mechanisms as possible. If one security mechanism fails, others might still protect your system.

11
Additional security considerations

This chapter covers

- Securing running applications on different standalone servers, inside different VMs and containers
- Running a container via a service versus as a child of the container engine via fork and exec
- Linux security features used to keep containers isolated from each other
- Setting up container image trust
- Signing images and trusting them

In this chapter, I review and demonstrate some additional security considerations when using Podman to run containers. Some of the content was covered in other chapters, but I think it is useful to concentrate on these features from a security perspective.

One of the most frequent problems I see with people running containers is that when the container process is denied some access, the user's first reaction is to run the container in --privileged mode, which turns off all security separation for your container. Understanding how to deal with the security features discussed in this chapter helps you avoid this.

11.1   Daemon versus the fork/exec model

Throughout the previous chapters, you have learned quite a bit about the problems of a daemon like Docker versus the fork/exec model employed by Podman.

11.1.1   Access to the docker.sock

Recall that Docker, by default, runs a daemon owned by the root user. This means any user who has access to the daemon can launch processes with full root access on the system. Docker recommends some users put their accounts into the docker group in the /etc/group. On some distributions, this allows you to access the /run/docker.sock without being root:

```
# ls -l /run/docker.sock
srw-rw----. 1 root docker 0 Jun 13 14:54 /run/docker.sock
```

You can run a Docker container similarly to how you have been running a Podman container:

```
$ docker run registry.access.redhat.com/ubi8-micro echo hi
Unable to find image 'registry.access.redhat.com/ubi8-micro:latest' locally|
latest: Pulling from ubi8-micro
4f4fb700ef54: Pull complete
b6d5e0581b2f: Pull complete
Digest: sha256:a519ab06c0287085c352af0d2b84f2a2b257d2afb2e554b8d38a076cd6205b48
Status: Downloaded newer image for registry.access.redhat.com/
ubi8-micro:latest
hi
```

This excites a lot of users, until they understand they can also launch a root shell on their system with a simple Docker command:

```
$ docker run -ti --name hack -v /:/host --privileged
➥ registry.access.redhat.com/ubi8-micro chroot /host
# cat /etc/shadow
...
```

At this point, you have a fully privileged root shell on the host system, in which you can hack the machine all you want. Not only that, but Docker defaults all logging to being file based. When you are done hacking the system, you can remove the log files and all records of your activity:

```
$ docker rm hack
hack
```

Using rootless Podman, you cannot do this, since when you run the container, the container processes are run as your user UID and only have access to the same files as any process in your account. One way administrators figure out if they have been hacked is by examining the logging system, including the audit logs.

11.1.2 Auditing and logging

One key feature of a Linux system is tracking what processes do when they are running on a system. When you log in to a Linux system, your UID is recorded by the kernel into the process data in /proc/self/loginuid. You can see this data by executing the following command:

```
$ cat /proc/self/loginuid
3267
```

All processes created by this first process after login maintain this field. Even if you use a setuid program, like su or sudo, your loginuid stays the same:

```
$ sudo cat /proc/self/loginuid
3267
```

Even when you launch a container, the loginuid stays the same. In this next example, you run a simple container in daemon mode that sleeps, then use podman inspect to get the PID of the sleep processes, and finally examine the loginuid of the containerized process:

```
$ podman run -d ubi8-micro sleep 20
1c55b9cfa0cd20c36da4b606415e190a6c20cc868d3486981c7713d41ee9ea6a
$ podman inspect -l --format '{{ .State.Pid }}'
119394
$ cat /proc/119394/loginuid
3267
```

Notice the containerized process is still running with your loginuid. This shows that the kernel can track which user launched a container process on the system via this field, as long as the container engine uses the fork/exec model. If you run this same test with Docker, you get very different results:

```
$ docker run -d registry.access.redhat.com/ubi8-micro sleep 20
df2302cf8c6385df2b86ccd3429166e0d8dd0c9f0d0139e98e6354809a04080e
$ docker inspect df2302cf8c6 --format '{{ .State.Pid }}'
120022
$ cat /proc/120022/loginuid
4294967295
```

Instead of showing your loginuid, you see 4294967295, which is $2^{32} - 1$. This is how the Linux kernel represents -1, the default loginuid for all processes started by the system, not by users who logged into the system. The reason for this is that Docker uses a client-server model, and the container process is a child of the Docker daemon as opposed to the Docker client. Since the Docker daemon was launched by systemd when the system booted up, all of its children processes have the -1 loginuid.

The kernel's audit subsystem records the loginuid of every process on the system when it completes an auditable event. For example, when a user logs in and out of a system, these events are logged. Modifying /etc/passwd and /etc/shadow are also loggable events.

Following is the USER_START audit log entry for when I logged into my system today. My UID 3267 is recorded along with my username:

```
# ausearch -m USER_START
type=USER_START msg=audit(1651064687.963:315): pid=2579 uid=0 auid=3267
➥ ses=3 subj=system_u:system_r:xdm_t:s0-s0:c0.c1023 msg='op=PAM:session_open
➥ grantors=pam_selinux,pam_loginuid,pam_selinux,pam_keyinit,pam_namespace,
➥ pam_keyinit,pam_limits,pam_systemd,pam_unix,pam_gnome_keyring,pam_umask acct=
➥ "dwalsh" exe="/usr/libexec/gdm-session-worker" hostname=fedora addr=?
➥ terminal=/dev/tty2 res=success'UID="root" AUID="dwalsh"
```

If you launched the container by using a Podman command, then the audit subsystem records your UID in the audit logs. If the container was launched via Docker, it records -1 as the loginuid. Imagine your system was hacked via a container. You need to go back and examine which user launched the container that hacked your system via the audit.log.

Let's show an example of this. First, become root, and set up a watch on the /etc/passwd file using auditctl:

```
# auditctl -w /etc/passwd -p wa -k passwd
```

Now run a --privileged container using Docker, which touches the host's /etc/passwd file:

```
# docker run --privileged -v /:/host registry.access.redhat.com/ubi8-
➥ micro:latest touch /host/etc/passwd
```

This simulated what would happen if a Docker container escaped confinement and was able to modify the host's /etc/passwd file. Now examine the audit.log, where there should be a record of the /etc/passwd modification. Notice that the audit log shows auid=unset. This is how the audit log represents the loginuid of the user that modified the /etc/passwd file. As you can see, because no user launched the Docker daemon directly, the audit log has no record of the user who launched the container:

```
# ausearch -k passwd -i
...
type=SYSCALL msg=audit(05/03/2022 08:24:52.885:464) : arch=x86_64
➥ syscall=openat success=yes exit=3 a0=AT_FDCWD a1=0x7ffef7a9ef75
➥ a2=O_WRONLY|O_CREAT|O_NOCTTY|O_NONBLOCK a3=0x1b6 items=2 ppid=6723
➥ pid=6743 auid=unset uid=root gid=root euid=root suid=root fsuid=root
➥ egid=root sgid=root fsgid=root tty=(none) ses=unset comm=touch
➥ exe=/usr/bin/coreutils
```

Now run the same command with Podman:

```
# podman run --privileged -v /:/host registry.access.redhat.com/
➥ ubi8-micro:latest touch /host/etc/passwd
```

Examine the audit.log for the Podman container that modifies the /etc/passwd file, and you see that auid=dwalsh. Because Podman follows the fork/exec model and was launched by a user who logged into the system and had a record in the loginuid, the audit.log can record which user launched a container that hacked the system:

```
# ausearch -k passwd -i
…
type=SYSCALL msg=audit(05/03/2022 08:25:42.466:480) : arch=x86_64
➥  syscall=openat success=no exit=EACCES(Permission denied) a0=AT_FDCWD
➥  a1=0x7fff3d5aef59 a2=O_WRONLY|O_CREAT|O_NOCTTY|O_NONBLOCK a3=0x1b6
➥  items=2 ppid=6978 pid=6986 auid=dwalsh uid=root gid=root euid=root
➥  suid=root fsuid=root egid=root sgid=root fsgid=root tty=(none) ses=1
➥  comm=touch exe=/usr/bin/coreutils
➥  subj=system_u:system_r:container_t:s0:c484,c845 key=passwd
```

> **NOTE** On current Fedora, the audit subsystem is disabled. You can enable it by removing /etc/audit/rules.d/audit.rules and regenerating the audit rules with the augenrules --load command.

This is one reason, back in 2014, I said access to the docker.sock via non-root processes is more dangerous than giving out the root process or sudo access, since both of those record the loginuid, meaning you can track what the user is doing on your system. When you give access to the root running docker.sock, you have no tracking data. Let's look into how you can protect the kernel and the filesystem from processes running within a container in the next section.

11.2 *Podman secret handling*

Often, when running a container, you need to provide a secret to the service running within the container. An example of this is a database tool that requires an administrator and password to control access. Another example is a service that requires a password to reach another service.

Developers of these applications do not want to hardcode the secret information into the image. The user of the container application must provide the secret. You can just provide the secret to the application via environment variables, but this means if you commit the image, the secret gets committed to the image.

Podman provides a secret mechanism, podman secret, which allows you to either add files or environment variables to a container without these secrets getting saved when you commit the container to an image. First, let's look at creating a secret.

> **Listing 11.1 Using secrets within a Podman container**

Add your secret data to a file.

```
$ echo "This is my secret" > /tmp/secret                 ←
$ podman secret create my_secret /tmp/secret             ←┐  Use podman secret
b5f27b90e9b3486fb5a78d1eb                                   │  create to name a secret
$ podman run --rm --secret my_secret ubi8 cat               │  based on the file.
```

```
/run/secrets/my_secret
This is my secret
```
Use the --secret option to leak the secret into the container.

You can also leak the secret into the container as an environment variable by adding the `--secret my_secret,type=env` flag:

```
$ podman run --secret my_secret,type=env --name secret_ctr ubi8 bash
  -c 'echo $my_secret'
This is my secret
```

If you were to commit this container to an image, the secret would not be saved inside the image.

Listing 11.2   The secret is not saved when the container is committed to the image.

```
$ podman commit secret_ctr secret_img
Getting image source signatures
Copying blob a9820c2af00a skipped: already exists
Copying blob 3d5ecee9360e skipped: already exists
Copying blob dc409efbefc4 done
Copying config 501812299f done
Writing manifest to image destination
Storing signatures
501812299f0c0cfbb032d144e6d2c2a41c5eadf229e7b76f6264ab74d9f6c069
$ podman image inspect secret_img --format
  '{{ .Config.Env }}'
[TERM=xterm container=oci PATH=/usr/local/sbin:/usr/local/
  bin:/usr/sbin:/usr/bin:/sbin:/bin]
```
Commit the secret_ctr into the secret_img image.

Inspect the image to view the committed environment variables, and notice the my_secret environment is not committed.

Table 11.1 lists all of the `podman secret` commands.

Table 11.1   `podman secret` commands

Command	Man page	Description
create	podman-secret-create(1)	Create a new secret.
inspect	podman-secret-inspect(1)	Display detailed information on one or more secrets.
ls	podman-secret-ls(1)	List all available secrets.
rm	podman-secret-rm(1)	Remove one or more secrets.

11.3   *Podman image trust*

In many situations, users of container images want to specify which container image registries and images they trust. The `podman image trust` command allows you to specify which registries you trust. It also allows you to specify registries to block.

The location of the trusted registry is determined by the transport and the registry host of the image. Using this container image—docker://quay.io/podman/stable—as an example, Docker is the transport, and quay.io is the registry host.

> **NOTE** Podman image trust is not available in remote mode, for example, on a Mac or Windows box. You have to execute the commands documented here on a Linux box. If you are using the Podman machine, use the `podman machine ssh` command to enter the VM. See appendixes E and F for more information.

The trust policy is defined in /etc/containers/policy.json, which describes a registry scope (registry and/or repository) for the trust. The trust policy can use public keys for signed images. The `podman image trust` command must be run as root.

The scope of the trust is evaluated from the most specific to the least specific. In other words, a policy may be defined for an entire registry. Or it can be defined for a particular repository in that registry or defined down to a specific signed image inside the registry. In the following example, you reject pulls from docker.io and then later specify only docker.io/library images are allowed for pulling.

The following list includes valid scope values that can be used in policy.json from most specific to the least specific:

```
docker.io/library/busybox:notlatest
docker.io/library/busybox
docker.io/library
docker.io
```

If no configuration is found for any of these scopes, the default value (specified by using `default` instead of `REGISTRY[/REPOSITORY]`) is used, as shown in the following listing. Table 11.2 describes the valid trust values used for registries.

Listing 11.3   Telling Podman to not pull images from a specific container registry

Use Podman image trust to set a more specific registry/repository for docker.io/library.

Use podman image trust to reject all images from the docker.io container registry.

Attempt to pull the alpine image from the container registry, and see that Podman rejects the image.

```
$ sudo podman image trust set -t reject docker.io       ◁
$ podman pull alpine                                      ◁
Trying to pull docker.io/library/alpine:latest…
Error: Source image rejected: Running image docker://alpine:latest
➥ is rejected by policy.
$ sudo podman image trust set -t accept
➥ docker.io/library
$ podman pull alpine                                      ◁
Trying to pull docker.io/library/alpine:latest…
Getting image source signatures
Copying blob 59bf1c3509f3 skipped: already exists
Copying config c059bfaa84 done
Writing manifest to image destination
Storing signatures
C059bfaa849c4d8e4aecaeb3a10c2d9b3d85f5165c66ad3a4d937758128c4d18
$ podman pull bitnami/nginx                               ◁
```

Podman can pull the docker.io/library/alpine image.

Images pulled from the rest of docker.io are rejected.

```
Resolving "bitnami/nginx" using unqualified-search registries
⮕ (/etc/containers/registries.conf.d/999-podman-machine.conf)
Trying to pull docker.io/bitnami/nginx:latest…
Error: Source image rejected: Running image docker://bitnami/nginx:latest
⮕ is rejected by policy.
```

Table 11.2   The trust type tells container engines like Podman which registries to trust.

Types	Description
accept	Images from the specified registry are allowed to be pulled.
reject	Images from the specified registries are not allowed to be pulled.
signBy	Images from the specified registries must be signed by the specified name.

If you examine the policy.json file, you see the entries added by the podman image trust command:

```
$ cat /etc/containers/policy.json
{
    "default": [
        {
            "type": "insecureAcceptAnything"
        }
    ],
    "transports": {
        "docker": {
            "docker.io": [
                {
                    "type": "reject"
                }
            ],
            "docker.io/library": [
                {
                    "type": "insecureAcceptAnything"
                }
            ]
…
```

You can use the podman image trust show command to show the current settings in an easier-to-view form:

```
$ podman image trust show
all          default                       accept
repository   docker.io                     reject
repository   docker.io/library             accept

repository   registry.access.redhat.com    signed      security@redhat.com
https://access.redhat.com/webassets/docker/content/sigstore
repository   registry.redhat.io            signed
⮕ security@redhat.com  https://registry.redhat.io/containers/sigstore
docker-daemon                              accept
```

Through the `accept` and `reject` flags, you can set up which registries you trust and which you reject. If you want to lock down where images on your production system come from, you can change the `default` policy for your system to `reject` images from any registry. All images you want to allow need to come from a specific registry:

```
$ sudo podman image trust set --type=reject default
$ podman image trust show
all          default                      reject

repository   docker.io                    reject

repository   docker.io/library            accept

repository   registry.access.redhat.com  signed     security@redhat.com
https://access.redhat.com/webassets/docker/content/sigstore
repository   registry.redhat.io           signed
➥ security@redhat.com  https://registry.redhat.io/containers/sigstore
docker-daemon                             accept
```

With these settings on your system, Podman accepts images from docker.io/library and signed images from registry.redhat.io. All images from other registries are rejected. Podman allows pulling of images directly from the `docker-daemon` as well.

Don't forget to restore the default policy.json:

```
$ sudo cp /tmp/policy.json /etc/containers/policy.json
```

Podman supports using signed images from container registries. Red Hat signs and ships its images. Let's look at how you, too, can sign images.

11.3.1 *Podman image signing*

One way of signing images is utilizing a GNU Privacy Guard (https://gnupg.org) key. Podman can sign images before pushing them to remote registries, referred to as *simple signing*. You can configure Podman and other container engines to require images to be signed with a particular signature. All unsigned images are rejected.

First, you need to create a GPG key pair or select a premade pair. You can generate new GPG keys by running `gpg --full-gen-key` and following the interactive dialog. Refer to the following web page for a description of creating keys: http://mng.bz/JV9V.

Following is an example of creating a simple key with default params. Make sure to use your own email address:

```
$ gpg --batch --passphrase '' --quick-gen-key dwalsh@redhat.com default
➥ default
```

Most container registries do not understand image signing; they just provide the remote storage for the container images. If you want to sign an image, you need to distribute the signatures yourself, usually using a web server. You can configure Podman and other container engines to retrieve signatures from this web service.

In the following examples, you will create a web service running on your local machine to demonstrate image signing. Podman is able to push and sign the image in a single command. Podman reads signature locations in the registries configuration file /etc/containers/registries.d/default.yaml.

Examine the default.yaml file to find the `sigstore-staging` flag and see the default location where Podman stores signatures:

```
sigstore-staging: file:///var/lib/containers/sigstore
```

The `sigstore-staging` flag tells Podman to store signatures in the /var/lib/containers/sigstore directory. When you want other users to use these signatures to verify your images, you need to put these images onto a web server. Now you are ready to test out simple signing, first signing the ubi8 image and then setting up Podman to pull the image using the signature to verify it.

SIGNING AND PUSHING THE IMAGE

Before starting this section, you should back up a couple of security files, so you can restore them later:

```
$ sudo cp /etc/containers/registries.d/default.yaml
➥ /etc/containers/policy.json /tmp
```

Let's pull an image from a registry and add a signature, then push it back to the registry. Make sure to use your own registry account, image, and previously created GPG key:

```
$ sudo podman pull quay.io/rhatdan/myimage
Trying to pull quay.io/rhatdan/myimage:latest…
…
2c7e43d880382561ebae3fa06c7a1442d0da2912786d09ea9baaef87f73c29ae
$ podman login quay.io/rhatdan
Username: rhatdan
Password:
Login Succeeded!
$ sudo -E GNUPGHOME=$HOME/.gnupg \
    podman push --tls-verify=false --sign-by dwalsh@redhat.com
➥ quay.io/rhatdan/myimage
…
Storing signatures
```

Look in the sigstore-staging directory /var/lib/containers/sigstore for the repository name rhatdan. You will see that there is a new signature available, created by the podman push command. Make sure to use your own registry account name:

```
$ sudo ls /var/lib/containers/sigstore/rhatdan/
'myimage@sha256=0460a9d13a806e124639b23e9d6ffa1e5773f7bef91469bee6ac88
➥ a4be213427'
```

Now that you have signed the image, you need to set up a web server to provide the signature and configure Podman and other container engines to use the signatures and signed images.

CONFIGURING PODMAN TO PULL SIGNED IMAGES

When configuring Podman to use signatures to verify images, you need to configure the system to retrieve the signatures. Usually, you share signatures on a web service. You can do this by configuring the `sigstore` flag in the /etc/containers/registries.d/default.yaml file to identify the website that stores signatures. Podman downloads these signatures from this website.

For this example, you will create a web service running on localhost at port 8000. Add the `sigstore: http://localhost:8000` web server to the default.yaml file. This will tell Podman to retrieve signatures from this web server when pulling images. Podman looks for a signature based on the name of the image along with its digest:

```
$ echo "  sigstore: http://localhost:8000" | sudo tee --append
➥ /etc/containers/registries.d/default.yaml
```

For this example, start a new server using `python3` inside the local staging signature store /var/lib/containers/sigstore:

```
$ cd /var/lib/containers/sigstore && python3 -m http.server
Serving HTTP on 0.0.0.0 port 8000 (http://0.0.0.0:8000/) ...
```

In another window, remove quay.io/rhatdan/myimage from local storage, since you want to pull with the signatures:

```
$ podman rmi quay.io/rhatdan/myimage
Untagged: quay.io/rhatdan/myimage:latest
Deleted: 2c7e43d880382561ebae3fa06c7a1442d0da2912786d09ea9baaef87f73c29ae
```

You need to set up image trust for the quay.io/rhatdan repository and assign the publickey.gpg public key to use when verifying images signed by dwalsh@redhat.com:

```
$ sudo podman image trust set -f /tmp/publickey.gpg quay.io/rhatdan
```

The previous Podman command adds the following stanza to the /etc/containers/policy.json file:

```
...
"transports": {
    "docker": {
        "quay.io/rhatdan": [
            {
                "type": "signedBy",
                "keyType": "GPGKeys",
                "keyPath": "/tmp/publickey.gpg"
            }
        ],
...
```

You have not created the `keyPath` file /tmp/publickey.gpg yet. Create it using the following GPG command:

```
$ gpg --output /tmp/publickey.gpg --armor --export dwalsh@redhat.com
```

Now you can pull the signed image:

```
$ podman pull quay.io/rhatdan/myimage
Trying to pull quay.io/rhatdan/myimage:latest...
...
Writing manifest to image destination
Storing signatures
2c7e43d880382561ebae3fa06c7a1442d0da2912786d09ea9baaef87f73c29ae
```

It worked! Still, you are not really sure if it used signatures. Prove it to yourself by attempting to pull another image from the repository, which you don't have signatures for, and it will fail:

```
$ podman pull quay.io/rhatdan/podman
Trying to pull quay.io/rhatdan/podman:latest...
Error: Source image rejected: A signature was required,
↪ but no signature exists
```

Make sure to restore all settings back to default:

```
$ sudo cp /tmp/default.yaml /etc/containers/registries.d/default.yaml
$ sudo cp /tmp/policy.json /etc/containers/policy.json
```

Also, stop the localhost web server started in another terminal. Table 11.3 describes the infrastructure you need to set up to allow simple signing to be used within your environment.

Table 11.3 Infrastructure required for simple signing

Requirements	Description
GPG private key	You need a GPG key pair, where the private key is used on the service that signs the images.
Signature web server	A web server has to run somewhere that has access to the signature storage.

Once you have the infrastructure set up to use simple signing, you will need to know the requirements of each client that uses and verifies the signatures. Table 11.4 lists each of these requirements.

Table 11.4 Client configuration required for simple signing

Requirements	Description
GPG public key (/tmp/publickey.gpg)	The public GPG key used for signing must be present on any machine that pulls the signed images.

Table 11.4 Client configuration required for simple signing *(continued)*

Requirements	Description
Client's sigstore configured	The signature web server has to be configured as a sigstore in a /etc/containers/registries.d/ *.yaml file on all systems, which need to pull the signed images.
Client's image trust configured	Image trust has to be configured on every container engine system that uses the images.

11.4 *Podman image scanning*

Podman is not an image scanner; it leaves this to other tools. But Podman does have a nice feature that makes it easier for a scanner to scan an image. Podman can directly mount an image that can be scanned. Scanners look at the mounted content of an image without having to execute any of the code in the image. Recall that you cannot mount containers or images in rootless mode, without first entering the user namespaces. Execute the podman image mount command to show the error:

```
$ podman image mount ubi8
Error: cannot run command "podman image mount" in rootless mode, must
➥ execute `podman unshare` first
```

In this next example, you first use podman unshare to enter the user namespace, and then you mount the ubi8 image. Finally, change the directory to the mount directory, and run a find command to locate all of the setuid binaries in the image. Notice that you use tools from the host operating system to scan the image:

```
$ podman unshare
# podman image mount
# mnt=$(podman image mount ubi8)
# echo $mnt
/home/dwalsh/.local/share/containers/storage/overlay/05ddfb76c5eb2146646c70
➥ e20db21a35dfec2215f130ce8bd04fce530142cfbd/merged
# cd $mnt
# /usr/bin/find . -user root -perm -4000
./usr/libexec/dbus-1/dbus-daemon-launch-helper
./usr/bin/chage
./usr/bin/mount
./usr/bin/umount
./usr/bin/newgrp
./usr/bin/gpasswd
./usr/bin/passwd
./usr/bin/su
./usr/sbin/userhelper
./usr/sbin/unix_chkpwd
./usr/sbin/pam_timestamp_check
```

Scanning an image with tools within the image is not safe, since a hacker of the image can modify the scanning tools. Podman makes it easy for scanners to do their jobs.

11.4.1 Read-only containers

I often talk about containers in production versus containers in development. When a containerized application is in development, it is useful to be able to write to the container image and potentially commit that image later. Although this is somewhat common, most people switch to using Containerfiles when it comes to actually building images. The bottom line is once developers hand off their software to quality engineering, they expect content to be treated as read only.

When running a container in production, I believe it makes sense to run the image in read-only mode. Imagine you are running an application that gets hacked. The first thing the hacker wants to do is to write the backdoor into the application; then, the next time the container or application starts, the container has the exploit in place. If the image was read only, the hacker is prevented from leaving a backdoor in place and is forced to start the cycle from the beginning.

The `--read-only` option prevents applications from writing content to the image and forces applications to only write content to either tmpfs filesystems or volumes added to the container. Sometimes you might want to block the container from writing anywhere on your system and only read or execute code within the container. Another benefit of running containers in read-only mode is that you catch errors where you did not know the container was writing to the image. Finally, writing on top of a copy-on-write filesystem, like overlayfs, is almost always slower than writing to a volume or a tmpfs:

```
$ podman run --read-only ubi8 touch /foo
touch: cannot touch '/foo': Read-only file system
```

One problem with running in rootless mode is that applications often expect to write to /run, /tmp, and /var/tmp. Podman manages this by automatically mounting tmpfs filesystems at those locations:

```
$ podman run --read-only ubi8 touch /run/foo
```

Because some users believe allowing any places for a containerized application to write, even on tmpfs mounts, is too insecure, Podman added a `--read-only-tmpfs` option. The `--read-only-tmpfs` option adds the /run, /tmp, and /var/tmp tmpfs when run in `--read-only` mode. If you want to disable this, you can use the `--read-only-tmpfs=false` flag:

```
$ podman run --read-only-tmpfs=false --read-only ubi8 touch /run/foo
touch: cannot touch '/run/foo': Read-only file system
```

11.5 Security in depth

In the security field, there is a common idea of *security in depth*. According to this notion, multiple layers or tools should be used to safeguard assets. The classic analogy for this is the security of an ancient castle, which would usually be built high on a hill, have multiple walls, have moats, and have even more security features. An attacker would need to break through all of these layers to get to the ruler.

Container security works in much the same way. Podman uses all of the security mechanisms provided by Linux, giving you security in depth.

11.5.1 *Podman uses all security mechanisms simultaneously*

Podman containers can run with all of the security mechanisms mentioned in this chapter. This means a hacked container needs to find a way to escape read-only filesystems, namespaces, dropped capabilities, SELinux, seccomp, and so on to gain access to your system.

In certain cases, you might need to loosen some security mechanisms to allow a container to run. Understanding how to deal with the security features discussed in this chapter is always better than just running your containers with the `--privileged` flag, which turns off all of your defenses.

Podman shoots for a reasonable amount of security wrapping for containers, but it needs to allow general-purpose containers to succeed. Understanding your container application's security requirements and the Podman security features allows you to ratchet up the security wrapping of your containers. If you know your container does not need to run as root, don't start it as root. If your container does not need any Linux capabilities, drop them. Rootless containers are better than rootful containers. Consider also running containers in read-only mode or inside of separated user namespaces. You have the ability to make your castle walls thicker around your containerized applications by simply employing these measures.

11.5.2 *Where should you run your containers?*

I'll leave you with one final thought. At the beginning of this chapter, I talked about the three pigs living in different types of shelters—standalone houses, duplexes, and condominium buildings—each slightly less secure than the last. Container security can do better than the pigs living in individual housing units, in that the units can be stacked together.

Imagine you had two different containers: a web frontend and a database with credit card data. If you wanted to make sure they were separate, you could put them together on the system inside containers or, better yet, put them in containers but put them into separate VMs, and then, finally, put the VMs on separate machines. You would be able to put your web frontend into a machine running a VM inside of a container inside of your DMZ exposed to the internet. You could do all this while putting your database inside of your private network, without limited network access to your web frontends. The possibilities are nearly endless.

Summary

- Container security has many different facets, including separation of running containers, trusting the images and registries, scanning the images, and so on.
- Defense in depth means your container tooling takes advantage of as many security mechanisms as possible. If one security mechanism fails, the others might still protect your system.
- Container security is all about protecting the Linux kernel and host filesystem from hostile container processes.
- Setting up and controlling the container images you run on your systems is critical. Do not allow your users to run random applications from the internet.

appendix A
Podman-related
container tools

This appendix describes the three tools that use containers/storage and containers/image libraries. These tools address the following functionalities:

- Moving container images between different container registries and storage
- Building container images
- Testing, developing, and running containers in production on a single node
- Running containers in production at scale

As the original creator of Podman, I recognized the need for specialized tools, each performing specific functionality rather than a one-size-fits-all monolithic solution.

From a security perspective, each of these four categories requires different security constraints. Containers running in production need to be run in a more secure environment than ones running in development and testing. Moving container images between registries requires no privileged access to the host you are running the command on—only remote access to the registries. You will have the least secure system with a monolithic daemon. If my containers need more access during builds, then in production, they get the same access as during builds.

Another critical problem with a monolithic daemon is that it prevents experimentation with the tools and doesn't allow them to go their own way. One example of this is when we proposed a change to the Docker daemon to allow users to pull different types of OCI content off of container registries. This change was denied, as it had little to do with Docker containers.

Similarly, when the monolithic daemon is modified for one product, it can negatively affect features of another one using that daemon. It could cause performance degradation or complete breakage. This happened when Kubernetes was being developed, since it relied on the Docker daemon as the container engine. But since Docker is monolithic and being developed for many other projects, many of its changes affected Kubernetes, leading to instability. It was obvious that Kubernetes needed a dedicated container engine for its workloads, and in December 2020 it was announced that Kubernetes will eventually use the newly developed standard, the Container Runtime Interface (CRI; see http://mng.bz/yaDq) to improve interaction between orchestrators and different container runtimes. I wrote a coloring book, *The Container Commandos* (figure A.1; https://red.ht/3gfVlHF), illustrated by Máirín Duffy (@marin), describing the container tools talked about in this appendix, based on superheroes.

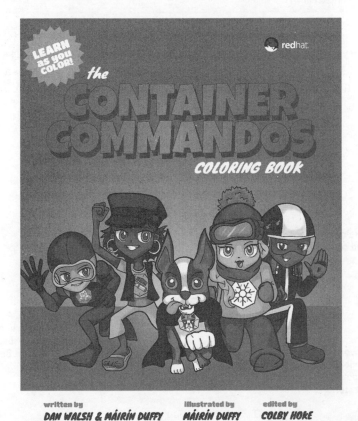

Figure A.1
The Container Coloring Book
(https://red.ht/3gfVlHF)

Finally, sometimes there are conflicting interests or release schedules in play. Having separate, independent tools allows releases to be deployed independently from all the others at their own pace to guarantee new features to their customers. Four projects were created for the distinct functions described in table A.1.

As you have already learned a great deal about Podman, you know now why it is included in this list. Podman is an excellent tool for understanding and developing

Table A.1   Primary container tools based on containers/storage and containers/image.

Tool	Description
Skopeo	Performs various operations on container images and image repositories (https://github.com/containers/skopeo)
Buildah	Facilitates a wide range of operations on container images (https://github.com/containers/buildah)
Podman	All-in-one management tool for pods, containers, and images (https://github.com/containers/podman)
CRI-O	OCI-based implementation of the Kubernetes Container Runtime Interface (https://github.com/cri-o/cri-o)

containers as well as pods and images. It encapsulates everything Docker CLI does but without locking everything under one central daemon. Because Podman works without a daemon and uses the operating system for sharing data, other tools can work with the same data stores and libraries. The rest of this appendix describes the rest of the tools, starting with Skopeo (figure A.2).

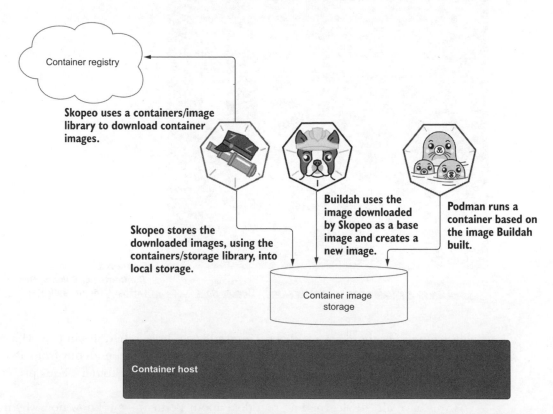

Figure A.2   Skopeo, Buildah, and Podman work together by sharing the same containers/storage images and containers/image library for pulling and pushing images.

A.1   Skopeo

While using container engines like Docker or Podman, if you want to inspect a container image in a registry, you are required to pull this image from the registry to your local storage. Only then can you examine it. The problem is that this image can be huge, and after inspecting it, you might realize it wasn't what you expected, and you wasted time pulling it. Because the protocol used to pull the image and inspect it is just a web protocol, a simple tool, Skopeo, was created to pull the image's detailed information and display it on the screen. *Skopeo* is the Greek word for *remote viewing*.

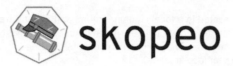

Execute the following `skopeo inspect` command to examine an image's detailed information in JSON form:

```
$ skopeo inspect docker://quay.io/rhatdan/myimage
{
  "Name": "quay.io/rhatdan/myimage",
  "Digest":
"sha256:fe798c1576dc7b70d7de3b3ab7c72cd22300b061921f052279d88729708092d8",
  "RepoTags": [
      "Latest",
      "1.0"
  ],
…
```

Skopeo was extended to also copy images off of registries. Eventually, Skopeo became the tool for copying images between different types of storage (transports). These types of storage became the transports defined in table A.2.

Table A.2   Podman-supported transports

Transport	Description
Container registry (docker)	This is the default transport. It references a container image stored in a remote container image registry website. Registries store and share container images (e.g., docker.io and quay.io).
oci	References a container image; compliant with the Open Container Initiative Format specification. The manifest and layer tarballs are located in the local directory as individual files.
dir	References a container image; compliant with the Docker image layout. It is very similar to the oci transport but stores the files using the legacy Docker format. As a non-standardized format, it is primarily useful for debugging or noninvasive container inspection.

Table A.2 Podman-supported transports *(continued)*

Transport	Description
`docker-archive`	References a container image in a Docker image layout, which is packed into a TAR archive.
`oci-archive`	References an image compliant with the Open Container Initiative Format specification, which is packed into a TAR archive. It is very similar to the `docker-archive` transport but stores an image in OCI format.
`docker-daemon`	References an image stored in the Docker daemon's internal storage. Since the Docker daemon requires root privileges, Podman has to be run by the root user.
`container-storage`	References an image located in a local container storage. It is not a transport but more of a mechanism for storing images. It can be used to convert other transports into `container-storage`. Podman defaults to using `container-storage` for local images.

Other container engines and tools wanted to use the functionality developed in Skopeo to copy images, so Skopeo was split in two: the command line, Skopeo, and the underlying library, containers/image. Splitting functionality into a separate library made it possible to build other container tools, including Podman.

The `skopeo copy` command is very popular for copying images between different types of container storage. One difference compared to Podman and Buildah, as you'll see in section A.2, is that Skopeo forces users to specify the transport for the source and destination. Podman and Buildah default to using the `docker` or `containers-storage` transport, depending on the context and command. In the following example, you will copy an image from a container registry using the `docker` transport and store the image locally using the `container-storage` transport:

```
$ skopeo copy docker://quay.io/rhatdan/myimage containers-storage:quay.io/
    rhatdan/myimage
Getting image source signatures
Copying blob dfd8c625d022 done
Copying blob 68e8857e6dcb done
Copying blob e21480a19686 done
Copying blob fbfcc23454c6 done
Copying blob 3f412c5136dd done
Copying config 2c7e43d880 done
Writing manifest to image destination
Storing signatures
```

Another command many Skopeo users use is `skopeo sync`, which lets you synchronize images between container registries and local storage.

Skopeo is mainly used for infrastructure projects to help provision multiple container registries—for example, copying images from a public registry to a private one. Table A.3 describes the most popular commands used with Skopeo. One of the first tools to take advantage of the containers/image library was Buildah.

Table A.3 Primary Skopeo commands and their description

Command	Description
`skopeo copy`	Copy an image (manifest, filesystem layers, or signatures) from one location to another.
`skopeo delete`	Mark the image name for later deletion by the registry's garbage collector.
`skopeo inspect`	Return low-level information about an image name in a registry.
`skopeo list-tags`	List tags in the transport-specific image repository.
`skopeo login`	Log in to a container registry (the same as `podman login`).
`skopeo logout`	Log out of a container registry (the same as `podman logout`).
`skopeo manifest digest`	Compute a manifest digest for a manifest file, and write it to standard output.
`skopeo sync`	Synchronize images between container registries and local directories.

A.2 Buildah

As you learned in section 1.1.2, creating a container image means creating a directory on disk and adding content to it to make it look like the root, /, directory on a Linux machine, called a rootfs. Originally, the only way to do this was with `docker build`, using a Dockerfile. While Dockerfiles and Containerfiles are excellent ways of creating recipes for your container images, a low-level building block tool that allowed other ways to build container images was needed—one that allowed breaking the image-build process into individual commands, letting you use other more powerful scripting tools and languages than Containerfile to build images. We created a tool called Buildah (https://buildah.io) to serve this purpose.

Buildah was designed to be that simple tool for building container images. It's built on top of the container/storage and container/image libraries, just like Podman and Skopeo. It has a lot of functionality similar to Podman. You can pull images, push images, commit images, and even run containers on images. What mainly differentiates Podman from Buildah is the underlying concept of a *container*. A Podman container is a long-lived one, a *running* container, while a Buildah container is just a temporary one, a *working* container, which will be used to create an OCI image.

NOTE Buildah is a Linux-only tool, not available on Mac or Windows. However, Podman embeds Buildah in the `podman build` command. Podman on

Mac and Windows uses the Buildah code on the server side, allowing those platforms to build using Containerfiles and Dockerfiles. See appendixes E and F for more information.

Buildah was designed to take the steps defined in a Dockerfile and make them available at the command line. Buildah wanted to simplify building a container image by allowing you to use all of the tools available within the OS to populate the image. You can add data to this directory via standard Linux tools, like cp, make, yum install, and so on. Then commit the rootfs into a tarball, add some JSON to describe what the creator of the image wanted the image to do, and finally, push this to a container registry. Basically, Buildah breaks down the steps you learned about in a Containerfile into individual commands you can execute from a shell.

> **NOTE** The name *Buildah* is a play on the way I pronounce *builder*. If you ever heard me speak, you'd notice I have a strong Boston accent. When the core team asked what I wanted to call the tool, I said, "I don't care, just call it *builder*." And they heard *Buildah*.

The first step when building a new container image is pulling a base image. In a Containerfile, this is done with the FROM instruction.

A.2.1 *Creating a working container from a base image*

The first command to look at is buildah from. It is equivalent to the Containerfile's FROM instruction. When executing buildah from IMAGE, it pulls the specified image from the container registry, saves it in a local container storage, and creates a working container based on this image. As mentioned previously, this container is similar to a Podman container, except it exists temporarily only to become a container image. In the following example, a working container is created based on an ubi8-init image.

Listing A.1 Buildah pulling an image and creating a Buildah container

```
$ buildah from ubi8-init
Resolved "ubi8-init" as an alias (/etc/containers/registries.conf.d/
➥ 000-shortnames.conf)
Trying to pull registry.access.redhat.com/                Pulls the image
➥ ubi8-init:latest…                              ◁──────   from the container
Getting image source signatures                           registry
Checking if image destination supports signatures
Copying blob adffa6963146 done
Copying blob 29250971c1d2 done
Copying blob 26f1167feaf7 done
Copying config 4b85030f92 done
Writing manifest to image destination
Storing signatures                       Outputs a new
ubi8-init-working-container    ◁──────   container name
```

Notice that the `buildah from` output looks the same as the `podman pull` output, except for the last line, which outputs the container name: `ubi8-init-working-container`. If you run the `buildah from` command again, you get a second container name:

```
$ buildah from ubi8-init
ubi8-init-working-container-1
```

Buildah keeps track of its containers and generates each one by incrementing a counter. Of course you can override the container name with the `--name` option. Next, you will add content to this container image.

A.2.2 Adding data to a working container

Buildah has two commands, `buildah copy` and `buildah add`, for copying the contents of a file, URL, or directory into the container's working directory. They map to the same functionality as the Containerfile's `COPY` and `ADD` instructions.

> **NOTE** It is somewhat confusing to have two commands that do almost the same thing. In most cases, I recommend you just use `buildah copy` and `COPY` inside a Containerfile. The main difference between the two is that `COPY` only copies local files and directories off of the host into the container image. The `add` command supports the use of URLs to pull remote content and insert it into your container. The `ADD` command also supports taking TAR and ZIP files and expanding them when copied into the container image.

The syntax of the `buildah copy` command requires you to specify the name of the container previously created by the `buildah from` command, followed by the source and, optionally, destination. If the destination is not provided, source data will be copied into the container's working directory. The destination directory will be created if it doesn't exist yet.

The following example copies the local html/index.html file (created previously in section 3.1) into the /var/lib/www/html directory in the container:

```
$ buildah copy ubi8-init-working-container html/index.html
➥ /var/lib/www/html/
```

If you would like to use more advanced tools like package managers to add content to your containers, Buildah supports running commands inside the containers.

A.2.3 Running commands in a working container

To run a command inside the working container, you need to execute `buildah run`. Under the hood, this command works exactly the same as the `RUN` instruction; it starts a new container on top of the current one, executes a specified command, and commits the result back to the working container. The syntax of `buildah run` requires you to specify the name of the working container followed by the command. In the following example, you install the `httpd` service within the container:

```
$ buildah run ubi8-init-working-container dnf -y install httpd
Updating Subscription Management repositories.
Unable to read consumer identity
This system is not registered with an entitlement server. You can use
➡ subscription-manager to register.
…
Complete!
```

To make sure you will have a running web server once the running container is created, the next command enables the Apache HTTP Server service:

```
$ buildah run ubi8-init-working-container systemctl enable httpd.service
Created symlink /etc/systemd/system/multi-user.target.wants/httpd.service ?
➡ /usr/lib/systemd/system/httpd.service.
```

Table A.4 shows the relationship between Containerfile instructions and Buildah commands.

Table A.4   Containerfile instructions mapped to Buildah commands

Instruction	Command	Description
ADD	buildah add	Add the contents of a file, URL, or directory to the container.
COPY	buildah copy	Copies the contents of a file, URL, or directory into a container's working directory.
FROM	buildah from	Creates a new working container, either from scratch or using a specified image as a starting point.
RUN	buildah run	Runs a command inside the container.

A.2.4 *Adding content to a working container directly from the host*

Up until now, you've seen how Buildah can perform the same commands you execute within a Containerfile, but one of Buildah's goals is exposing the container image rootfs directly to the host. This allows you to use commands available on your host machine to add content to the container image, without requiring the commands to be present inside the container image.

The `buildah mount` command allows you to mount a working container's root filesystem directly on your system and then use tools like cp, `make`, `dnf`, or even an editor to manipulate the contents of the container's rootfs.

If you run Buildah as root, you can simply execute the `buildah mount` command. But in rootless mode, this isn't allowed. Recall from section 2.2.10, where you learned about the `podman mount` command, that you must first enter the user namespace. Similarly, the `buildah unshare` command creates a shell running in the user namespace. Once you are in the user namespace, you can mount the container. In the following example, using what you have learned so far, you will use commands from your host's operating system `grep` to add content to the container:

```
$ buildah unshare
# mnt=$(buildah mount ubi8-init-working-container)
# echo $mnt
/home/dwalsh/.local/share/containers/storage/overlay/133e1728eac26589b07984
➥  e3bdf31b5e318159940c866d9e0493a1d08e1d2f6a/merged
# grep dwalsh /etc/passwd >> $mnt/etc/passwd
# exit
```

Now you can check if your changes were actually applied inside a working container:

```
$ buildah run ubi8-init-working-container grep dwalsh /etc/passwd
dwalsh:x:3267:3267:Daniel J Walsh:/home/dwalsh:/bin/bash
```

After you are done populating the content of the working container, it's time to specify other instructions from the Containerfile. These will describe your intentions as the container image creator.

A.2.5   *Configuring a working container*

You probably noticed in table A.3 that there are a lot of missing Containerfile instructions. Containerfile instructions like LABEL, EXPOSE, WORKDIR, CMD, and ENTRYPOINT are used to populate the OCI image specification.

Now, using the buildah config command, you can add a port to expose (EXPOSE) and mark a location inside the container rootfs as a volume (VOLUME), which will be used as the website root directory:

```
$ buildah config --port=80 --volume=/var/lib/www/html
➥  ubi8-init-working-container
```

You can inspect the corresponding OCI image specification fields using the buildah inspect command:

```
$ buildah inspect --format '{{ .OCIv1.Config.ExposedPorts }} {{
➥  .OCIv1.Config.Volumes }}' ubi8-init-working-container
map[80:{}] map[/var/lib/www/html:{}]
```

Table A.4 shows the relationship between Containerfile instructions and Buildah config options. You can also refer to table A.5 for additional information on these instructions.

Table A.5   Containerfile instructions mapped to Buildah config options

Instruction	Option	Description
MAINTAINER	--author	Sets contact information of the image author
CMD	--cmd	Sets a default command to run within a container
ENTRYPOINT	--entrypoint	Sets a command for a container that will run as an executable
ENV	--env	Sets the environment variable for all subsequent instructions

Table A.5 Containerfile instructions mapped to Buildah config options *(continued)*

Instruction	Option	Description
HEALTHCHECK	--healthcheck	Specifies a command to check if a container is still running
LABEL	--label	Adds key-value metadata
ONBUILD	--onbuild	Sets a command to be run when the image is used as the base for another image
EXPOSE	--port	Specifies a port that the container will listen on at run time
STOPSIGNAL	--stop-signal	Sets the stop signal to be sent when the container is stopped
USER	--user	Sets the user to be used when running the container and for all subsequent RUN, CMD, and ENTRYPOINT instructions
VOLUME	--volume	Adds a mount point and marks it as a volume for external data
WORKDIR	--workingdir	Sets the working directory for all subsequent RUN, CMD, ENTRYPOINT, COPY, and ADD instructions

Once you have finished adding content to the Buildah container image and adding configuration to the OCI image specification, you need to create an image from the working container.

A.2.6 *Creating an image from a working container*

The working container you've been building so far can be used to create the OCI-compliant image using the buildah commit command. This command works in the same way as the podman commit command you learned about in section 2.1.9. Inputs for this command are the working container name and an optional image tag; if a tag is not specified, the image will have no name:

```
$ buildah commit ubi8-init-working-container quay.io/rhatdan/myimage2
Getting image source signatures
Copying blob 352ba846236b skipped: already exists
Copying blob 3ba8c926eef9 skipped: already exists
Copying blob 421971707f97 skipped: already exists
Copying blob 9ff25f020d5a done
Copying config 5e47dbd9b7 done
Writing manifest to image destination
Storing signatures
5e47dbd9b7b7a43dd29f3e8a477cce355e42c019bb63626c0a8feffae56fcbf9
```

You can see the image using buildah images:

```
$ buildah images
REPOSITORY                          TAG       IMAGE ID       CREATED         SIZE
quay.io/rhatdan/myimage2            latest    5e47dbd9b7b7   2 minutes ago   293 MB
registry.access.redhat
➥  .com/ubi8-init                   latest    4b85030f924b   5 weeks ago     253 MB
```

Because Podman and Buildah share the same container image storage, you can see the same images with podman images:

```
$ podman images
REPOSITORY                       TAG        IMAGE ID       CREATED        SIZE
quay.io/rhatdan/myimage2         latest     5e47dbd9b7b7   4 minutes ago  293 MB
registry.access.redhat
➡ .com/ubi8-init                 latest     4b85030f924b   5 weeks ago    253 MB
```

You can even run a Podman container on the image:

```
$ podman run quay.io/rhatdan/myimage2 grep dwalsh /etc/passwd
dwalsh:x:3267:3267:Daniel J Walsh:/home/dwalsh:/bin/bash
```

A.2.7   Pushing an image to a container registry

Similarly to Podman, Buildah has the buildah login and buildah push commands, which allow you to push images to container registries, as shown in the following example:

```
$ buildah login quay.io
Username: rhatdan
Password:
Login Succeeded!
$ buildah push quay.io/rhatdan/myimage2
Getting image source signatures
Copying blob 3ba8c926eef9 done
Copying blob 421971707f97 done
Copying blob 9ff25f020d5a done
Copying blob 352ba846236b done
Copying config 5e47dbd9b7 done
Writing manifest to image destination
Copying config 5e47dbd9b7 done
Writing manifest to image destination
Storing signatures
```

> **NOTE**   You can also use podman login and podman push or even skopeo login and skopeo copy to accomplish the same task.

Congratulations! You have successfully built an OCI-compliant container image manually by using simple shell commands rather than using a Containerfile. Additionally, if you want to create an image using an existing Containerfile or Dockerfile, you can use the buildah build command.

A.2.8   Building an image from Containerfiles

You can use the buildah build command to build an OCI-compliant image from a Containerfile or a Dockerfile. Buildah includes a parser that understands the Containerfile format and can perform all tasks using previously described commands automatically. In the next example, use the Containerfile from section 2.3.2:

```
$ cat myapp/Containerfile
FROM ubi8/httpd-24
COPY index.html /var/www/html/index.html
```

You can build your container image using this Containerfile by executing the following command:

```
$ buildah build ./myapp
STEP 1/2: FROM ubi8/httpd-24
Resolved "ubi8/httpd-24" as an alias (/home/dwalsh/.cache/containers/
➥ short-name-aliases.conf)
Trying to pull registry.access.redhat.com/ubi8/httpd-24:latest
...
Getting image source signatures
Checking if image destination supports signatures
Copying blob adffa6963146 skipped: already exists
...
STEP 2/2: COPY html/index.html /var/www/html/index.html
COMMIT
Getting image source signatures
Copying blob 352ba846236b skipped: already exists
...
bbfcf76c994c738f8496c1f274bd009ddbc960334b59a74953691fff00442417
```

You've probably noticed that this output matches precisely the output of the podman build command. This is because the podman build command uses Buildah.

A.2.9 *Buildah as a library*

Buildah was designed to not only be used as a command-line tool but also to be a Golang-based library. Buildah is being used in a few different tools, such as Podman and the OpenShift image builder. Buildah allows these tools to internally build OCI images. Every time you do a podman build, you are executing the Buildah library code. Having learned how to build container images using Buildah, copy images between container storages using Skopeo, and manage and run containers on the host using Podman, let's talk about how all these tools are used in the Kubernetes ecosystem.

A.3 *CRI-O: Container Runtime Interface for OCI containers*

When Kubernetes was being developed, it used the Docker API internally to run containers. Kubernetes relied on features of Docker that changed from release to release, sometimes breaking Kubernetes. At the same time, CoreOS wanted their alternative container engine, called RKT (https://github.com/rkt/rkt), to work with Kubernetes. Kubernetes developers decided, then, to split out the Docker functionality and use a new API called the Container Runtime Interface (CRI; http://mng.bz/yaDq). This interface allows Kubernetes to use other container engines in addition to Docker.

When Kubernetes wants to pull a container image, it calls out to a remote socket via the CRI and asks the listener to pull an OCI image for it. When it wants to launch a Pod/Container, it calls out to the socket and asks it to launch the container.

NOTE CoreOS was eventually acquired by Red Hat, and the RKT project has ended. Kubernetes has deprecated Docker as a container runtime.

Red Hat saw the CRI as an opportunity to develop a new container engine, which they ended up calling the Container Runtime Interface for OCI containers (CRI-O; https:// cri-o.io/). CRI-O is based on the same containers/storage and containers/image libraries as Skopeo, Buildah, and Podman and can be used in conjunction with these tools. CRI-O's primary objective is replacing the Docker service as the container engine for Kubernetes.

CRI-O is tied to Kubernetes releases. When a new version of Kubernetes is released, the version numbers are synchronized. CRI-O is optimized for Kubernetes workloads; the engineers working on it understand what Kubernetes is trying to do and are making sure CRI-O does it in the most efficient way possible. Since CRI-O has no other users, Kubernetes doesn't have to worry about breaking changes in CRI-O.

NOTE CRI-O is the core technology used with Red Hat's OpenShift Kubernetes-based product. OpenShift uses Podman to install and configure CRI-O before Kubernetes starts running. The OpenShift image builder embeds Buildah functionality to allow users to build images within their OpenShift clusters.

appendix B
OCI runtimes

This appendix describes the primary OCI runtimes used with container engines like Podman. As discussed in chapter 1, the OCI runtime (https://opencontainers .org) is the executable launched by container engines, including Podman, used to configure the Linux kernel and subsystems to run the kernel; its last step is launching the container. The OCI runtime reads the OCI runtime specification JSON file and then configures the namespaces, security controls, and cgroups and eventually starts the container process (figure B.1).

In this appendix, you'll learn the four main OCI runtimes in use. The --runtime option allows you to switch between different OCI runtimes. In the next example, you will run the same container command twice, each time with a different runtime. In the first command, you run the container with a runtime, crun, defined in the containers.conf, so you don't need to specify the path to the runtime.

Listing B.1 Podman running with the alternate OCI runtime `crun`

```
$ podman --runtime crun run --rm ubi8 echo hi
hi
```
> The --runtime option tells Podman to use the crun OCI runtime, rather than the default.

The default runtime is defined under the [containers] table in the containers.conf file on the Linux machine.

Listing B.2 Modifying the default OCI runtime

```
$ grep -iA 3 "Default OCI Runtime" /usr/share/containers/containers.conf
# Default OCI runtime
#
#runtime = "crun"
```
> Podman defaults to crun on most systems; on some older distributions, like Red Hat Enterprise Linux, Podman defaults to runc.

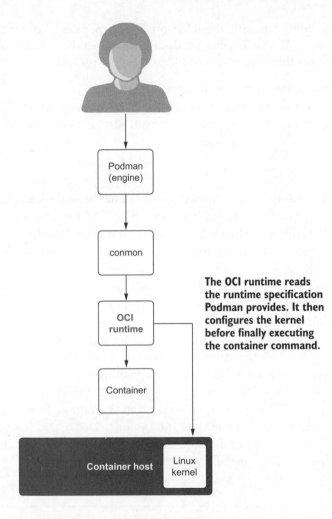

The **OCI** runtime reads the runtime specification Podman provides. It then configures the kernel before finally executing the container command.

Figure B.1   Podman executes the OCI runtime to launch the container.

In the second example, you use the full path of the OCI runtime, /usr/bin/runc:

```
$ podman --runtime /usr/bin/runc run –rm ubi8 echo hi
hi
```

If you want to permanently change the default OCI runtime, you can set the runtime option in the [engine] table in the containers.conf file in your home directory:

```
$ cat > ~/.config/containers/containers.conf << EOF
[engine]
runtime="runc"
EOF
$ podman --help | grep -- runc
   --runtime stringPath to the OCI-compatible binary used to run containers.
    (default "runc")`
```

NOTE The --runtime option is only available on Linux. podman --remote, and therefore Podman, on Mac and Windows, does not support the --runtime option, so you need to set the containers.conf file on the server side.

See the podman(1) man page for more information: man podman.

OCI runtimes are continuously being developed and experimented with. You can expect innovation to happen in this space going forward. The first container runtime developed, and the de facto standard, is runc.

B.1   *runc*

runc is the original OCI runtime (https://github.com/opencontainers/runc). When the OCI originally formed, Docker donated runc to the OCI to serve as the default implementation of an OCI runtime. The OCI continues to support and develop runc. It is written in Golang and also includes the libcontainer library, which is used in many container engines and Kubernetes.

The runc website states that runc, and all of the OCI runtimes, is a low-level tool not designed to be used directly by the end user. It is recommended to be launched by container engines like Podman or Docker.

Recall that the container engine's job is pulling the container images to the host, configuring and mounting the root filesystem (rootfs) to be used within the container, and, finally, writing the OCI runtime JSON file before launching the OCI runtime.

The OCI runtime specification describes only the content of the JSON file used by OCI runtimes. Because every OCI engine supports the runc command line, the other OCI runtimes adopted the same CLI commands and options. This makes it easier for one runtime to replace another when launched by the container engine. Table B.1 shows the commands supported by runc and therefore all OCI runtimes.

Table B.1   runc commands

Command	Description
checkpoint	Checkpoints a running container
create	Creates a container
delete	Deletes any resources held by the container often used with detached containers
events	Displays container events, such as OOM notifications, CPU, memory, and IO usage statistics
init	Initializes the namespaces and launches the process
kill	Sends the specified signal (default: SIGTERM) to the container's init process
List	Lists containers started by runc with the given root
pause	Suspends all processes inside the container
ps	Displays the processes running inside a container

Table B.1 `runc` commands *(continued)*

Command	Description
`restore`	Restores a container from a previous checkpoint
`resume`	Resumes all processes that have been previously paused
`run`	Creates and runs a container
`spec`	Creates a new specification file
`start`	Executes the user-defined process in a created container
`state`	Outputs the state of a container
`update`	Updates container resource constraints

`runc` continues to be developed and has a very active community. The problem with `runc` is that it is written in Golang. Golang was not designed to be a small, often-executed application that needs to start quickly and fork/exec a command and exit quickly. Fork/exec is a heavy operation in Golang, and although `runc` attempts to work around this, it ultimately sacrifices a bit of performance. The *a bit* can accumulate over time though, so `crun` performs much better at scale.

B.2 crun

`runc`, being written in Golang, is a very heavy executable—12 megabytes in size. Golang is a great language, but it doesn't take advantage of shared libraries. Golang executables take up considerably more memory because of this. The size of `runc` causes it to be somewhat slower loading during container start. Another problem with Golang is that it does not support the fork/exec model all that well; it is slower than fork/exec in other languages (e.g., C). This lack of speed is more important when you are starting and stopping hundreds or thousands of containers—for example, on a Kubernetes cluster. Container engines like Podman, also written in Go, generally run for a much longer time, so the startup time is not as important. OCI runtimes like `runc` execute for a very short time and exit quickly.

Giuseppe Scrivano, a contributor to `runc` and Podman, understood these deficiencies in `runc` and wanted to write a compatible OCI runtime in the C language. He created a very lightweight OCI runtime called `crun`.

`crun` describes itself as "*a fast and lightweight OCI runtime.*" (https://github.com/containers/crun) It supports all of the same commands and options as `runc`, and the `crun` executable is many times smaller than `runc`. Execute the `du -s` command to compare sizes:

```
$ du -s /usr/bin/runc /usr/bin/crun
14640    /usr/bin/runc
392    /usr/bin/crun
```

crun, being written in C, supports fork and exec much better than Golang and, therefore, is much quicker when launching a container.

This also makes it plug in easily to other libraries on the system, and there is some experimentation on using crun as a library for processing the OCI runtime JSON file and launching different types of containers (e.g., WASM and Windows containers on Linux). crun also has potential for launching KVM-separated containers based on libkrun.

crun is now the default OCI runtime used by Podman in Fedora and in Red Hat Enterprise Linux 9. runc continues to be supported and is the default OCI runtime in Red Hat Enterprise Linux 8.

crun and runc are the two primary OCI runtimes for managing traditional containers that use namespace separation. Both these projects work fairly closely together. When bugs or problems are found in either OCI runtime, they are quickly fixed in both. See the crun(1) man page for more information: man crun.

B.3   *Kata*

OCI runtimes are also written to use VM separation, with the primary example of this being Kata Containers. The Kata Container project (https://katacontainers.io) advertises itself as the following: "*The speed of containers, the security of VMs. Kata Containers is an open source container runtime, building lightweight virtual machines that seamlessly plug into the container's ecosystem.*"

Kata containers use VM technology for launching each container, which is very different from launching a VM and running Podman within it. A standard VM has an init system, which launches all sorts of services, like logging systems, cron, and more. On the other hand, a Kata container launches a micro OS, which runs only the container and its support services (figure B.2). As its only purpose is launching the container, when the container exits, this VM goes away.

I believe running containers within VM/hypervisor separation gives you better security separation than traditional container separation, where containers communicate directly with the host kernel. A VM-separated container has to first break out of containment inside of the VM, then find a way to break out of the hypervisor—only then to face attacking the host kernel.

While VM-separated containers are more secure, this does come with some downsides. There is a decent amount of overhead in starting a Kata container, configuring the hypervisor, launching the kernel and other processes within the VM, and then

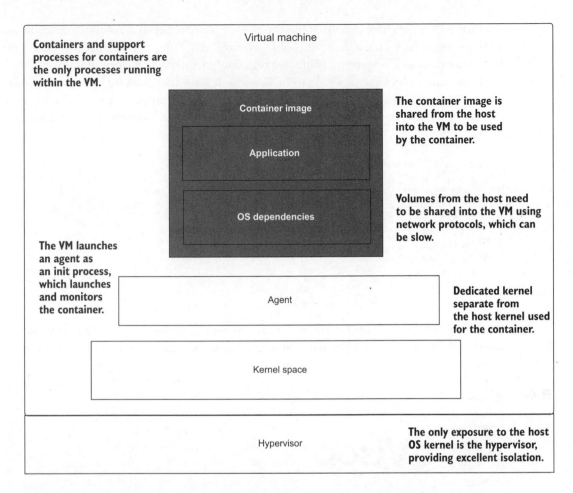

Figure B.2   Kata containers launches a lightweight VM, which only runs the container.

finally the container. The VM's memory, CPU, and so on have to be preallocated and are difficult to change. Running Kata within a VM in the cloud is often not allowed, or is at least more expensive, because most of the cloud vendors frown on nested virtualization.

Finally, and most importantly, VM-separated containers by their very nature have difficulties sharing content with other containers and the host operating system. The biggest problem is with volumes.

While sharing content with the host machine in traditional containers is just a bind mount, in VM-separate containers, bind mounts do not work. Since the processes on the host and in the container are running with two different kernels, you need a network protocol to share content. Kata containers originally used NFS and Plan 9 networked filesystems. Reading/writing data over these networked filesystems is considerably slower than native filesystem reads and writes you get with a bind mount.

Virtiofs is a new filesystem that has the properties of a network filesystem but allows VMs to access files on the host. It is able to show major improvements in speed over the network-based filesystems, while still remaining under heavy development.

Kata containers have two ways to be launched. Kata traditionally has an OCI command line, `kata-runtime`, based on the `runc` command supported by Podman. You can see the paths defined in containers.conf, on the Linux machine, by searching for #kata:

```
$ grep -A 9 '^#kata' /usr/share/containers/containers.conf
#kata = [
#  "/usr/bin/kata-runtime",
#  "/usr/sbin/kata-runtime",
#  "/usr/local/bin/kata-runtime",
#  "/usr/local/sbin/kata-runtime",
#  "/sbin/kata-runtime",
#  "/bin/kata-runtime",
#  "/usr/bin/kata-qemu",
#  "/usr/bin/kata-fc",
#]
```

The bottom line on Kata containers is that you get better security with a performance overhead. You can choose between these OCI runtimes with your workload's needs in mind.

B.4 *gVisor*

The last OCI runtime I cover in this appendix is gVisor (https://gvisor.dev/). The gVisor website advertises itself as "an application kernel for containers that provides efficient defense-in-depth anywhere."

gVisor includes an OCI runtime called `runsc` and works with Podman and other container engines. The gVisor project calls itself an application kernel, written in Golang, that implements a substantial portion of the Linux system call interface. It provides an additional layer of isolation between running applications and the host operating system. Google engineering wrote the original versions of gVisor and claims that the bulk of the containers Google Cloud run use the gVisor OCI runtime.

gVisor is somewhat similar to VM-isolated containers in that gVisor intercepts almost all system calls from within the container and then processes them. gVisor describes itself as an application kernel for containers written in Golang, limiting the access to the host kernel. At the same time, it does not have the same problem of a nested virtualization as Kata.

However, gVisor introduces a performance penalty with additional CPU cycles and higher memory usage. This may introduce increased latency, reduced throughput, or both. gVisor is also an independent implementation of the system call surface, meaning many of the subsystems or specific calls are not as optimized as more mature implementations.

appendix C
Getting Podman

Podman is a great tool for working with containers, but how do you get it installed on your system? What packages are required to make it work? This appendix covers installing or building Podman on your system.

C.1 Installing Podman

Podman is available for almost all Linux distributions via their package managers. It is also available on Mac, Windows, and FreeBSD platforms. The official podman.io site, https://podman.io/getting-started/installation, is regularly updated with new instructions on how to install Podman for different distributions. Most of the content in this appendix originates from the podman.io site, as seen in figure C.1.

C.1.1 macOS

Because Podman is a tool for running Linux containers, you can use it on a macOS desktop only if you have access to a Linux box, running either locally or remotely. To make this process somewhat easier, Podman includes a command, `podman machine`, to automatically manage VMs.

HOMEBREW
The Mac client is available through Homebrew (https://brew.sh/):

```
$ brew install podman
```

Podman has the ability to install a VM and run a Linux instance on your machine using the `podman machine` command. On a Mac, you must execute the following commands to install and start the Linux VM to successfully run containers locally:

```
$ podman machine init
$ podman machine start
```

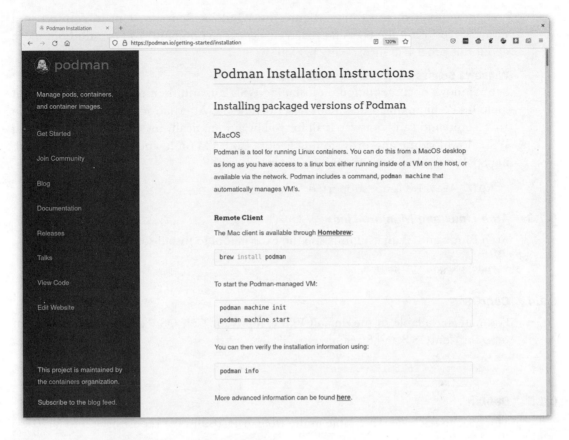

Figure C.1   Podman installation instructions website

Optionally, you can use the `podman system connection` command to set up SSH connections to remote Linux machines running the Podman service.

You can then verify the installation information using

```
$ podman info
```

The Podman command is running natively on the Mac but communicating with an instance of Podman running within the VM.

C.1.2   *Windows*

Because Podman is a tool for running Linux containers, you can use it on a Windows desktop only if you have access to a Linux box, running either locally or remotely. On Windows, Podman can also utilize the Windows Subsystem for Linux system.

WINDOWS REMOTE CLIENT

You can retrieve the latest Windows Remote client on the https://github.com/containers/podman/releases site.

Once installed, you can configure the Windows Remote client to connect to a Linux server using the `podman system connection` command. You can find out more about this process at http://mng.bz/M0Kn.

WINDOWS SUBSYSTEM FOR LINUX (WSL) 2.0

See Windows documentation on installing WSL 2.0, and then pick a distribution that includes Podman, including many described below. Alternatively, the `podman machine init` command can bootstrap it all for you by automatically installing and configuring WSL, downloading and provisioning Fedora Core VM on it, and creating corresponding SSH connections for the Podman remote client.

NOTE WSL 1.0 is not supported.

C.1.3 *Arch Linux and Manjaro Linux*

Arch Linux and Manjaro Linux use the `pacman` tool to install software:

```
$ sudo pacman -S podman
```

C.1.4 *CentOS*

Podman is available in the default Extras repos for CentOS 7 and in the AppStream repo for CentOS 8 and Stream:

```
$ sudo yum -y install podman
```

C.1.5 *Debian*

The `podman` package is available in the Debian 11 (bullseye) repositories and later:

```
$ sudo apt-get -y install podman
```

C.1.6 *Fedora*

```
$ sudo dnf -y install podman
```

C.1.7 *Fedora-CoreOS, Fedora Silverblue*

Podman comes preinstalled on these distributions. There is no need to need to install it.

C.1.8 *Gentoo*

```
$ sudo emerge app-emulation/podman
```

C.1.9 *OpenEmbedded*

BitBake recipes for Podman and its dependencies are available in the meta-virtualization layer (http://mng.bz/aPzB). Add the layer to your OpenEmbedded build environment, and build Podman using

```
$ bitbake podman
```

C.1.10 openSUSE

```
sudo zypper install podman
```

C.1.11 openSUSE Kubic

The openSUSE Kubic distribution has Podman built in. There is no need to need to install it.

C.1.12 Raspberry Pi OS arm64

The Raspberry Pi OS uses the standard Debian repositories, so it is fully compatible with Debian's arm64 repository:

```
$ sudo apt-get -y install podman
```

C.1.13 Red Hat Enterprise Linux

RHEL7

Make sure you have a RHEL7 subscription, then enable the extras channel and install Podman:

```
$ sudo subscription-manager repos --enable=rhel-7-server-extras-rpms
$ sudo yum -y install podman
```

> **NOTE**   RHEL7 is no longer receiving updates to the Podman package except for security fixes.

RHEL8

Podman is included in the `container-tools` module along with Buildah and Skopeo:

```
$ sudo yum module enable -y container-tools:rhel8
$ sudo yum module install -y container-tools:rhel8
```

RHEL9 (AND BEYOND)

```
$ sudo yum install podman
```

C.1.14 Ubuntu

The `podman` package is available in the official repositories for Ubuntu 20.10 and newer:

```
$ sudo apt-get -y update
$ sudo apt-get -y install podman
```

C.2   Building from source code

I usually advise people to get the packaged versions of Podman because successfully running Podman on Linux requires having additional tools installed, such as conmon (container monitor), `containernetworking-plugins` (network configuration), and `containers-common` (general configuration). While the process of building Podman from the source code is not very complicated, the list of dependencies differs from one Linux distribution to another. You can always check the latest instructions on the following Podman page: http://mng.bz/gRDE.

C.3   *Podman Desktop*

There is also a GUI, Podman Desktop, for browsing, managing, and inspecting containers and images from different container engines, available at https://github.com/containers/podman-desktop. Podman Desktop offers the capability to connect to multiple engines at the same time and provides a unified interface. This is a relatively new project under heavy development, so expect some rough edges.

To provide some background, in September 2021, Docker Inc. announced they will begin charging for the previously free version of Docker Desktop on macOS. The Docker announcement has caused many people to switch and look for a replacement.

Summary

- Podman is a tool for running Linux containers, so it runs only on Linux.
- Podman is available in default package repositories of most major Linux distributions.
- Podman is available as a remote client on Mac and Windows, which connects to either a local or remote Linux box.
- Podman provides a special command for Linux VM management on macOS and Windows.
- Podman can be built from source code, but it requires many other tools to run successfully.
- Podman Desktop is an alternative for the popular Docker Desktop.

appendix D
Contributing to Podman

My favorite thing about open source is the community effort. It is great to be able to contribute to a project and, better yet, get people to contribute to your project. The analogy I like to use comes from the *Grimms' Fairy Tales* story "The Elves" (https://sites.pitt.edu/~dash/grimm039.html):

> *A shoemaker, through no fault of his own, had become so poor that he had only leather enough for a single pair of shoes. He cut them out one evening, then went to bed, intending to finish them the next morning. Having a clear conscience, he went to bed peacefully, commended himself to God, and fell asleep. The next morning, after saying his prayers, he was about to return to his work when he found the shoes on his workbench, completely finished.*

The story goes on to describe a couple of elves that come by each night and finish the shoes. I see this as the way open source works. Basically, the people doing little contributions, bug reporting, bug fixes, document fixes, feature requests, and publicizing the project are all the elves. Sometimes I even go to bed, and when I wake up I'll find someone has fixed the problem I was attempting to deal with the night before! And sometimes the elves grow up to be maintainers. Some small contributions over time grow, and these developers end up being core members of the Podman team. Some we even hired.

D.1 Joining the community

Each small change helps make the project better. When I talk to college students about open source, I tell them about the unique opportunities they have, which were not around when I was a student. They can make a contribution to a software project or product and then list it on their resume. When interviewing a student for an internship or a job, having a few github.com contributions on a resume is very impressive.

Podman and its underlying technologies are always looking for new contributions (figure D.1). No contribution is too small—from a spelling mistake in a man page up to a full-blown feature. You don't have to be a software developer to contribute. We are always looking for help on documentation, web design for podman.io, as well as software help. Many great ideas come from users of the product. Just reporting a bug or reporting what you don't like can lead to fresh ideas that improve the project. I often ask people who have set up complicated environments using Podman to blog about it, so others can learn.

Figure D.1   Podman's Community page (https://podman.io/community)

Podman is an inclusive community, as are all of the github.com/containers projects. The code of conduct statement for the containers project at http://mng.bz/5mEB states the following:

> *As contributors and maintainers of the projects under the https://github.com/containers repository, and in the interest of fostering an open and welcoming community, we pledge to respect all people who contribute through reporting problems, posting feature requests, updating documentation, submitting pull requests or patches, and other activities to any of the projects under the containers umbrella.*

D.2 Podman on github.com

Issues, discussions, and pull requests reside on the github.com/containers/podman repository (figure D.2). As of this writing, the project has over 1,200 forks and 12,000 stars. The bottom line is it is a very active project.

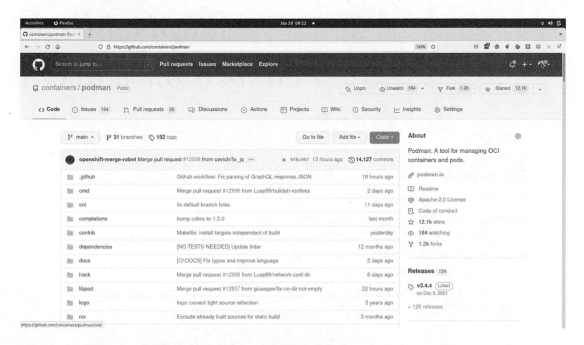

Figure D.2   Podman's github page (github.com/containers/podman)

You can also communicate directly with the core maintainers on IRC on the #podman channel on libera.chat. The IRC channel is also linked to #podman:matrix.org (https://matrix.to/#/#podman:matrix.org) on Matrix and the Podman Discord (https://discord.com/invite/x5GzFF6QH4) for web access.

There is also a low-volume mailing list you can join by sending an email to podman-join@lists.podman.io. Finally, you can follow @podman_io on Twitter or follow me @rhatdan.

appendix E
Podman on macOS

This appendix covers

- Installing Podman on macOS
- Using the `podman machine init` command to download a VM with a Podman service installed
- Using the `podman` command to communicate with the Podman service running in the VM
- Starting or stopping the VM with the `podman machine` start/stop commands

Podman is a tool for launching Linux containers. Linux containers require a Linux kernel. As much as I'd love to convince the world to move to the Linux Desktop like I use, most users work on macOS and Windows operating systems—perhaps even you. If you use the Linux Desktop, hooray! And if you don't use a macOS machine, feel free to skip this appendix.

Because you did not skip this appendix, I'll assume you want to create Linux containers without having to `ssh` into a Linux box. You likely want to use native software development tools and keep development local.

One way to achieve this would be running Podman as a service on a Linux box and using the `podman --remote` command to communicate with this service. Podman provides the `podman system connection` command to configure how Podman communicates with a Linux box. However, the problem with this approach is that it is a meticulous process and requires a number of manual steps. Please refer to this web page for an updated tutorial on this process: http://mng.bz/69ro.

A better way would be using a new command, `podman machine`, which encapsulates all these steps and improves your experience with managing a Linux box to be used for `podman-remote`. In this appendix, you'll learn how to install Podman on macOS and then use the `podman machine` commands to install, configure, and manage the VM to allow you to use the native Podman client to launch containers.

The first step to launching Podman on a macOS is installing it. The macOS client is available through Homebrew (https://brew.sh/).

> **NOTE** Homebrew describes itself as "… the easiest and most flexible way to install the UNIX tools Apple didn't include with macOS" (https://docs.brew .sh/Manpage).

Homebrew is the best way to get open source software installed on your macOS. If you do not currently have Homebrew installed on your macOS, open a terminal, and install it with the following command at the prompt:

```
$ /bin/bash -c "$(curl -fsSL
➥ https://raw.githubusercontent.com/Homebrew/install/HEAD/install.sh)"
```

Now run the following `brew` command to install a trimmed-down version of Podman, with only `--remote` support, into the /opt/homebrew/bin directory:

```
$ brew install podman
```

If you don't have access to a Linux VM or a remote Linux server, Podman allows you to create a locally running VM using the `podman machine` command. It makes this easy by creating and configuring a VM with a Podman service enabled.

> **NOTE** If you have an existing Linux machine, you can use the Podman system connection commands to set up connections to those machines.

E.1 Using podman machine

The `podman machine` commands allow you to pull a VM from the internet and start it, stop it, or remove it. This VM is preconfigured with the Podman service. Additionally, this command creates the SSH connection and adds this information to the `podman system connection` datastore, greatly simplifying the process of setting up a `podman-remote` environment. Table E.1 lists all of the `podman machine` subcommands used to manage the life cycle of the Podman virtual machine. The first step is initializing a new VM in your system using the `podman machine init` command, described in the following section.

Table E.1 Podman machine commands

Command	Description
init	Initialize a new virtual machine.
list	List virtual machines.
rm	Remove a virtual machine.
ssh	ssh into a virtual machine. This is useful for entering the virtual machine and running the native Podman commands. Some Podman commands are not supported remotely, and you might want to change some configurations inside the VM.
start	Start a virtual machine.
stop	Stop a virtual machine. If you are not running containers, you might want to shut down the VM to save system resources.

E.1.1   *podman machine init*

The podman machine init command downloads and configures a VM on your macOS system (figure E.1). By default, it downloads the latest released fedora-coreos image (https://getfedora.org/en/coreos) if it was not downloaded before. Fedora CoreOS is a minimal operating system designed to run containers.

NOTE   The VM is relatively large and takes a few minutes to download.

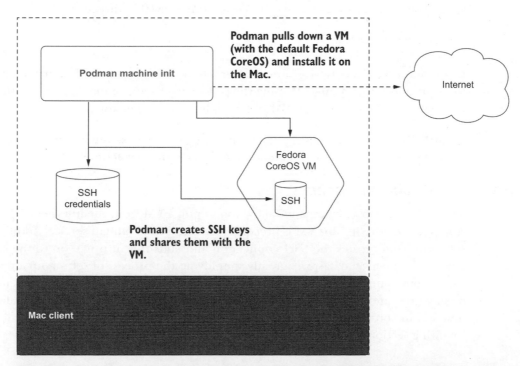

Figure E.1   The podman machine init **command pulling the VM and configuring the SSH connections**

Listing E.1 Podman downloading a VM onto the Mac and preparing it for execution

```
$ podman machine init
Downloading VM image: fedora-coreos-35.20211215.2.
➡ 0-qemu.x86_64.qcow2.xz
[========>----------------------------------------------] 111.0MiB /
➡ 620.7MiB
Downloading VM image: fedora-coreos-35.20211215.2.0-qemu.x86_64.qcow2.xz: done
Extracting compressed file
```

> **Podman finds and downloads the latest fedora-coreos qcow image onto your system.**

> **After downloading the image, Podman decompresses the image and configures qemu to be ready to execute it. It also configures the SSH connection to the Podman system connection datastore.**

Podman preconfigures the VM with the amount of memory, disk size, and CPUs for it to use. These values can be configured using `init` subcommand options. Table E.2 describes these options.

Table E.2 Podman machine `init` command options

Option	Description
`--cpus uint`	Number of CPUs (the default is 1)
`--disk-size uint`	Disk size in GB (the default is 10). This is an important setting to consider, since it limits the number of containers and images allowed to be used within the VM. If you have the space, I recommend increasing the field.
`--image-path string`	Path to qcow image (the default is `testing`). Podman has two built-in Fedora CoreOS images it can pull: `testing` and `stable`. You can also select other OSs and VMs to download, but the VMs must support CoreOS/Ignition files (https://coreos.github.io/ignition/).
`--memory integer`	Memory in MB (the default is 2048). The VM requires a certain amount of memory to run, and depending on the containers you want to run within the VM, you might need more.

Once `podman machine init` finishes downloading and installing the VM, you can view the VM with the `podman machine list` command. Notice the * indicates the default VM to be used. The `podman machine` command currently only supports running one VM at a time:

```
$ podman machine list
NAME                     VM TYPE   CREATED        LAST UP        CPUS
➡ MEMORY     DISK SIZE
podman-machine-default*  qemu      2 minutes ago  2 minutes ago  1
➡ 2.147GB    10.74GB
```

In the next section, you'll examine the automatically created SSH connection.

E.1.2   *Podman machine SSH configuration*

The podman machine init command provides the OS with the Ignition config, which includes an SSH key for the core user. Then Podman adds SSH connections on the client machine for the rootless and rootful modes, configures the user account, and adds required packages and configurations within the VM. The SSH configuration allows password-less SSH commands to the core and root accounts from the client. The podman machine init command also configures the Podman system connection information (see section 9.5.4). The system connection database is configured for both the rootful user and the rootless user within the VM. If no previous connections are present, the podman machine init command will make the newly created connection a default one.

You can examine all the connections using the podman system connection list command. The default connection, podman-machine-default, is the rootless connection:

```
$ podman system connection list
Name                          URI
Identity                                        Default
podman-machine-default
➥   ssh://core@localhost:50107/run/user/501/podman/podman.sock
➥   /Users/danwalsh/.ssh/podman-machine-default   true
podman-machine-default-root
➥   ssh://root@localhost:50107/run/podman/podman.sock
➥   /Users/danwalsh/.ssh/podman-machine-default   false
```

Sometimes containers you want to execute require root privileges and cannot run in rootless modes. For this, you can modify the system connection to default to the rootful service using the podman system connection default command:

```
$ podman system connection default podman-machine-default-root
```

View the connections again to confirm the default connection is now podman-machine-default-root:

```
$ $ podman system connection list
Name                          URI
➥  Identity                                       Default
podman-machine-default
➥   ssh://core@localhost:50107/run/user/501/podman/podman.sock
➥   /Users/danwalsh/.ssh/podman-machine-default   false
podman-machine-default-root
➥   ssh://root@localhost:50107/run/podman/podman.sock
➥   /Users/danwalsh/.ssh/podman-machine-default   true
n-machine-default ssh://root@localhost:38243/run/podman/podman.sock
```

Now all Podman commands connect directly to the Podman service running within the root account. Change the default connection back to the rootless user using the Podman system connection default command again:

```
$ podman system connection default podman-machine-default
```

If you attempt to run a Podman container at this point, it fails because the VM is not actually running. You need to start the VM.

E.1.3   Starting the VM

After adding a VM and setting a specific connection as a default one, try running a podman command:

```
$ podman version
Cannot connect to Podman. Please verify your connection to the Linux system
using `podman system connection list`, or try `podman machine init` and
`podman machine start` to manage a new Linux VM
Error: unable to connect to Podman. failed to create sshClient: Connection
to bastion host (ssh://root@localhost:38243/run/podman/podman.sock)
failed.: dial tcp [::1]:38243: connect: connection refused
```

As the error points out, the VM is not running and must be started.

   You start a single VM using the podman machine start command. Podman only supports running one VM at a time. By default, the start command starts the default VM. If you have multiple VMs and want to start a different VM, you can specify the optional machine name:

```
$ podman machine start
INFO[0000] waiting for clients...
INFO[0000] listening tcp://127.0.0.1:7777
INFO[0000] new connection from @ to /run/user/3267/podman/
➡ qemu_podman-machine-default.sock
Waiting for VM …
macOShine "podman-machine-default" started successfully
```

You are now ready to begin running Podman commands on the Linux box that runs the Podman service. Run the podman version command to confirm the client and server are configured correctly. If not, the Podman commands should instruct you on configuring the system:

```
$ podman version
Client:
Version:      4.1.0
API Version:  4.1.0
Go Version:   go1.18.1
Built:        Thu May  5 16:07:47 2022
OS/Arch:      darwin/arm64
Server:
Version:      4.1.0
API Version:  4.1.0
Go Version:   go1.18
Built:        Fri May  6 12:16:38 2022
OS/Arch:      linux/arm64
```

Now you can use the Podman commands you learned in the previous chapters directly on macOS. When you are done working with containers in the VM, you probably should shut it down to save resources.

NOTE   Podman is supported on M1 arm64 machines as well as the x86 platforms. `podman machine init` downloads the matching architecture VM, allowing you to build images for that architecture. Support for building images on other architectures is being worked on as of this writing.

E.1.4   *Stopping the VM*

The `podman machine stop` command allows you to shut down all containers within the VM as well as the VM itself:

```
$ podman machine stop
```

When you need to start using containers again, launch the VM with the `podman machine start` command.

NOTE   All of the `podman machine` commands work on Linux as well and allow you to test different versions of Podman at the same time. Podman on Linux is the complete command; therefore, you need to use the `--remote` option to communicate with the Podman service running within the VM launched by the Podman machine. On non-Linux platforms the `--remote` option is not required, since the client is preconfigured in `--remote` mode.

Summary

- Linux containers require a Linux kernel, meaning running containers on a macOS requires a virtual machine running Linux.
- Podman on a macOS is not running containers locally on the macOS. The Podman command is actually communicating with the Podman service running on a Linux machine.
- The `podman machine init` command pulls down and installs a Fedora CoreOS VM onto your platform, which is running the Podman service.
- The `podman machine init` command also sets up the SSH environment required to allow the Podman remote client to communicate with the Podman server inside the VM.

appendix F
Podman on Windows

This appendix covers

- Installing Podman on Windows
- Using the `podman machine init` command to create a Fedora-based WSL 2 distribution running Podman
- Using the `podman` command on Windows to communicate with the Podman service running in the WSL 2 instance
- Starting or stopping the WSL 2 instance with the `podman machine` start/stop commands

Podman is a tool for launching Linux containers. Linux containers require a Linux kernel. As much as I'd love to convince the world to move to the Linux desktop like me, most users work on Mac and Windows operating systems—perhaps even you. If you use the Linux desktop, hooray! And if you don't use a Windows machine, feel free to skip this appendix.

Because you did not skip this appendix, I'll assume you want to create Linux containers without having to `ssh` into a Linux machine and create the container there. You likely want to use native software development tools and keep their software local to their machines.

On Linux, Podman can be run as a service allowing remote connections to launch containers. Then, from another system, the `podman --remote` command can be used to communicate with the remote Podman service to launch a container.

Further, you can use `podman system connection` to configure `podman --remote` to communicate with a remote Linux machine running the Podman service over SSH, without providing a URL to every command. The problem with all of this is that someone has to configure the remote machine with the correct version of the Podman service, and then you have to configure the SSH session.

Realizing that this experience is not optimal for new users of Podman on a Windows desktop, Podman added a new command: `podman machine`. The `podman machine` command makes it easy to create and manage a WSL 2-based Linux environment with Podman preinstalled and configured. The Podman command on Windows is actually a thinned down Podman command with only `podman --remote` support. In this appendix, you'll learn how to install Podman onto your Windows machine, and then use the `podman machine` commands to install, configure, and manage the WSL 2 instance.

F.1   First steps

The `podman machine` command on Windows accepts all the same commands as those used on Linux and Mac, with very similar behavior. Still, there are a few differences, since the underlying backend on Windows is based on Windows Subsystem for Linux (https://docs.microsoft.com/en-us/windows/wsl/) instead of the VM, as in the other operating systems.

WSL 2 involves using the Windows Hyper-V hypervisor; however, unlike a standard VM-based approach, WSL 2 shares the same VM and Linux kernel instance across every Linux distribution instance installed by the user. As an example, if you create two WSL 2 distributions, and you run `dmesg` on each instance, you see the same output, since the same kernel is hosting both.

> **NOTE** WSL 1 doesn't work with Podman; you must upgrade your Windows machine to an OS version that supports WSL 2. For x64 systems, you will need Windows version 1,903 or higher, with build 18,362 or higher. For arm64 systems, you will need Windows version 2004 or higher, with build 19,041 or higher.

Running Podman with WSL 2 enables efficient resource sharing between the host and all running instances in exchange for less isolation. Keep in mind the `podman machine` command shares the same kernel with any other distributions you have running, and be cautious when manipulating any kernel-level setting (e.g., network interfaces and netfilter policy) in any distribution because you may unintentionally affect containers executed by Podman.

F.1.1   Prerequisites

Podman for Windows requires Windows 10 (build 19,041 or later) or Windows 11. As WSL 2 uses a hypervisor, your computer must have virtualization instructions enabled (e.g., Intel VT-x or AMD-V). Additionally, the hypervisor requires second-level address translation (SLAT) support. Finally, your system must either have internet connectivity or an offline copy of all software to be fetched by the `podman machine`.

NOTE If at any time you experience the errors 0x80070003 or 0x80370102
(or any error indicating the VM cannot be started), you most likely have virtualization disabled. Check your BIOS (or WSL 2 instance) settings to verify
VT-x/AMD-V/WSL 2 instance and SLAT are enabled.

While not required, installing Windows Terminal (as opposed to the standard CMD
command application or PowerShell) is strongly recommended (future versions of
Windows 11 include it by default). In addition to having modern terminal features,
like transparent cut and paste and tiled screens, it also offers direct WSL and Power-
Shell integration, making it easy to switch between environments. You can install it via
the Windows store or `winget`:

```
PS C:\Users\User> winget install Microsoft.WindowsTerminal
```

F.1.2   Installing Podman

Installing Podman is straightforward. Go to the Podman site or the Podman GitHub
repository, and download the latest Podman MSI Windows Installer in the Releases
section (figure F.1; https://github.com/containers/podman/releases).

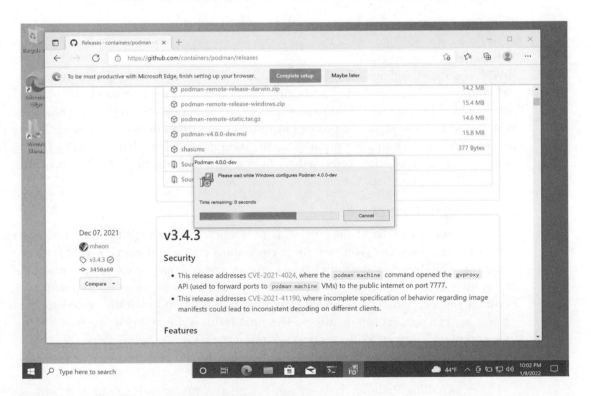

Figure F.1   Downloading and running the Podman installer

After running the installer, open a terminal (use the `wt` command if you installed Windows Terminal as recommended), and execute your first `podman` command (figure F.2).

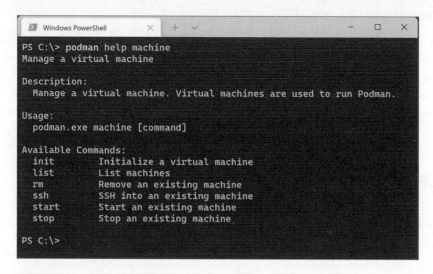

Figure F.2   Podman commands running within the Windows Terminal

AUTOMATIC WSL INSTALLATION

If WSL is not installed on your Windows system, Podman installs it for you. Simply execute the `podman machine init` command (as illustrated in figure F.3) to create your first machine instance, and Podman prompts you for permission to install WSL. The WSL install process requires a reboot but resumes execution of the machine creation process. (Be sure to wait a few minutes for the terminal to relaunch and install.) If you prefer a manual installation, refer to the WSL installation guide: https://docs.microsoft .com/en-us/windows/wsl/install.

F.2   *Using podman machine*

The setup and use of the Linux environment is made easy through the use of `podman machine` commands. On Windows, these commands create and manage a WSL 2 distribution, including downloading a base Linux image and packages from the internet and setting everything up for you. The WSL 2 distribution is preconfigured with the Podman service, and SSH connection configuration is automatically added to the `podman system connection` datastore. The final result is the ability to easily run Podman commands on your Windows desktop as if it was a Linux system. Table F.1 lists all of the `podman machine` commands used to manage the lifecycle of the WSL 2-backed Linux environment.

After installing Podman (see section F.1.2), the first step is creating a WSL 2 machine instance on your system. You will use the `podman machine init` command, described in the following section.

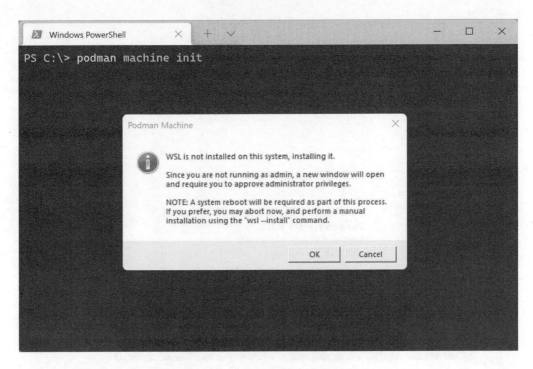

Figure F.3   The `podman machine init` **starts the WSL installation.**

Table F.1 `podman machine` **commands**

Command	Description
`init`	Initialize a new WSL 2-based machine instance.
`list`	List WSL 2 machines.
`rm`	Remove a WSL 2 machine instance.
`set`	Set an updatable WSL machine setting.
`ssh`	`ssh` into a WSL 2 machine instance. This is useful for entering the WSL 2 instance and running the native Podman commands. Some Podman commands are not supported remotely, and you might want to change some configurations inside the WSL 2 instance.
`start`	Start a WSL 2 machine instance.
`stop`	Stop a WSL 2 machine instance. If you are not running containers, you might want to stop to save system resources.

F.2.1   podman machine init

As shown in figure F.4, you can use the `podman machine init` command to automate the installation of a WSL 2-based Linux environment that hosts a Podman service for running containers. By default, `podman machine init` downloads a known compatible

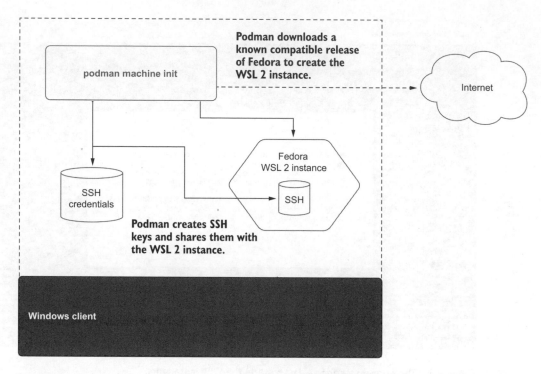

Figure F.4   The `podman machine init` command creating the WSL 2 distribution and configuring SSH connections.

release of Fedora to create the WSL 2 instance (https://getfedora.org). Fedora is used, since it is well integrated with Podman and is the operating system used by most of the Podman core developers.

NOTE   In addition to the base image, a number of packages must be downloaded and installed, which can take several minutes to complete.

The following shows the condensed output from running the `podman machine init` command:

```
PS C:\Users\User> podman machine init
Downloading VM image: fedora-35.20211125-x86_64.tar.xz: done
Extracting compressed file
Importing operating system into WSL (this may take 5+ minutes on a new WSL
➥ install)...
Installing packages (this will take awhile)...
Fedora 35 - x86_64                                  5.5 MB/s │  79 MB    00:14
Complete!
Configuring system…
Generating public/private ed25519 key pair.
Machine init complete
To start your machine run:
        podman machine start
```

Table F.2 explains the `init` options that allow you to customize the default settings.

Table F.2 `podman machine init` **command options**

Option	Description
`--cpus uint`	Not used
`--disk-size uint`	Not used
`--image-path string`	On Windows, this option refers to the Fedora distribution number (e.g., 35). As with Linux and Mac, you can also specify an arbitrary URL or filesystem location with a custom image, but Podman expects a Fedora-derived layout.
`--memory integer`	Not used
`--rootful`	Determines whether this machine instance should be rootful or rootless

> **NOTE** The physical limits specified in table F.2 (e.g., CPU, memory, and disk) are currently ignored on Windows, since the Windows Subsystem for Linux (WSL) backend dynamically resizes and shares resources across distributions. If you need to constrain resources, you can configure those limits in your users' .wslconfig file. However, they apply globally to all WSL 2 distros, since they share the same underlying VM.

F.2.2 Podman machine SSH configuration

The `podman machine init` command creates an account within the WSL 2 instance. By default, the user in Fedora is user@localhost. Podman configures SSH on the client machine and the new user account and root within the WSL 2 instance. The SSH configuration allows for passwordless SSH commands to the `user` and `root` accounts from the client. The `podman machine init` command also configures the Podman system connection information (see section 9.5.4). The system connection database is configured for both the rootful user and rootless user within the WSL 2 instance. If you do not have any existing connections, the `podman machine init` command creates and sets as a default one of the rootless user connections to your WSL 2 instance.

You can examine all of the connections using the `podman system connection list` command. The default connection, podman-machine-default, is the rootless connection:

```
PS C:\Users\User> podman system connection ls
Name                             URI                         Identity
⮕ Default
podman-machine-default           ssh://user@localhost:57051..  podman-machine-
⮕ default  true
podman-machine-default-root      ssh://root@localhost:57051..  podman-machine-
⮕ default  false
```

Sometimes containers you want to execute require root privileges and cannot run in rootless modes. You can change the default connection to rootful by switching the default mode for the created machine instance. Modify the default to rootful service using the `podman machine set` command:

```
PS C:\Users\User> podman machine set --rootful
```

View the connections again to confirm the default is now `podman-machine-default-root`:

```
PS C:\Users\User> podman system connection ls
Name                            URI                             Identity
➡ Default
podman-machine-default          ssh://user@localhost:57051..
➡ podman-machine-default  false
podman-machine-default-root   ssh://root@localhost:57051..
➡ podman-machine-default  true
```

Now all Podman commands connect directly to the Podman service running within the root account. Change the default connection back to the rootless user using the `podman machine set` command again:

```
PS C:\Users\User> podman machine set --rootful=false
```

If you attempt to run a Podman container at this point, it fails because the machine instance is not actually running. You need to start the machine instance.

F.2.3 *Starting the WSL 2 instance*

Attempting to execute the `podman version` command fails because the WSL 2 instance is not started:

```
PS C:\Users\User> podman version
Cannot connect to Podman. Please verify your connection to the Linux system
using `podman system connection list`, or try `podman machine init` and
`podman machine start` to manage a new Linux Linux VM
Error: unable to connect to Podman. failed to create sshClient: Connection
to bastion host (ssh://root@localhost:38243/run/podman/podman.sock)
failed.: dial tcp [::1]:38243: connect: connection refused
```

As the error points out, the virtualized Linux environment (the WSL 2 machine instance) is not running and must be started.

You start a single WSL 2 instance using the `podman machine start` command. By default, it starts the default WSL 2 instance: `podman-machine-default`. If you have multiple WSL 2 instances and want to start a different WSL 2 instance, you can specify the optional machine name for the `podman machine start` command:

```
PS C:\Users\User> podman machine start
Starting machine "podman-machine-default"
This machine is currently configured in rootless mode. If your containers
require root permissions (e.g. ports < 1024), or if you run into compatibility
issues with non-podman clients, you can switch using the following command:
        podman machine set --rootful
```

```
API forwarding listening on: npipe:////./pipe/docker_engine
Docker API clients default to this address. You do not need to set
DOCKER_HOST.
Machine "podman-machine-default" started successfully
```

You are now ready to begin running Podman commands on the host that communicates with the Podman service running in the WSL 2 instance. Run the `podman version` command to confirm the client and server are configured correctly. If not, the Podman commands instruct you on how to configure the system:

```
PS C:\Users\User> podman version
Client:        Podman Engine
Version:       4.0.0-dev
API Version:   4.0.0-dev
Go Version:    go1.17.1
Git Commit:    bac389043f268e632c45fed7b4e88bdefd2d95e6-dirty
Built:         Wed Feb 16 00:33:20 2022
OS/Arch:       windows/amd64
Server:        Podman Engine
Version:       4.0.1
API Version:   4.0.1
Go Version:    go1.16.14
Built:         Fri Feb 25 13:22:13 2022
OS/Arch:       linux/amd64
```

Now you can use the Podman commands you learned in the previous chapters directly on Windows. Make sure you understand that Podman on Windows is equivalent to `podman --remote` talking remotely to the Podman service within the WSL 2 instance.

F.2.4   *Using podman machine commands*

After your machine instance is running, you can perform Podman commands in your PowerShell prompt as if running within Windows:

```
PS C:\Users\User> podman run ubi8-micro date
Thu Jan  6 05:09:59 UTC 2022
```

STOPPING THE WSL 2 INSTANCE

When you are done using containers on your system, you might want to shut down the WSL 2 instance to save on system resources. Use the `podman machine stop` command to shut down all containers within the WSL 2 instance as well as the WSL 2 instance:

```
PS C:\Users\User> podman machine stop
```

When you need to start using containers again, launch the WSL 2 instance with the `podman machine start` command.

> **NOTE** All of the `podman machine` commands work on Linux as well and allow you to test different versions of Podman at the same time. Podman on Linux

is the complete command; therefore, you need to use the `--remote` option to communicate with the Podman service running within the WSL 2 instance launched by the `podman machine` command. On non-Linux platforms, the `--remote` option is not required, since the client is preconfigured in `--remote` mode.

LISTING MACHINES

You can list the available machine instances using the `podman machine ls` command. The values returned by this command on Windows reflect current active usage, as opposed to fixed resource limits, as is the case on Mac and Linux. Disk storage reflects the disk space currently allocated to each machine instance. The CPU values convey the number of CPUs on the Windows host (unless limited by WSL) repeated per machine instance. The returned memory values are also repeated (with slight variation from sampling variability) and reflect the total amount of memory used by the Linux kernel for all distributions in use (since it is shared). In other words, for total usage, you sum the disk sizes but not memory and CPU.

```
PS C:\Users\User> podman machine ls
NAME                    VM TYPE       CREATED        LAST UP   CPUS
➡ MEMORY       DISK SIZE
podman-machine-default  wsl           3 days ago     Running   4
➡ 528.4MB      845.2MB
other                   wsl           4 minutes ago  Running   4
➡ 524.5MB      778MB
```

USING PODMAN AT THE WSL PROMPT

In addition to the `podman machine ssh` command, you can also access the `podman machine` guest using the WSL prompt. If you are running Windows Terminal, the `podman machine` guests (names prefixed by Podman) are in the down-arrow dropdown. Alternatively, you can drop into a WSL shell from any PowerShell prompt by using the `wsl` command and specifying the backing distribution name. For example, the default instance created by `podman machine init` is `podman-machine-default`. You can use either approach to manage the guest and execute Podman commands inside a full-featured Linux shell environment:

```
PS C:\Users\User> wsl -d podman-machine-default
[root@WIN10PRO /]# podman version
Client:        Podman Engine
Version:       4.0.1
API Version:   4.0.1
Go Version:    go1.16.14

Built:         Fri Feb 25 13:22:13 2022
OS/Arch:       linux/amd64
```

UPDATING FEDORA

Since the Windows machine implementation is based on Fedora, not Fedora CoreOS, fixes and enhancements are not automatic. They must be explicitly initiated on the guest using Fedora's package management command: `dnf`. Further, upgrading to a new version of Fedora requires exporting any data you need to preserve and using `podman machine init` to create a second machine instance (or replacing the existing one after a `podman machine rm` command).

> **NOTE** Currently, it is difficult to run Fedora CoreOS inside of WSL, so it was decided to default to Fedora. If Windows support for CoreOS changes in the future, `podman machine` will move to Fedora CoreOS.

As an example, to pull the latest packages for the version of Fedora running on the podman guest, perform the following command:

```
PS C:\Users\User> podman machine ssh dnf upgrade -y
Warning: Permanently added '[localhost]:52581' (ED25519) to the list of
known hosts.
Last metadata expiration check: 1:18:35 ago on Wed Jan  5 21:13:15 2022.
Dependencies resolved.
…
Complete!
```

ADVANCED STOPPING AND RESTARTING

Normally, to stop and restart Podman, you would use the respective `podman machine stop` and `podman machine start` commands. Stopping the machine is the preferred approach, since system services can come to a clean stop. However, in some cases, you may wish to force a hard restart of the WSL facilities, including the shared Linux kernel, which stays active even after a machine stop. To kill all processes associated with a WSL distribution, use the `wsl --terminate <machine name>` command. To shut down the Linux kernel, killing all running distributions, use the `wsl --shutdown` command. After these commands are issued, you can use a standard `podman machine start` command to relaunch your instance:

```
PS C:\Users\User> wsl --shutdown
PS C:\Users\User> podman machine start
Starting machine…
Machine "podman-machine-default" started successfully
```

Summary

- Linux containers require a Linux kernel, meaning running containers on a Mac or Windows platform requires a VM running Linux.
- Podman on Windows does not run containers locally on Windows. The Podman command is actually `podman --remote` communicating with the Podman service running on a Linux machine backed by WSL 2.

- The `podman machine init` pulls down and installs a virtual Linux environment onto your platform, which runs the Podman service.
- The `podman machine init` command also sets up the SSH environment required to allow the Podman remote client to communicate with the Podman server inside of the WSL 2 instance.
- Podman on Windows with WSL is the full Podman command. WSL is running the Podman commands under the Linux kernel, even though it feels like it is running natively on the Windows machine.

index